THE GREAT
EARTHQUAKE

THE GREAT EARTHQUAKE

America Comes to Messina's Rescue

Salvatore J. LaGumina

<teneo> // press

YOUNGSTOWN, NEW YORK

To my Sicilian-born parents,
Maria Madonia and Giacomo LaGumina

TABLE OF CONTENTS

LIST OF PLATES

FOREWORD

The immense debt of civilization to Italy, the warm and stead-
fast friendship between that country and our own, the affection
for their native land felt by great numbers of good American citizens who are immigrants from Italy; the abundance which God
blessed us in our safety; all these should prompt us to immediate
and effective relief.
> —Theodore Roosevelt, president of the United States, in a
> letter to Congress requesting approval for humanitarian
> assistance to Italy, January 1909.

When the greatest natural disaster the world had ever known struck
southern Italy in the final days of 1908, President Theodore Roosevelt,
with the support of Congress and the American people, chose to render
assistance on a scale the world had never seen. In a dispatch that began
"[w]ith all possible haste," President Roosevelt diverted to Sicily and to
Calabria the Great White Fleet, which was, at the time, in the Mediterranean nearing the end of a global tour designed to demonstrate America's
assent to the world stage. Our ships and our sailors carried badly needed

food, water, medicine, blankets, and other supplies to aid survivors left homeless, orphaned, widowed, alone, and in shock.

The destruction from the initial earthquake in the Strait of Messina and the subsequent tidal wave that swept both Sicily and Calabria was unimaginable. In Messina, a vibrant port city of one hundred and fifty thousand people before the earthquake, only fifteen thousand survived; the American consul general in Messina and his wife were among the dead. In Reggio, a city of fifty thousand, only ten thousand survived. It would take days before the true extent of the devastation was known, but President Roosevelt, keenly aware of America's debt—indeed, the world's debt—to Italy for its contributions to civilization, understood that America had an obligation to respond immediately with money, supplies, and even flesh and blood.

Under the command of Admiral Charles S. Sperry, the ships of the Great Flight Fleet sailed into Messina and Reggio, and under the command of U.S. Naval attache' Reginald Belknap, our sailors stayed in Italy for more than six months. From January to June 1909, they buried the dead; administered to the survivors; and built houses, hospitals, schools, and entire villages. They ate, drank, worked, and slept among the Italians of Sicily and Calabria. They earned the love and gratitude of a nation and the admiration of the world. It was, to be sure, the world's first major effort of humanitarian assistance—an act by our sailors not of combat but of charity and compassion, a model for many such efforts by the United States to come.

One hundred years after the earthquake, Salvatore LaGumina tells a story that has unfortunately been forgotten. Using first-hand accounts from survivors and witnesses, including American sailors, Italian peasants, priests, and journalists, he vividly recounts the utter destruction caused by the earthquake and tidal wave and the subsequent aid rendered by the U.S. Navy. At the same time, his narrative is gripping, disturbing, and inspiring. We owe an immense debt of gratitude to him for helping us remind ourselves of the force for good that our nation is, has always been, and always will be.

I, personally, am especially grateful to Professor LaGumina for having brought this story to my attention while I was still serving as the assistant secretary of the navy. As an Italian American whose grandparents came from Sicily and Calabria, this story is especially poignant. And it held many lessons for my tenure as assistant secretary, a time when our navy and Marine Corps again responded with compassion to multiple natural disasters—a tsunami in Indonesia, an earthquake in Pakistan and India, and a hurricane in New Orleans.

G. K. Chesterton once said, "The true soldier fights not because he hates what is in front of him, but because he loves what is behind him." The good, the truth, and the beauty of America that lies behind our soldiers, sailors, airmen, and marines today as they fight to preserve our freedom and administer to the victims of modern earthquakes and tsunamis, is the same good, truth, and beauty that lay behind them and inspired their compassion 100 years ago in Italy.

Let us read their story and stand proud.

The Honorable Richard Greco Jr.,
The Assistant Secretary of the Navy
Financial Management and Comptroller
2004–2006

PREFACE

Salvatore LaGumina's gripping account of the devastating 1908 earthquake and tsunami in Italy and the valiant reconstruction effort led by the U.S. Navy, published 100 years later, is at once an Italian story, an American story, and an Italian American story. For the Italian—the citizen of the country that gave the world the Renaissance; accounting; modern banking; the piano; and giants like Dante Alighieri, Michelangelo, Leonardo da Vinci, Gaetano Filangieri, and Enrico Fermi—it was a moment of naked vulnerability, profound courage, and sheer stamina. It was a moment of anguish, witness to the worst suffering imaginable for a human being: the sudden, violent, and senseless loss of mothers, fathers, children, and friends—rich and poor alike. But it was also a moment of truth and goodness, witness to the best qualities of man—pure love of neighbor and love of God, rendering comfort and aid to the dying, the grieving, and the needy.

For the American, the citizen of a young country painstakingly built by immigrants from many nations, it was a moment of greatness—the ascendance of a nation to the world stage, a nation come of age not to conquer, not to dominate, not to colonize, but to serve as a beacon of liberty for all people wanting to be a part of a grand and noble experiment of self-governance, hard work, and meritocracy. It was a moment of leadership by example, a tradition set forth by our founding fathers and carried on by every president and generation that has followed. It was a moment of great charity. In the aftermath of the 1908 earthquake, the United States acted not out of self-interest but out of a humble sense of responsibility and duty to a friendship that has roots in the time of the very foundation of our nation. Eighteenth-century Italian philosophers Filippo Mazzei and Gaetano Filangieri were friends of Thomas Jefferson and Benjamin Franklin, and by the accounts of Jefferson and Franklin, Mazzei and Filangieri inspired their thoughts and words, even the very Declaration of Independence and the immortal truth, "All men are created equal."

For the Italian American, the story is a continuation of a centuries-old, proud legacy of contribution to the world. As President Roosevelt cited in his letter requesting that Congress authorize aid for earthquake and flood-ravaged Italy, civilization owes an immense debt to Italy. Indeed, Italy helped teach the world to see. Christopher Columbus saw beyond flat horizons, igniting exploration and globalization. Galileo Galilei saw beyond the senses, enabling modern science; Guglielmo Marconi saw beyond the limitations of the wire, making possible the radio, television, and every wireless-communication device we enjoy today. St. Thomas Aquinas, St. Claire, and Padre Pio saw beyond the temptations of this world to help us focus on the next world. As Italian Americans, we are the heirs of anonymous artists and cobblers, bakers and shoemakers, whose inventions of hand and mind, art and science, flood the world's churches, town squares, shops, and libraries; we are the heirs of a creative genius that continues throughout the world wherever Italians are present and breathe the inspiration of sweat and tears of our mothers and fathers, grandmothers and grandfathers, whose very act of emigrating to the United States—many penniless, orphaned, and still in shock after the earthquake and tidal wave—was an act of courage, wisdom, and humility; it was an act of virtue, gaining us, as Italian Americans, a happy inheritance.

Let us be proud. As Italians, let us be proud of our courage to overcome what seemed insurmountable. As Americans, let us be proud of our sailors and the aid they rendered to a suffering people. As Italian Americans, let us make our forebearers proud that we took our inheritance and used it honorably and virtuously in our adopted country, making good on their sacrifices. It is only in this way that we can, like our ancestors in Italy, contribute to the future of civilization.

Lawrence Auriana,
Chairman of the Board
Columbus Citizens Foundation

ACKNOWLEDGMENTS

It is my happy duty to thank a number of people for their assistance in writing this book. Dr. Frank Alduino more than extended himself in suggesting and helping with research in the National Archives. Hon. Richard Greco, former assistant secretary of the navy, was a valuable source of information and encouragement. I deeply appreciate the support rendered by Lawrence Auriana, Joseph Camilletti, Dr. Mario Mignone, and Prof. Marcello Saija of the University of Messina who also made available important visual material. Prof. David Crugnola and the library staff at Nassau Community College were also most helpful in locating and making available vital research material.

My wife Julie helped more than she knows by her kind understanding, wonderful support, and proof reading of the manuscript. It was her suggestion that we visit an antique store in Vermont that led me to discover Reginald Belknap's fine book *American House Building in Messina and Reggio*, which launched me into the project. She also established contact with some of the people who provided testimony of the earthquake's impact on their families.

I should like to extend my appreciation also to my publisher Teneo Press, as well as Dr. Paul Richardson and Toni Tan—they have all been most cooperative and accommodating.

THE GREAT
EARTHQUAKE

INTRODUCTION

Natural disasters in the form of floods, cyclones, earthquakes, tsunamis, hurricanes, landslides, and volcanic eruptions occur throughout the world thousands of times a year. Since most of them are of a short duration and localized in terms of harm to people and property, they elicit limited response on the part of the general public and, for the most part, go unreported. There are times, however, when the fury and ferocity of an event are so deep, so searing, and so harmful that they leave in their wake immeasurable levels of distress, pain, and sorrow. The resultant grief and unhappiness are, furthermore, long lasting and, accordingly, capture the world's attention for protracted periods of time. The tsunami catastrophe in Indonesia in 2004, Hurricane Katrina in 2005, and the earthquakes of Myanmar and China in 2008 are recent examples of such events. Thus, Hurricane Katrina—the worst natural calamity in U.S. history, which caused the death of many people and wreaked extensive property damage in New Orleans, one of the nation's most colorful cities—continues to be cited in newspaper reportage. At this writing, we still lack a full, final tally of casualties, as well as reliable cost estimates for reconstruction.

Recurring earthquakes, floods, and other calamities have been the bane of certain geographic areas, such as southern Italy and Sicily. Those regions have been long identified with periodicity of disasters—none, however, packing the wallop of what occurred on December 28, 1908: the worst natural disaster in recorded European history, and until that time, the most disastrous in world history. The devastation and destruction that characterized that occurrence dwarfed all others in the width and scope of the area involved and the number of casualties it caused. It was also a phenomenon that evoked sympathy throughout the world as nation after nation sought to bring relief and aid to the stricken nation. For the Italian nation—which had only recently become united, yet still was struggling with the lingering force of regionalism—this would prove to be its most severe test, one that would try the mettle of the purported integration. How it dealt with the natural catastrophe would effectively validate its claim to be regarded as among the great world powers. For other nations, the Great Earthquake was to be of great consequence, as it afforded a concerted opportunity to demonstrate their commitment to humanitarian impulses. For the United States, this event would be of singular meaning—one that saw it respond swiftly, generously, and extensively to people in need.

Ties between the United States and Italy on social, cultural, and literary levels had been intimate for decades, even before unification, while political interaction between the two had a shorter history that at times had been strained—as in the aftermath of the 1891 lynching of eleven Italian immigrants. Additionally, trade and commerce between the two nations was modest, although increasing, as was the presence of Italian immigrants in America, especially in large eastern cities like New York. These background factors and more came into play in the aftermath of the Great Earthquake—they collectively form the building blocks to reconstruct the event a century later.

The frantic creativity unleashed by this natural disaster will be examined in an effort to make historical sense of the Great Earthquake. It is hoped that the narratives in this monograph, along with their analysis against a background of historical events, will help us to better understand not only the power of an earthquake in itself, but also its impact on society. The mass emergency that constituted the Messina upheaval presented society with great pragmatic and symbolic challenges. This monograph will examine and analyze the impact of the Great Earthquake on Italy, as well as the responses of civil leaders, the monarchs, the Church, and the extensive aid rendered by outside nations. Together, they were confronted with a populace collectively consumed with apocalyptic visions—a mood of a people that seemed on the verge of a social breakdown, and one that desperately needed the reestablishment of order. The plight of the survivors/victims and their efforts at coping with the trauma of the disaster will be reviewed, along with their resiliency and determination in the face of adversity. This work will also appraise the role played by Italian Americans who experienced grave sorrow over the travail that befell their homeland—a legacy that endures.

Above all, this study will delve into the recovery and recuperation of Messina and other affected areas by examining the level and extent of aid proffered by the United States from the highest levels of government, to the particularly significant role played by the United States Navy. Simply put, the amount of assistance offered by the United States in terms of money, people, and genuine sympathy was extraordinary. It constitutes a chapter of American history that best demonstrates, in a remarkable way, the great humanitarian role that a military arm can and did display—one that showed America at its best.

CHAPTER 1

AMERICA AND ITALY

By the end of the nineteenth century, the United States had acquired considerable diplomatic experience in dealing with the major European nations of England, France, and Germany—albeit sometimes against a background of hostility. In contrast, United States relations with Italy were more circumscribed—in part because Italy was a latecomer among the family of European nations (having achieved final unification in 1870), and in part because it was "the smallest and the weakest of the great powers,"[1] not to be regarded as a major force relative to England, France, and Germany. For decades following Italian unification, cordiality characterized official relations between the United States and Italy, which only became strained in the 1890s following the lynching of eleven Italians in New Orleans in 1891. These men were Sicilian immigrants who had been accused of killing the city's police chief; they were tried and found not guilty. The tension over this ugly incident persisted for some time until a compensation package for families of the victims brought about a resolution.

Until the 1880s, contact between ordinary Americans and Italians was quite limited because of the relatively small number of Italian immigrants living in the country. Italian newcomers, furthermore, had come primarily from the north—an area whose people historically enjoyed higher socioeconomic standards than those in the south, were better educated and knowledgeable about America, and accordingly provoked favorable comments from observers. However, the arrival of massive numbers of poverty-stricken newcomers emanating from southern Italy—largely illiterate and not inclined to become permanent citizens—served to harden attitudes about these new arrivals, as Americans soon considered them a distinctly undesirable element. The bifurcation that prevailed was so pronounced that it found its way into official immigration designations of preferable northern Italians, in invidious comparison to unattractive southern Italians.

AMERICAN PERCEPTIONS

In truth, Americans knew little about southern Italians who were seen "huddled in their depressing ghettoes" that set them off as "part of another culture, strange, distant and virtually invisible."[2] The immigration of millions of southern Italians—whose dark, coarse, and swarthy features stood in contrast to lighter-skinned and leaner northern Italians—made Americans believe that their country was becoming the dumping ground for disagreeable and unwanted people. Americans saw these newcomers as excessively clannish, extremely ignorant, and regrettably disinclined to make America their permanent residence—rendering them ill prepared for democracy.

Of course, Americans of upper-class deportment who expressed disdain for all forms of productive work—especially any type of manual labor—seldom mingled with these people and consequently saw them from a different perspective. These American exemplars of the Victorian era sought self-respect from immediate peers and saw Italy from a dissimilar viewpoint; they indulged in a romantic view of Italy as a land of unsurpassed beauty enriched by classical art, majestic buildings, historic churches, and admirable Italian culture. Partakers of "the grand tour" of Europe, they regarded holidays and protracted stays in Italy as indispensable; they were unabashed admirers of the other Italy—the Italy of magnificent cathedrals, impressive palaces, exquisite gardens, fabulous panoramic views, estimable cuisine, and complaisant peasants. This was the predominant perspective of American travelers of upper-class deportment—such as architects like Sanford White and Charles McKim who went to Italy to study its architecture—while to numberless aspiring artists, studying Italian painting in its Italian setting was indispensable. One of America's most noted sculptors of the late nineteenth and early twentieth centuries, William Couper, stayed in Italy for more than twenty years learning the neoclassic and idealistic style he incorporated into his works. John Singer Sargent—the most successful portrait painter of his era, as well as a gifted landscape painter and watercolorist—studied in Italy where, in fact, he was born. Morgan Russell, the American synchronist painter, also spent time in Italy.

LITERARY PERSONAGES

The literary establishment likewise sought out and intermingled with their Italian counterparts from the beginning of the golden age of American literature. Washington Irving, for example, visited and imbibed Sicilian culture as early as 1804. Among the literary lights of the second half of the nineteenth century who expressed great empathy with Italian history and culture were William Dean Howells, Edith Wharton, and Francis Marion Crawford.[3]

Howells—called the "dean of American literature" who had enormous influence on American literary tastes—was clearly enamored of things Italian, a manifest Italophile throughout his career. He served as American consul to Venice where he studied Italian literature, traveled extensively in Italy, and left a deft portrait of the attractions that Italy (and especially Rome) had for foreigners.

The trouble is that Italy is full of very living Italians, the quickest-witted people in the world, who are alert to seize every chance for bettering themselves financially as they have bettered themselves politically. For my part, I always wonder they do not still rule the world when I see how intellectually fit they are to do it, how beyond any other race they seem still equipped for their ancient primacy. Possibly it is their ancient primacy which hangs about their necks and loads them down. It is better to have too little past, as we have, than too much, as they have. But if antiquity hampers them, they are tenderer of its vast mass than we are of our little fragments of it; tenderer than any other people, except perhaps the English, have shown themselves; but when the time comes that the past stands distinctly in the way of the future, down goes the past, even in Italy...

Beyond the tenements, the generous breadth of the new streets has been bordered by pleasant stucco houses of the pretty Italian type, fleetingly touched but not spoiled by the taste of the art nouveau, standing in their own grounds, and not so high-fenced but one could look over their garden-walls into the shrubs and flowers about them. Like suburban effects are characteristic of the new wide residential streetson the hither side of the Tiber, and on both shores the streets expand from time to time into squares, with more or less tolerable new monuments...Rome grows, and as Italy prospers, it will grow more and more, for there must forever be a great and famous capital where there has always been one. The place is so perfectly the seat of an eternal city that it might well seem to have been divinely chosen because of the earth and heaven which are more in sympathy there than anywhere else in the world. The climate is beyond praise for a winter which is mild without being weak; there is a summer of tolerable noonday heat, and of nights deliciously decline from the temperature of October to the lowest cool; the spring is scarcely earlier than in our latitudes, but the fall is a long, slow level of January without the vicissitudes of other autumns. The embrowning or reddening or yellowing leaves turn sere, but drop or cling to their parent boughs as they choose, for there is seldom a frost to loosen their hold, and seldom a storm to tear them away.[4]

The legendary American writer Edith Wharton found her travels to Italy so utterly enthralling that she recorded her exultation in its fabled gardens in her book *Italian Backgrounds*:

> But to those who first see Syracuse in the month of March—the heart of the Sicilian spring—it must appear preeminently as one vast unbounded garden. The appeal of architecture and history pales before the vast glory of loosened soil...
>
> There are gardens everywhere, gardens of all kinds and classes, from the peasant's hut hedged with pink geraniums to the villa with its terraced sub-tropical growth; but most wonderful, most unexpected of all, are the famous gardens of the quarries.[5]

The celebrated Mark Twain (Samuel L. Clemens) visited and worked in Italy more than once, where he made extensive use of his experience as a reporter and writer. Along with a number of American authors and artists, he was a passionate lover of Italy, and, indeed, it was to Italy that he had brought his wife in hopes that the climate would help her ailing health. William Roscoe Thayer was an American author and editor whose ardor for Italy was so fervent that he adopted it as a second home. He graduated from Harvard where he was a classmate of Theodore Roosevelt, and wrote extensively about Italian history. His writings deeply influenced Wharton. Italy was also a must in the itinerary of Henry Adams, whose *The Education of Henry Adams* reflects time he spent in Rome, including his meeting Giuseppe Garibaldi. Another Harvard product who spent a good deal of his life in Italy was Bernard Berenson from Boston, who settled in Italy with his wife Mary and became the foremost student and scholar of Italian Renaissance art, winning renown as a man of letters and the world's leading authority on Italian painting.

Foremost among well-bred American families with a fondness for Italian culture were the Crawfords and the Howes, both of whom lived in Italy for many years. For example, Francis Marion Crawford—of proper Bostonian patrician lineage but born in 1854 in Bagni di Lucca, Italy, educated at Harvard, and a descendent on one side of his family of Revolutionary War hero General Francis Marion (popularly known as the "Swamp Fox")—was a brilliant scholar. No less prestigious was his maternal heritage—he was the son of Louisa Cutler Ward and the nephew of Julia Ward Howe, the American poet, whose stirring Civil War song "Battle Hymn of the Republic" established her as an icon among American poets. Crawford made Italy his permanent home where he became a prolific writer of more than forty romance and adventure novels and popular histories set in Italy, which became very popular. He found many estimable attributes about Italians and Italy that were conveyed in his writings.

> The true Italian peasant in his native environment I have always found to be a most amiable character, hard working, and honest according to his lights…Italy is really the easiest country to live in, and is under most excellent police protection. During all of my long residence there I have never had any trouble with anything approaching interference on the part of the Camorra and my home is in the reputed Camorra district.[6]

Mary Crawford Fraser, Francis' sister and also a writer, related a chronicle of many family members, relatives, and in-laws partaking in vacations in Rome—including that of her legendary aunt Julia Ward Howe. The daughter of a wealthy New York City family, Julia Ward traveled extensively, especially to Italy where she met her future husband and where at least one of her children was born.

Maud Ward Howe, Julia's daughter and Crawford's cousin and member of the upper-crust social set, was still another American devoted to Italian culture who spent years in Italy—along with her husband, the artist John Elliott. Elliott—a renowned artist whose works ranged from miniatures and portraitures to pastel illustrations for children's fairy tales to grander oils on canvas—received a commission in 1904 to produce a large mural for the National Museum of Washington. This led to another sojourn to Italy for the Elliotts where, for an extended period, they occupied the apartments of Mrs. Elliott's cousin. Finally, Elliott completed his great mural painting *Diana of the Tides*, slated to adorn a wall in the

National Museum on Christmas Day in 1908. Both Maud and John were in Italy on the eve of the historic 1908 earthquake.

SICILIAN ATTRACTIONS

Although less well known than the more celebrated novelists, there were other remarkable American visitors to be found in the peninsula in late 1908—some of them in Rome, while others sojourned in Sicily. Cities like Taormina on the fabled island, for example, situated high on the cliff side of the northeastern coast, had for years been an upscale destination for the leisure class who delighted in walking the cobbled streets lined with hotels, restaurants, and shops, and who reveled in enjoying Taormina's heights where one would be rewarded by Italy's most beautiful and commanding views of blue waters of the Ionian and Tyrrhenian seas. There, too, one could attend opera in the extraordinary and charming 2,500-year-old Greek amphitheater, 420 feet above sea level and sitting on seats hewn in the rocks in a semicircular fashion. Poets and actors, painters and famous society figures, as well as the frivolous, flocked to Taormina, making it a must on their grand Italian tours.

Still other Americans, such as Katherine Davis of the influential Bement family of Delaware, spent their winters in cities like Syracuse— also renowned for its Greek ruins. Destined to become a woman prominent in government service, Davis was in Italy in 1908. Also present in Italy at the time while visiting her parents, who lived in Florence, was Alice Fitzgerald, a glamorous young debutante who shocked her family by spurning the life of the idle rich to join the nursing profession. While in the course of time she would achieve worldwide fame in her chosen profession—organizing nursing schools and introducing public health nursing—she would be called upon to play a meaningful role dealing with catastrophe in Italy.

PARADOX

American visitors of aristocratic bent expended much time and money in furthering their understanding and appreciation for the finer achievements in Italian art, architecture, painting, and landscape. For the most part, however, they did not display the same level of interest in the lives of the poor, ordinary, and landless Italian peasants. The historian H. Stuart Hughes explains the dichotomy as "a paradox—a paradox concealing a profound misunderstanding. For Americans, Italy is a land that seems greatly familiar; actually it is little known." Notwithstanding that Hughes' opinion was written in the mid-twentieth century, it has applicability to earlier times. "This again is a long standing situation—the mixture of familiarity and strangeness, of admiration and contempt, in the American attitude toward Italy, dates back to the earliest contacts between Americans and Italians."[7]

The reality was that at the beginning of the twentieth century, Italy was a poor and backward nation that—while home to historic vestiges of antiquity and offering spectacular views and wonderful cuisine—was also deceptive. One-third of the country was mountainous, another third mostly hills, with only about a third available for agriculture. Even this description is deceiving because clay soil, rather than rich black loam, covers much of southern Italy, providing even less land for cultivation. It is estimated that clay soil accounts for three-quarters of Sicily's agricultural base. A virtual lack of natural resources and historic regionalism constituted further obstacles. The Italian peninsula also suffers from natural disasters. In addition, until the twentieth century, the south suffered from the scourge of malaria. Against this background, Italy was portrayed as "a land of mass resignation."[8]

ITALIAN GOVERNMENT

Upon entering the twentieth century, Italy's government was that of a constitutional hereditary monarchy, with the official head of state enjoying considerable power. King Victor Emmanuel III had ascended the throne in 1899 following the assassination of his father, King Humbert, at the hands of anarchists. By comparison to his father, Emmanuel was depicted as more intelligent, more highly educated, and in closer touch with modern ideas.[9] This was a view shared by American diplomats like Lloyd C. Griscom who described Emmanuel as a voracious reader: "He read everything that came his way—he was even wading through each fat volume of the *Cambridge Modern History* as it was published."[10]

Italy also had a representative government in the form of a parliament that exercised power over day-to-day affairs. Although there were political parties representing various shades of the political spectrum, liberalism predominated in the early postunification period, to be followed by nationalism—each tainted with scandals, corruption, and fraud. Thus the political situation in the Italy of the late nineteenth and early twentieth centuries was one of a country struggling to adjust to its status as a unified nation. "Italy is made, now we must make Italians,"[11] was an expression underscoring the hard reality that unification would not instantly erase or even diminish centuries-old regional loyalties and differences. Nor would it end the inferior status of the south vis-à-vis the north. Added to this mix was the position of the Catholic Church that refused to accept an Italian government that had expropriated its lands and privileges. The pope described himself as "prisoner of the Vatican" and instructed Catholics not to vote or accept public office.[12] Although some aspects of church–state relations were relaxed in ensuing years, the "prisoner" status endured into the new century.

Thus the prevailing social, economic, political, and religious conditions in the new Italian nation insured that government leaders faced formidable challenges. Italy's fragile democracy was additionally buffeted when it embarked upon imperialist ventures that ended disastrously and further served to convince foreign observers of the country's fundamental weakness. That damaging perception was to plague the country for many years. For decades following unification, several prime ministers enjoyed only short tenures. One prime minister who served intermittently was Giovanni Giolitti, who has inspired conflicting interpretations of his role. One of the major liberal reformers of late nineteenth- and early twentieth-century Europe, Giolitti emerged not as a transitional figure who would lead fledgling Italy into modern democracy, but as a staunch adherent to nineteenth-century elitist liberalism, trying to navigate the new tide of mass politics. Some described him as "an opportunist. A hardened skeptic, he had no belief in the honesty or sincerity of anyone, and was finally convinced that every man had his price—money for this one, office for that, decorations for the other."[13] However, others saw Giolitti as a shrewd leader who needed all of his guile to bring disparate groups to work for common goals in a country divided by numerous fissures. Giolitti was at the helm of the Italian government as 1908 neared its end.

During the late nineteenth century, Italian agriculture was under severe stress. In addition to archaic methods of farming, highly inefficient landholding systems, and absentee landlords, the free play of the market economy would hurt the backbone of the economy; namely, Sicilian products became less competitive with foreign goods. The resultant strain intensified the struggle for survival. The failing agrarian system understandably found many ready to look to the United States for an opportunity to improve their lot. Sicilian enclaves emerged in communities ranging from Buffalo, New York, to Ybor City, Florida, where they found employment in Buffalo's industries (especially railroads) and where in Florida they were mainstays of cigar manufacturing.[14]

THE IMMIGRATION PHENOMENON

By the late nineteenth and early twentieth centuries, Italy had begun to experience massive emigration—indeed, it acquired a reputation as the classic emigrating nation, a standing that was to endure for the next century and a half. Although the causes of the outflow were a combination of "push/pull" factors, there can be little doubt that economic hardship considerations were the principal cause, especially for southern Italians. Ironically, because unification did not bring a surcease of the problem of earning a livelihood in that geographic area, not surprisingly, migrants sought their future elsewhere—even if only temporarily. It is estimated that perhaps 3 million people left Sicily—more than any other single Italian region. Emigration patterns in Sicily, however, were quite varied—those who lived along the seaports and coasts or in the Aeolian Islands were much more accustomed to seeing and mixing with people from different countries and accordingly were more inclined to emigrate, while those deep within the island were insulated from that experience and presumably less likely to depart. Nevertheless, due to repeated failure to improve Italy's agriculture system, the notion of emigration affected even the latter locales. One study showed that by the end of the nineteenth century, 99 percent of the land in inland Sicily belonged to 1 percent of the population.

> [E]very morning at dawn, in front of the church, the *gabelloto* Mafioso (Mafia-type middleman) chose, among the poor daily workers (*jurnateri*), those who had the right to work that day…
>
> Inhabitants of this type of Sicily were immediately ready to leave. No family was particularly attached to the land, and there was no hope for the future.[15]

That escaping "la miseria"—their only lot in Italy being feebly eking out a living—was the prime motive for emigrating is borne out in numerous personal testimonies, such as that of Saverio Rizzo.

> I was born in the town of Cimigliano, Italy, which I left at the age of sixteen in 1903. I was preceded to America by two of my brothers, one of whom was killed in a mining accident in New Jersey.
>
> Most of the men who had emigrated from my town had intended to return, expecting to remain in America for perhaps five or six years simply to earn money. Cimigliano, however, had no industries and there was a scarcity of work and a certain amount of poverty.[16]

Although Saverio earned only a meager $3 a week, it seemed enormous. "To me three dollars a week seemed a fortune. Converted to Italian money, I was going to earn triple the amount my father was earning at home. What I did not know was that there was also triple the cost of living."[17]

HERITAGE OF DISASTER

Vulnerability to natural disasters was the lot of Italians from time imme-
morial. Disease in the form of malaria plagued the country into the
twentieth century, while periodic earthquakes exacted a heavy toll of life.
Geologically, Sicily was, as one writer put it, "as restless as it has been
politically and socially. At least twice it was connected, with the Italian
mainland, and once probably with Africa, so that African animals entered
it. The Straits of Messina, only two miles wide, and one hundred and
fifty fathoms deep, are Nature's record of an earthquake rupture between
Italy and Sicily."[18]

The Catania Earthquake of 1693, for example, killed probably 60,000
in Catania, Sicily, and 93,000 in Naples. The Calabria Earthquake of
1783 was estimated to have cost the lives of 50,000, while the 1905 Calabria Earthquake obliterated twenty-five villages in the Calabria region,
killing about 5,000 people. A plague in 1740 claimed the lives of 40,000
in Messina while the cholera epidemic of 1854 numbered 16,000 victims. Notwithstanding these disasters, Messinese proved themselves so
resilient a people that Messina elicited acclaim in a guidebook since "at
present day the town is again in prosperous condition."[19]

GUIDEBOOKS

The Baedeker travel guide informed prospective travelers to Messina
about basic geographical, sociological, and historical facts: it had a population in 1896 of 80,000 in the city and a total of 141,000 when its
environs were included, and it was Italy's busiest port as some 4,000
steamboats used the harbor facilities annually.[20] Readers learned that
even though Messina's collection of antiquities was small due to prior
natural disasters, there were wonderful sights and sites for travelers to
see and enjoy. Among the more appealing were the public gardens of
Flora (Villa) where one could enjoy music on summer evenings, the
university that housed some antiquities and valuable manuscripts, the
"quay" that bustled with steamboat activity, and magnificent churches

such as the Cathedral of Matrice—an imposing edifice that was begun during the Norman period of the eleventh century and completed by King Roger II in 1254, which contained sarcophagi of monarchs and a classical Renaissance altar.[21] Messina claimed several handsome streets such as Via Garibaldi, on which was located the municipal palace, and Corso Vittorio Emanuele, previously known for its row of palaces all of uniform height—but since the earthquake of 1873, none was higher than two stories. In short, it was regarded as an exceptionally beautiful city. For many veteran travelers, there was no more beautiful a sight than the Straits of Messina. Many a correspondent used the most lavish words to describe the high, snow-capped mountain line on the horizon from which hills terraced with olives descend toward the bay. The bay at dawn, with its unmatched array of glimmering green, blue, and pink surfaces, also regularly evoked the most superlative description.

The guidebook suggested that visitors take a journey to nearby Faro, a fishing village located at the narrowest part of the Strait of Messina (3,600 yards) that afforded charming glimpses of the sea and the opposite coast of Calabria. At this point, the waters are very turbulent as currents run in such diverse directions as to form whirlpools. From that vantage point, they could see the glittering town of Palmi across the strait and Scilla—famous for the "Charybdis" legend that can be traced to Homer's *Odyssey*, specifically Odysseus' journey home when he was forced to navigate a narrow strait. In Greek mythology, Charybdis, the daughter of Poseidon and Gaia, is a sea monster who swallows huge amounts of water three times a day and then belches them back out again, creating whirlpools. According to the myth, Charybdis lies on one side of a narrow channel of water while another sea monster, Scylla, lies on the other side of the strait. The two sides of the strait are within an arrow's range of each other, so close that sailors attempting to avoid Charybdis will pass too close to Scylla, and vice versa. Thus the phrase "between Scylla and Charybdis" came to mean being in a state where one is between two dangers, and where moving away from the one will cause one to be in danger of the other. To the Messinese, the location of Charybdis was in the Strait of Messina. This corridor of sea was seen as a halo of charm and mystery—a great mythological patrimony that evolved over the centuries with numerous elaborations and variations. It was no wonder why the Strait of Messina was regarded as a bewitched and dangerous area.[22] The strait was also characterized by the phenomenon of the *fata morgana*, which sometimes, under certain climatic conditions, makes it appear as if the shadows thrown off by the houses and lights of Messina stretch out over the water to join those given off from the Calabrian shores, making everything seem like one immense city.

By the end of the nineteenth century, wealthy travelers from European countries and the United States, who undoubtedly read and were influenced by Baedeker's popular guidebooks, had become accustomed to spending winters in various Italian cities and towns. What could be better than to escape the rigors of harsh winter weather in much more salubrious climates—in settings that overflowed with wonderful sights amidst a marvelous culture steeped in history? In Italy they could imbibe in cultural pursuits to satisfy unique individual tastes. They learned Italian and became acquainted with peculiar Italian customs. They also found entertaining the celebration of holidays like Christmas, replete with its delightful and enchanting Italian customs, as well as the marvelous gustatory treats for which Italy was famous. Christmas in Messina in 1908 was, indeed, fulfilling to visitors who expected to bask in its glow for several days to come.

ENDNOTES

1. *New York Times*, December 23, 1897.
2. Alexander DeConde, *Half Bitter, Half Sweet: An Excursion Into Italian-American History* (New York: Charles Scribner's Sons, 1971), 79.
3. Ibid., 129–130.
4. William Dean Howells, *Roman Holidays and Others (Whitefish, MT: Kessinger Publishers, 1908)*, 14, 38, 39.
5. Edith Wharton, *Italian Villas and Their Gardens* (New York: C. Scribners, 1905), 134–135.
6. *New York Times*, May 12, 1907.
7. H. Stuart Hughes, *The United States and Italy* (New York: W. W. Norton and Company, 1953), 3–4.
8. Ibid., 34.
9. Luigi Villari, *Italy* (New York: Charles Scribner's Sons, 1929), 102, 114.
10. Lloyd C. Griscom, *Diplomatically Speaking* (New York: The Literary Guild of America, Inc., 1940), 296. For more on Griscom's diplomatic career, see Salvatore Prisco, "Griscom and Trade Expansion," *Diplomacy & Statecraft* 18, no. 3 (September 2007): 539–549.
11. Michael Huyssenne, *Modernity and Secession* (New York: Berghahn Books, 2006), 172.
12. Corrado Ricci and Ernesto Begni, eds., *Vatican : Its History Its Treasures* (1915; repr., Whitefish, MT: Kessinger Publishing, 2003), 546.
13. Villari, *Italy*, 108.
14. Gary Mormino and George Pozzetta, *The Immigrant World of Ybor City* (Champagne, IL: University of Illinois Press, 1987), 22–36.
15. Marcello Saija, "A Study of Sicilian Emigration," *Arba Sicula* 26, nos. 1–2 (Spring and Summer 2005): 46–67.
16. Salvatore J. LaGumina, *The Immigrants Speak* (Staten Island, New York: Center for Migration Studies, 1979), 5.
17. Ibid., 8.
18. Maude Howe, *Sicily in Shadow and in Sun* (Boston: Little, Brown, and Company, 1910), xi.
19. Karl Baedeker, *Southern Italy and Sicily, Handbook For Travel* (London: Dulau & Co., 1880), 311. A similar claim was made in the 1896 edition.
20. Baedeker, *Southern Italy and Sicily*, 314.
21. Ibid., 313–314.

22. See Rosa Santoro, *The Damned Charm of Scylla and Charybdis*, http://www.google.com/search?q=cache:aN0OQ2W8uAUJ:home.um.edu.mt/medinst/mmhn/rosa_santoro.pdf+The+Damned+Charm+of+Scylla+and+Charybdis+%22santoro%22&hl=en&ct=clnk&cd=1&gl=us.

CHAPTER 2

AN APPALLING UPHEAVAL

CHRISTMAS IN MESSINA

December 27, 1908—the feast of St. Barbara—found Messina enjoying a rather tranquil day. Although the day brought rain and wind, city inhabitants followed habitual pursuits. To opera lovers, it was a time for a display of customary grace and good manners highlighted by beautiful ladies wearing the latest hairstyles and clothing typical of the belle époque as they proceeded to the Victor Emmanuel Theatre to hear Hungarian soprano Paola Koralek and tenor Angelo Gamba singing the immortal melodies of Verdi's *Aida*—Gamba was soon to be killed by the earthquake. Others, meanwhile, preferred to remain at home, perhaps listening to poetry or visiting family. For their part, Calabria's residents were celebrating the inauguration of a new and modern electric plant to illuminate the city.

It was a mild day, and although Messinese had thronged the city's ninety-one churches on Christmas Day, they were still anticipating the enjoyment of La Befana—a character in Italian folklore similar to Saint

Nicholas or Santa Claus, whose name is derived from the festival of Epiphany. She visits children on the eve of January 6 to fill their socks with candy if they are good or a lump of coal if they are bad. Some indulged in the unique Italian custom of *la passeggiata*—the evening stroll in which elegant women took to their meandering and men relaxed in the town square—no one remotely aware of the lurking turmoil. Except for those whose duties required them to be up during the night, all inhabitants of Messina, Reggio, and Calabria were asleep when, at 5:20 a.m. on December 28, 1908, virtually without warning, the earthquake struck with lethal ferocity. In actuality, measuring devices in Messina recorded a tremor ten minutes earlier—those awakened by it described it as a deep rumbling noise like the peal of thunder or the explosion of many bombs. This was followed a few seconds later by a rough, jolting movement.[1]

Several vessels near Messina were conscious of the rumble as the ships quivered as though they had lost their screws or run aground or struck a major piece of wreckage. In most places, the sea first receded for a few minutes from the usual level and then flooded the coast with at least three big waves. Sea-level oscillations lasted for many hours. The earthquake reached its maximum intensity on the Calabrian coast near Pellaro, where run-up heights as large as thirteen millimeters were observed, and in Sicily at Giardini Naxos and at Sant'Alessio. Seamen saw thousands of dead fish piling up on a corner of the harbor. Gushing waters flooded the lower parts of Messina and washed away lighthouses and cottages into the sea. On the coast of Calabria, the waves were more serious, flooding houses and ruining buildings and leaving a trail of twisted railway lines and distorted land surfaces. The sea waves spread east to Syracuse and even impacted the island of Malta, 120 miles farther away, where it was reported that, due to turbidity and slump in the submarine canyon, a cable parted.

This was the fourth-largest earthquake ever recorded, and the strongest ever to hit Messina and all of Europe. The violent earthquake, which lasted thirty-two seconds, came in the darkness of night—during the Messina winter, the sun rises towards 7:30 a.m.—fomenting turbulent waters in the strait into huge waves of upwards of forty feet high that came crashing down three to four blocks inland, crushing and devastating everything in their path. Many homes had been constructed with seemingly strong walls made up of round stones probably removed from beds of nearby streams and piled on top of one another in the belief that such solid partitions could withstand the tremors of a heaving earth. Sadly, this proved to be a mistaken belief because the stones were easily loosened by the water's force, causing the collapse of houses, with concomitant violent destruction of human life. Some buildings, however—such as the Vittorio Emmanuele Theatre and even ancient churches constructed with especially thick walls that used and fitted large squared stones—remained intact and were able to resist the earthquake magnificently. The extent of damage to the palazzata—the splendid row of baroque palaces two miles long that lined the semicircular sickle-shaped harbor fronting the strait—was deceptive. At first seemingly spared, in fact what remained were only the outer walls graced with exquisite sculptures—facades behind which were empty shells.

Saturated in melodramatic overtones and overdramatic flourishes, the following account nevertheless provides some notion of the cruelty wrought by the disaster.

> Men, woman and children again had a battle with the most diabolical forces of nature.
>
> The wave, fifty feet high, rolled back three blocks from the shore line and in its waters thousands met that death they had so miraculously escaped in the vortex of falling walls and crashing masonry.
>
> Hundreds of half dressed men, women and children who had fled from their homes to the streets were caught in the onrush of waters and drowned or injured.
>
> In a moment it had receded, carrying with it many of its unhappy victims while the bodies of others strewed the strand.
>
> Flames began making their way slowly over the devastated area in an inexorable advance. Imprisoned and pinioned human beings, unable to extricate themselves, burned alive, hundreds were dying of their injuries, while many were starving.[2]

Added to this was an all-pervading stench, a phenomenon all the journalists who visited Messina in the quake's aftermath commented about. Awareness of the smell of putrefaction that hung around the area led a student of the subject to conclude that "the smell of Messina was the smell of a loss of cultural control, of the breakdown of social distinction between life and death. Messina stank of the dissolution of the categories Italians lived by."[3] Even a month later, journalist Luigi Barzini, on board a ship in the harbor, was aware of the indefinable and penetrating scent from the city. "The smell is subtle, and it may be that we wouldn't notice it if we didn't know it so well. We will have it in our memories for the rest of our lives. It pursues us and we sense it everywhere."[4]

The two major cities on either side of the Messina Strait—Messina and Reggio di Calabria—suffered the destruction of over 90 percent of their buildings. Telegraph lines were cut and railway lines were damaged, hampering relief efforts. To make matters worse, the major quake on December 28 was followed by hundreds of smaller tremors over succeeding days, bringing down many of the remaining buildings and injuring or killing rescuers. The impact on the shoreline was so severe that even veteran sailors could barely recognize its contours because long stretches of the coast had sunk several feet into the Messina Strait.

SURVIVAL STORIES

Although the death rate was extremely high, there were many who survived and recounted their personal recollections of where they were, what they were doing, and their first reactions—as, for example, those on board trains. One young seminary student, Teodoro Rositani, who walked eleven miles to escape from Reggio, had a terrible tale to tell of danger, survival, and reunion in the first moments of the earthquake, in which he lost a sister.

> I was in a train waiting to go to San Giovanni, when the carriage was literally lifted off the tracks, the station crumbling to the ground before our eyes. We were soon climbing the heaps of rub-

bish all that was left of the station, guided by the cries of distress. We dragged forth the family of the stationmaster, all of whom were badly injured.

Meanwhile the shocks continued and the sea gathered itself into a wall of water, destroying everything it touched. The sun had risen before we had completed our work of rescue of the station.

We were roused from our work by the shouts and found ourselves in the embrace of the rest of our companions, who had escaped from the seminary. In our joy of the reunion we all fell on our knees and gave thanks for our escape, praying also for the less fortunate townspeople.[5]

His presence on board a train on the morning of December 28 may have saved the life of Giuseppe Cutroneo, but there would be no reunion with his family. Cutroneo, in the cattle business, awoke at 4:15 a.m. and boarded the last coach car to take him from Messina to Milazzo where, as was his custom, he would purchase his cattle.

Of a sudden the car shot up in the air, falling with a crash on one side. A deafening roar filled my head. The air became suffocating. My body seemed to grow numb all at once. I don't know how long I lay in a sort of stupor before I realized there was hole over me, through which I climbed out.

The spectacle again stupefied me. I thought the world had come to an end and that I was in purgatory. I could not at first recognize what I saw as Messina. Still the earth trembled and quakes came intermittently, each one toppling over walls that been cracked or left standing by the first shock. I looked back at the station. It had collapsed; the train shed had fallen on the forward part of the train and crushed in almost flat.

Somehow, he found his was back home:

I found only a heap of bricks, twisted iron and wood splinters where I used to live. The five stories had tumbled into a heap fifteen feet high. My house was a four room flat on the first floor. It had been buried at the bottom. Without thinking how impossible the task, I began to dig in the ruins. Down below I could hear moans, and they made me work like a madman.

> I would sometimes think I heard my wife's cry, and I would yell
> down into some crevice. "Floria! Floria! Here is your Giuseppe!"
> And then I would call to my children—to Diego, my six-year old
> little boy; to Tony, who was four, and Natalina, the baby.[6]

Cutroneo stayed for two more days, surviving on the food given him by Russian sailors. When he realized that all was lost, he, along with 200 others, left Messina for Palermo on the *Regina Marguarita* where he hoped to get a ship to take him to New York where his father lived. Some refugees were so scantily clad that they hid in the hold of the ship for most of the voyage, while others resorted to extreme measures in desperation. Men wore women's clothes and women wore men's garments. Penniless, he was helped by a well-dressed Palermo citizen who, like many others in the city, took pity on the refugees and gave him the $38 passage money. He arrived in the new country with only eighty cents but once again found other generous and sympathetic people who gave him a few more dollars.

Re d'Italia, a 6,500 ton, 430-feet-long ship that brought Cutroneo to America, was a Lloyd Sabaudo liner that carried 1,400 steerage passengers, some who had left before the disaster. One of them was Joseph Polifoni of Pittsburgh who having just finished visiting his mother, father, and brothers, left Messina for Naples on December 27—he soon would become terribly disconsolate when he could find out nothing about his family. After news of the earthquake, the ship made a stop at Palermo where it took on board hundreds of survivors, including dozens of injured who had fled their homes in such haste that they did not have their passports.[7]

Not a respecter of social classes, the earthquake impacted people across the social spectrum. The marquis Vincenzo Genoese, a refugee from Palmi, for example, was awakened by a tremendous roar on the morning of the earthquake, recalled that the house whirled around like the wings of a windmill. The walls of his dwelling cracked, and through them came a cloud of suffocating dust. Stunned, but uninjured, when the marquis realized he could not use the collapsed stairs to gain the streets, he resorted to descending instead from a third-story window by means of a rope. Finding it difficult to walk, owing to the fact that the streets were filled with debris, he nevertheless assisted in dragging eighty-six persons from beneath the ruins, all of them dead—their faces showing the agony they had suffered.

Paolo Riza, mayor of Capriolo, was in Messina on a pleasure trip that fateful morning when the floor of his room fell and threw him, half-conscious, into a mass of rubbish. His body became lodged in a niche in a wall, where he was pinioned by a heavy beam, and to make matters worse, a carpet covered his face, threatening to suffocate him. He managed to move the carpet with his teeth until he made an opening in the folds allowing him to breathe. The man lay in this position for five hours, expecting death at any moment. Once, hope sprang up in his breast when he was able to call the attention of a passerby, only to be disappointed when the man ran away. Finally, the hotel proprietor helped him escape. Another tragic episode occurred in Reggio when Demetrio Tripepi, mayor of the town, disappeared and was presumed to be lost, but was rescued by his frantic family who dug without rest in the ruins. The family's joy was short lived because the severely injured man died soon afterward.[8]

Sometimes an agonizing number of days were to pass before rescue came. Five days following the earth tremor, actress Flora Parini was lying half buried when she heard the voice of an Italian lieutenant who was also buried in debris nearby. He pleaded with her to call for help for both of them, reminding her that he had seen her performing recently and had vigorously applauded her singing. Happily, sailors soon rescued both of them. At the same time, it was reported that, at the risk of her own life and without any other aid, the mother superior of the St. Vincent Military Hospital saved Col. Minicci and his daughter from their home that had collapsed. The rescued officer was so grateful that he covered her hands with kisses. On January 14, thirteen days after the earthquake, soldiers found a mother with two small children still alive.[9]

RELIGIOUS INSTITUTIONS

Religious institutions suffered great damage—for example, in one institution, seven of twenty-one nuns perished, as did forty-nine of sixty of its students. Of twenty-one nuns at the Convent of San Vincenzo di Paola, only seven remained alive—all continued to engage in nursing the wounded. The Capuchin monks at Reggio who escaped death also worked heroically in rescuing the less fortunate. From the town of Scylla, which was virtually completely annihilated, two priests were able to escape with their lives only because they happened to be in the vault of the church, the most formidable portion of the building, when the church collapsed. In Morabito, the Bishop and other priests, "with touching courage and devotion have done much to preserve order by the example of calmness and self-denial they have given their people. They are busy carrying comfort and consolation to the dying and bereaved."[10]

SALVEMINI

Among the more prominent casualties of the Messina Earthquake was that of the family of Gaetano Salvemini, one of Italy's leading Socialist intellectuals. Honored as a brilliant historian and then as a future foremost anti-Fascist who taught at the University of Messina and later at Harvard University, he became the most celebrated political exile to America during the Fascist era of the 1920s and 1930s. Salvemini and family were residents of Messina at the time of the disaster. As it happened, he came home late the night of December 27 while the family was already fast asleep. He too went to sleep, but when awakened by ringing electric bells and desperate, howling dogs, he jumped out of the window as the walls of the five-storey building tumbled down. For days, Salvemini and his brother Ugo groped among ruins in search of bodies of the family—never finding all of them. He kept hoping against hope: "[W]henever he heard about the survival of a little boy as the same age as Ughetto, who was three, he hurried to the place or sent a telegram, only to come back every time disappointed." His wife, five children, and a sister all perished. He continued his historical pursuits, but confessed: "I go ahead, work, make speeches…in short, and go on living. I have on my table some letters that my wife, my sister, or the children wrote. They are like their voices. And when I have read one of them, I have to stop, because a great fit of weeping overcomes me, and I should like to die."[11]

Rossi

Not then prominent but destined to become successful in America was Anthony T. Rossi, another earthquake survivor, who was born in Messina in 1900. The earthquake killed his brother. Anthony was twenty-one years old when he came to the United States with two suitcases and $30. He worked for a time in various occupations and owned a few small businesses, one of which sold gift boxes of Florida fruit. In 1947 he founded Tropicana Products, whereupon he proceeded to invent and patent a pasteurization process to aseptically pack pure, chilled juice in glass bottles, allowing it to be shipped and stored without refrigeration. For the first time, it was possible to offer consumers over a widespread area the fresh taste of orange juice made from 100 percent fruit. Soon thereafter, he also devised a method of freezing pure, whole citrus juice for storage and shipping. He also became a very religious Protestant, making annual trips back to Sicily where, in 1966, he helped fund a church and mission. In the United States, he established the Aurora Foundation, which has funded Christian educational institutions, Christian missions, and other charities.

Unusual Outcomes

Peculiar reactions in the midst of this set of cataclysmic circumstances were perhaps inevitable. One example was that of an old woman who was extricated from the wreckage of the Church of San Francisco, not realizing that she had been buried for a week. She explained that she thought she was entombed in the church after having died a natural death and was living in the hereafter.

Humor found its way to intrude even in the midst of the utter catastrophe. The marquis Semmola, for instance, found himself imprisoned in a Messina cellar that was well stocked with provisions. When the rescue party approached the cellar in an attempt to extricate him, he told them to devote their efforts to saving his children. "Don't think of me," called out the marquis, "I am in a bar with plenty to eat and drink."[12]

One of the truly miraculous stories of survival was that of Marietta who was pregnant and awaiting a child when her house collapsed around her. Because her bed was under a solid arch in the bedroom, she was spared, but deeply embedded in the ruins. The situation was desperate because the house remains were so precarious that unless great care was taken, the remaining walls would crumble and crush the woman under the arch.

Through a hole in the wreckage, food and water were somehow lowered to her. Finally, five days later, the would-be rescuer came by with a piece of bread and three dried figs he had found in the ruins for her when, as he described it, "I made the usual signal; there was no answer…I put my ear to the hole; what did I hear? A sharp thin voice that wailed and wailed but said no word." The woman had borne her first child. On the eighth day, they extricated her and her baby boy:

> [S]trong as a young bull, for we had fed the mother and her milk had not failed. Miracles? Ah, well, that is as one believes. I myself put the two of them on the train for Taormina. There be many rich *forestieri* [foreigners] at Taormina; I doubt not they have cared for Marietta; they have great charity, those *forestieri* of Taormina. They have charity, and they understand us a little, those who live among us here in Sicily; they shared our calamity, they knew our people.[13]

SHOCK

Every survivor told of experiencing extreme shock and stupefaction as the result of the rupture of the earth. The testimony of Dr. Dentice, chief of the governor's cabinet, is a case in point. He happened to be awake at the moment the quake struck and, while his house did not fall, it was severely shaken and flung him from his bed before he could get to his feet. He called to the others, and all managed to get downstairs, while the shaking continued with ever-increasing violence. They were delayed slightly in leaving by an injury to an old aunt, whom they were obliged to half drag, half carry, with them. While thus engaged, they experienced the last and worst paroxysm of the earth's upheaval—ironically, the delay probably spared them their lives because they would have been right under falling masonry. Their house was near a small square to which they hastened and stood in utter darkness for two hours, listening to the death throes of the dying city. When asked about the effect upon him and his companions during that time, he replied:

> We did nothing. We stood silent in the rain dull, dazed, half-stupefied. I do not remember feeling any keen emotion, not even of fear. I think we all passed into a condition of submissive indifference. With the slow coming of daylight, our faculties awakened. The gloom revealed little until actual sunrise, and then we strove to make our way to the lower part of the town and the sea front.
>
> We found, to our astonishment, that we were prisoners. Every street leading from the square was piled twenty feet high with impassable ruins. We imagined that we alone were the victims of this isolation, and we looked for the speedy coming of soldiers or relief parties. We had no suspicion of the truth until two hours later, when I saw a priest a little distance down one street. I shouted to him to know what was the situation elsewhere.[14]

A medical doctor studying the psychological effects of an earthquake in Messina concluded that the effects of the severe earthquake on the population immediately produced a clinical syndrome he labeled "earthquake neurosis." However, the duration of the pathological manifestation was said to be brief, as in acute illnesses, and it soon disappeared without leaving any trace.[15] In what seems to be an astoundingly hasty conclusion, another medical professional wrote in 1916, "Thus, five or six months after the Messina Earthquake there was not a single person suffering from a neurosis caused by the earthquake"—saying essentially that traumatic neurosis is cured rapidly.[16] These judgments obviously seem myopic; among other issues, it appears impossible to trace all those who were scattered to far-off places as a consequence of the destruction, which makes no allowance for long-range impact.

Many survivors rushed to the shoreline to get away from ubiquitous and unrelenting signs of destruction. Dispirited and cold, they resorted to instincts of elemental survival such as roasting seabirds that had been killed by the tempest and cast upon the beach. Others had the strangest objects packed in sacks. There were examples of the cold hearted and avaricious—along the corner wall of a house lingered a callous man selling bread at exorbitant prices, amid a chorus of curses.

Desperate people staring death in the face either recoiled or retreated into their cowering selves, giving the impression that they did not seem to care. Some observers were struck by and critical of the attitude of those survivors who seemed incapable of helping themselves or others. In fact, they were bewildered—they were in shock. Asked about Messina and Reggio, they could make only desolate gestures or stare out as if uncomprehending.

SEA DESTRUCTION

Reggio Calabria was the region most devastated by the rising sea. Its seafront appeared to be completely swept away, while the harbor was so choked with wreckage from vessels of every kind that it remained for a time inaccessible by sea or by land.

> With the horrible inrush of the sea, the swallowing up of boats, the crushing of ships and the destruction of bridges and walls, the sea became almost instantly covered with debris containing

refuse of every description dotted with human bodies. When day dawned the entire shoreline of the surrounding country was utterly changed in appearance. The coastline was greatly altered, while of all the magnificent houses along the shore only a few tottering ruins remained. From these ruins from time to time there sprang jets of flame and smoke.[17]

One report told of a tidal wave at Catania that sank 500 boats and severely damaged a number of vessels and steamers, while at Messina a ferryboat moored at one of the docks seemed suddenly to be thrown high into the air. It landed on top of the dock and was left hanging there by the receding waters. A Russian vessel lying in the harbor was then hurled farther into the street.

The travail of a prospective sea journey by a chemist from Messina provided a vivid if exaggerated account of the turmoil. He had risen early on December 28 and was crossing the strait from Messina to Reggio at 5:30 on Monday morning.

> The boat had reached the middle of the strait when he suddenly became aware, as he stood on the deck, that the sea was greatly agitated. The next moment a great chasm opened in the water, and the boat dropped seemingly forty or fifty feet. Pulco believes that it touched bottom. Then it was picked up by a huge wave and hurled high up on a mountain of water, only to descend into the trough again, where it again appeared to strike the bottom. Most of the people on board were swept off and drowned. The boat was badly wrecked, but it floated ashore. Pulco was still on board.[18]

The earthquake scene left a chaotic jumble of plaster wall fragments, broken wooden fixtures, and stones. Everywhere it was impossible to pass through most streets. Standing walls had fallen out, exposing one tier of rooms above another in which nothing seems to have been disturbed: pictures were left hanging straight on the wall, lamps remained on tables, and vases and flowers on mantelpieces. Vultures could be seen congregating to prey on the corpses, a grisly reminder that Messina was a vast morgue of the dead. Among the more ghastly sights was that of buzzards feeding on the dead bodies. Soldiers were ordered to kill on sight any starving cats and dogs—who now sought the flesh of the dead—caught feeding.

PRISONERS ON THE LOOSE

The problem of prisoners who were released or escaped from crumbling city prisons was particularly acute. Although the earthquake killed outright many of the 650 inmates in one Messina prison, as it did the local police chief who lay within the ruins of his office, a number of prisoners did escape. These criminals resorted to their baser inclinations and joined with other malefactors to rob not only palaces but also ordinary citizens of Messina. Mutilations of fingers, hands, and ears in order to get hold of rings, earrings, and other jewels was perpetrated in the pursuit of their disgraceful activity. The desecration of the helpless dead, their offences against nature, and their absolutely repugnant and loathsome behavior elicited rebuke and condemnation from General Francesco Mazza, officer in charge of troops that were brought in to impose martial law. Mayhem reigned for two days, even after the imposition of martial law.

> What especially preoccupies me is the succession of thefts since the first day of the disaster. Hundreds of native and foreign malefactors have poured into the devastated district searching among the ruins for bodies to despoil or treasure to sack. The dead have been found with fingers cut off to remove rings and with ears torn to remove pendulants.[19]

AFTERMATH

While Messina's fires were not on the scale of those experienced in San Francisco in 1906, there were, in fact, hundreds of fires due to kerosene stoves that had overturned and flared up like matches. Those who could flee from their crumbling homes seeking escape in neighborhood streets and the waterfront, did so, but they could not run away from the sound of death amidst the falling houses and tottering towers—the groans of the dying. Nor could they flee the yawning cracks in front of them in the shaking earth. Terror and despair gripped all of Messina. Desperate survivors frantically sought to distance themselves from the frightening scenes in the densely built areas of the city. Those who personally experienced the horror of the natural disaster best described it—as the following words of a woman survivor who underwent the ordeal of being awakened by the quake reveal:

> We were all sleeping in my house when we were awakened by an awful trembling which threw us out of our beds. I cried out that it was an earthquake, and called to the others out to save themselves, while I quickly pushed a few clothes into a valise. The shocks continued, seeming to grow stronger. The walls cracked and my bureau split in two and crashed to the floor, nearly crushing me. My hands trembled so that I could scarcely open the doors.
>
> To increase the terror a rainstorm, accompanied by hail, swept through the broken windows. Finally, with my brother and sister, I succeeded in gaining the street, but soon lost them in the mad race of terror-stricken people who surged onward, uttering cries of pain and distress. During the terrible flight chimneys and tiles showered down upon us continuously. Death ambushed us at every step.
>
> Instinctively I rushed toward the waterfront, but there found the grand promenade transformed into a muddy, miry lake, in which I slipped and often fell. I learned afterward that I was rescued by a soldier and carried to a train.[20]

The account of another refugee from the disaster further reveals what took place.

> Infernal is the only word that will adequately describe the fearful and terrible scene. When the first shock came most of the city was fast asleep. I was awakened by the rocking of the house. Windows swayed and rattled and crockery and glassware crashed to the floor. The next moment I was violently thrown out of my bed to the floor. I was half stunned, but knew the only thing to do was to make my way outdoors.

The streets were filled. Everybody had rushed out in their nightclothes, heedless of the rain falling in torrents. Terrified shrieks arose from all sides and we heard heartrending appeals for help from the unfortunates pinned beneath the ruins.

Walls were tottering all around us, and not one of my party expected to escape alive. My brothers and sisters were with me, and in a frenzy of terror we groped our way through the streets, holding our own against the panic-stricken people clambering over piles of ruins, until we finally reached a place of comparative safety. I was struck down and badly injured by a piece of furniture that fell from the upper story of a house.

All along the road we were jostled by scores of fleeing people, half clad like ourselves. The houses seemed to be crashing to the street in whatever way we turned.

Suddenly the sea began to pour into the town. It seemed to me that this must mean the end of everything. The oncoming waters rolled in a huge wave, accompanied by a terrifying roar.

The sky was aglow with the reflection of burning palaces and other buildings and, as if this was not enough, there suddenly shot up into the sky a huge burst of flame, followed by a crash that seemed to shake the whole town. This probably was the gas works blowing up.

Eventually we reached the principal square of Messina. Here we found 2,000 or 3,000 utterly terrified people assembled. None of us knew what to do. We waited in an agony of fear. Men and women prayed and groaned and shrieked. I saw one of the big buildings fronting on the square collapse. It seemed to me that scores were buried beneath the ruins. Then I lost consciousness, and remember no more.[21]

A doctor resident of Messina described his escape from a third-floor bedroom where he was sleeping by gripping the roof of a neighboring house. He also told of fleeing to the pier where he saw a ferryboat that was docked suddenly thrown into the air and onto the pier.

The scene was similar in nearby small towns and villages. Indeed, some unfortunate towns, such as the fishing village of Faro, were completely obliterated. With cries of lamentations and prayers rending the air, thousands abandoned their homes to pray, even in the face of a terrific rainstorm. As in past times of extreme danger, people sought the help and mercy of Almighty God. Imploring God and their saints, townspeople of Prizzo, Cotrone, Santa Severina, and Piscopio—believing they were doomed—braved even the danger of collapsing walls to enter their churches where they proceeded to carry out images of the saints. Meanwhile, in an attempt to allay people's fears, Cardinal Nava, archbishop of Catania, promised that the body of St. Agatha would be carried in procession where people could plead for her intercession in this time of danger. According to tradition, in the seventeenth century, St. Agatha, the patron saint of deliverance from all scourges, answered pleas of an alarmed people and saved them by diverting away from Catania the stream of lava from a fearful eruption of Mount Etna. Thus they once again bore images of the saints in procession through the open country, invoking St. Agatha and the mercy of God. Over the next few days, there were further reports of the populace in a state of great excitement because an apparition of St. Agatha "like an angelic dream," had been seen on Mt. Etna. Convinced that it was through her intercession that Catania had been spared the latest catastrophe, the faithful were seen to "kneel in prayer and beat their breasts as penance for their sins."[22] In the mountainous regions inland, the population had taken refuge in grottos and caves where peasants and priests, soldiers and persons of gentle birth were living in common. For the time being, their bed was the ground and the fires they burned kept them safe from wild animals.

CUT OFF FROM THE WORLD

On December 29, after railroad connections between Messina and the Sicilian capital of Palermo were restored, the first trains brought survivors into Palermo. One passenger was a woman in torn clothing, the widow of Messina's chief of police who tried frantically to save her husband and children—in vain. Others gave frightening accounts of the horror that befell ninety guests of the Trinacria Hotel—patronized exclusively by foreigners and one of Messina's best accommodations—that was destroyed, undoubtedly killing all, except the proprietor. Although the suddenness of the hotel's collapse caught people unawares, many visitors tried to escape by jumping out of the windows and likely either were killed by falling masonry or drowned in a huge wave that swept over the hotel.

The steamer *Washington*, in the Strait of Messina at time the earthquake struck, shuddered as if it had gone aground. Conditions in the water were so severe that the ship captain was unable to see either the Messina lighthouse or Calabrian shore because of prevailing heavy fog. Nevertheless, he soon engaged in a rescue effort of those refugees in small boats that swarmed his ship seeking escape from ravaged Messina. For some of those who were rescued, the tragedy was sadly unending. Francesco Loiacono, one of the rescued and injured Italians who was unconscious when put aboard ship, became delirious upon regaining consciousness when he realized his wife and babies were left behind in the destroyed city. He yelled for the ship to bring him ashore as rescuers tried but were unable to quiet him. Seemingly bereft of his senses, he jumped overboard to return to his family, swam for a while, and then disappeared under the water.[23]

Prior to modern times and the development of rapid communication, the plight of unfortunate victims of natural disasters such as floods, earthquakes, and famines may have remained unknown for days or weeks. With the advent of the telephone and wireless radio, however, people would learn of such calamities almost immediately. Although, by 1908, small Sicilian and Calabrian villages were without electricity and would not become electrified for years to come, the major towns and cities, as well as ships in Messina Harbor, did have use of telephone and wireless technology at the time of the earthquake. Nonetheless, word about what had occurred was not instantaneous. Unfortunately, owing to the fact that telegraphic and telephonic communication facilities were almost completely destroyed, news of the terrible earthquake did not reach other regions of Italy for many excruciatingly long hours, compelling Messina, Reggio, and the surrounding areas to confront their ordeal in lonely isolation for a period of time. Absence of radio communications from government ships in the Messina Harbor led worried authorities in Rome to call the naval team in Naples to find out if it had any information, an inquiry that was conducted but yielded only a tragic silence, thereby rendering the situation even more ominous.

FIRST REPORTS

On the afternoon of December 29, the *Journal of Italy*—the earliest Roman paper to publish about the event, and dated, of course, the day before—voiced serious concerns that no news had arrived from Messina until late afternoon, notwithstanding the existence of a radio telegraph station in Messina with a direct line to Rome's Monte Mario Radio Station. Since the installation of Marconi radio/telegraph stations in Italian military vessels in 1904, it was expected that there would be instant communication in the event of an emergency.[24] However, there had been no word from the ten-vessel, radio-equipped First Torpedo Squadron stationed at Messina, nor the cruiser *Piedmont* that also was equipped with telegraphic devices. At 8:00 a.m. on the morning of the earthquake, the torpedo ship *Sappho* managed to create a passageway to Messina to begin the first relief work activity—picking up some 400 wounded survivors and transporting them to Milazzo. The first news about Messina was dispatched by the *Spica*, a torpedo boat that went streaming along the coast from point to point, always frustrated to find the wires down, until it reached Nicotera, a charming small town on the Tyrrhenian Sea, where the telegraph wires were intact and word about the calamity was sent out finally at 17:25 (5:25 p.m.) to the outside world. A cheerless postscript of the message stated that Commandant Passino of the torpedo fleet, after heroically trying to rescue other victims, went to aid his own family at his damaged home where he became a victim—crushed, as were all members of his family in the ruins of their residence.

The first Italian soldiers to become involved in the rescue effort were personnel from the Eighth Regiment of the Bersaglieri, stationed in Palermo. Unfortunately, this was to be a time of anguish and sorrow for many of the soldiers because they were from Sicilian garrisons with Sicilian officers. Scores of them had lost close relatives or friends—in one particularly agonizing case, an officer reported the loss of seventeen close relatives including his wife, mother, father, brothers, and sisters.[25] Despite the heartbreaking personal losses, they toiled on, landing on the afternoon of the 29th, and promptly began to set up field kitchens where they baked bread in the streets to feed the starving population. Italian authorities determined that the soldiers, which altogether numbered 5,000, should be deployed in taking refugees out of Messina and placing them on steamers that would then distribute them among different Italian cities.

CATASTROPHE IN REGGIO

However tardy the word about what had befallen Messina, it was even more baleful for Reggio, from which there was no word for more than a day. With normal telephone and wireless communications destroyed, Reggio Calabria sent a financier on horseback along the Ionian Sea on the southern coast,, who rode for ten hours before being able to reach a town with a working telegraph to send a telegram to Rome which dramatically confirmed the gravity of the horror to authorities. Nevertheless, for the Italian general public, vagueness surrounded earthquake news for a few days—indeed, it was not until several days later that Italian newspapers provided extensive photographic coverage.

Forsaken for two whole days, bitterness mounted against a perception that all the help seemed to go to Messina while Calabrians remained the prey of hunger, thirst, and cold. With barely fifty homes left standing, virtually the entire civic administration and the police were gone, and Reggio's streets were piled with corpses being devoured by ravens—Reggio's scenes of painful cruelty were not bearable. Some 2,000 people—haggard, starving, and tired—escaped to the hills along the Calabrian coast and took a last look at the dying cities. A young priest who had also escaped from Reggio tried to counter their despair. He blessed them and then, turning to Reggio, he cried, "Peace to the dying, peace to the dead. Men, women, and children knelt to the ground, and raising their hands to heaven, prayed for the deliverance of the multitude."[26] Partial surcease of the travail was provided when Monsignor Morabito, bishop of the diocese, arrived on New Year's Day with a cart filled with food that he distributed along with words of comfort. Unfortunately, the scope of the devastation was so immense that a great deal more was required.

"A state of frightful anarchy prevails here. Mobs of ruffians roam among the ruins, giving full vent to their vilest instincts."[27] These were the terrifying words contained in a newspaper correspondent's depiction of the stark condition of Reggio where widespread pillaging among wrecked stores and banks was taking place—giving readers a sense of the gravity of the situation. Italian soldiers suffered their share of casualties, but those soldiers who survived utilized their training and discipline to good advantage, carrying out patrols and protecting property. On occasion, they were forced to open fire on the wretched dregs of society—the escaped prisoners who sought to exploit society in the midst of its sorrow. The military assumed control of the city in an attempt at organized rescue, as the army commandeered general storage magazines to prevent looting and undertook the task of distributing rations.

The personal intervention of the king began to change the situation when he assigned the highly regarded explorer Admiral Umberto Cagni—who, in 1900, reached the uppermost latitude in Alaska up to that time—to supervise rescue operations. Arriving at the scene on the Italian battleship *Napoli*, Cagni immediately took over the city's main piazza where he began organizing assistance, deploying sailors to set up a temporary hospital camp where the injured could be treated and medicine dispensed to the many wounded. The most seriously injured were placed on board the warship. After dividing the city into several zones, Cagni then assigned troops from the Twenty-Second Infantry Division and the Second Bersaglieri, along with Italian Navy personnel and local police, to provide public security.

WERE REPORTS EXAGGERATED?

Because of the scarcity of accurate information, some were inclined to discount early reports as hyperbole brought on by emotion—a view that was shared even by a renowned scientist. A case in point was Dr. William

Hobbs, head of the Department of Geology at the University of Michigan, who happened to be in Italy attending a scientific conference at the time of the tragedy. "There is no doubt in my mind that the reports are exaggerated. I have several times visited towns that have been shaken with disturbances and I have found that things were not so bad as the papers had reported."[28] Accordingly, a *New York Times* editorial chided sensationalist treatment of the catastrophe "right here in New York, where, in the offices of some organs of publicity, inventive minds and fluent pens have supplemented the governable dynamics of nature, and have amplified with plausible fancies and tale already sufficiently abounding in horrors."[29] Hobbs' observations were made two days after the earthquake amidst an atmosphere of exaggerated reports that the Lipari Islands had disappeared, as well as other fantasies. With more time to analyze the event a couple of months later, he published a more considered article that showed some modification, although he continued to point out overstatements contained in his initial reports such as a reputed huge water wave from the Strait of Messina that was, in reality, "much less formidable than first reported." Hobbs explained that "[i]n a general way, experience has shown that a great earthquake renders a district comparatively immune from destructive shocks for a period usually measured at least in decades." Hence he stated that the greatest of the last earthquakes in the vicinity was that of 1783, whereas the 1894, 1905, and 1907 earthquakes were measurably smaller; the December 28, 1908, earthquake "rather confirm[s] than contradicts the general principle which has been established."[30]

PERRET'S OBJECTIVE VIEW

Among the first to visit the scene of horror was the remarkable Frank A. Perret of Brooklyn, New York, who, after studying physics and establishing himself in the field of electricity—the Perret electric motor was named after him—went to Italy for his health in the early 1900s. There, he began to work with Professor R. V. Matteucci, the director of the Volcanological Laboratory, and he also studied volcanic eruption sites in

Mt. Vesuvius, Mt. Etna, Stromboli, and the Strait of Messina. Recognized as one of the worlds' leading volcanologists, he is said to have predicted the great seismic disturbance in Sicily almost to the day and, even though he was away at the time, he rushed back to Italy three days before the terrible earthquake. That Perret was on board the German liner *Therapia*, the first foreign vessel to reach the Messina scene of disaster, was fortuitous in that he left for posterity valuable observations from the perspective of science and objectivity. His report was also able to dispel rumor that the Aeolian Islands had disappeared. Perret's chilling description of what he witnessed shortly after the eruption in Messina provides a dramatic picture of what occurred when the waters came out of the sea.

> [Thus] came the dread demon of the earthquake—came with a curious singing sound of a far-off wind-storm, till with a rumble and a roar it reached the cities of the strait, throwing the solid ground into a series of stony waves, lifting the houses bodily, then tossing to and fro, almost as a terrier shakes a rat, and ending some places with a rotary twist more terrifying than all the rest. The building, fair to look upon, but built of rubble and weakened by the strains of previous earthquakes, collapsed amidst suffocating clouds of dust into a hideous conglomeration of beams, girders, mortar, and stone, crushing or imprisoning the inmates, and falling into streets and wounding many of those who had escaped. Whatever had been a village or a city was now a ruin and hecatomb—in half a minute forty towns destroyed and over a hundred thousand dead.[31]

Perret explained that the destruction was an undulating vibration of the ground because of some sudden movement of underground strata that was likely triggered by a volcanic explosion. The effected shape took an elliptical form about fifteen miles north and south of Messina. He also stated that while it was a great earthquake, it was not the greatest ever recorded. Perret concluded that the event demonstrated the utter unpredictability of such phenomena.[32]

With unusual promptitude, in 1910 Mario Baratta, the foremost historian of Italian earthquakes, provided—under auspices of the Italian Geographical Society—a detailed account of the severe earthquake, carefully estimating the extent of the damage and the number of lives lost in different localities. Through interviews and questionnaires distributed among the survivors of the disaster, Baratta managed to define the time intervals between the arrival of the earthquake for about thirty villages and cities along the coast of Sicily and Calabria. His work in measuring seismic risk was regarded as exceptional, as was his study in outstanding detail of the Messina Earthquake in providing accurate reconstructions of the event along with cartographic and photographic materials.

A DANTEAN INFERNO

The first news reports with stories about the utter madness surrounding the earthquake area were very vague and confusing, leading to speculation that the extent of damage was exaggerated. However, it soon became evident that that was not the case; an Italian officer on the scene told a reporter from an Italian American newspaper that not even Dante could describe the horrors in Messina.[33] Comparison to Dante's inferno was, in fact, appropriate. The Seventh Circle of *The Inferno* is described as a steep, shattered terrain that was caused by an earthquake that shook hell just before Christ descended there. Messina's inhabitants were convinced that the heavy storm had broken into their lethargy and confronted them with the appalling reality that they were staring into the jaws of death. Broken, bloodied, and battered, terrified and demented people roamed the streets in tattered clothing or nude, screaming, cursing, or praying—admixture of the decent and the depraved, the sowers of harmony and the disseminators of discord, the humble and hardworking and society's outcasts. (Sleeping in the nude apparently was not unusual, but customary for Messina residents.) They included those who had sinned but prayed for forgiveness before their deaths, and those who were violent against their neighbors tried to justify their sins and remained unrepentant.

Scenes of anguish and horror at Messina would not let up, conjuring reminiscences of the biblical depiction of the plagues suffered by Pharaoh in Egypt, including weird scenes of clouds of crows descending upon the area. "They have crossed the sea in response to some mysterious intuition of the disaster" to further torment tortured survivors who processed naked through the streets bearing the images of saints. Desperately in need of the essentials of life, they fought over scarce morsels of food in anticipation of being plunged into absolute darkness at night. Twilight presented terribly eerie scenes. Shrouded in plaster, white outlines of ghastly shapes lay about, some seemingly leaning against walls, some clinging to the earth, others half coming out and half effaced within the dim light, all exhibiting attitudes of pain, abandonment, and despair. Nighttime was also the preferred moment for thieves and malefactors to gather around banks and palaces they planned to rob, or to steal from the dead and dying. As the sacking of the city took place, revolver shots rang out, further frightening survivors in the ruins. "Ghoul-like figures flitted in the semi-darkness, risking their lives among the tottering ruins, not to assist the agonized sufferers, but in fiendish striving to profit by the disaster that had overwhelmed their city."[34]

The testimony of Swedish-born Axel Munthe, who was passionate about Italy and spent a great deal of his life there, is instructive. Regarded as an expatriate, a humanist, and an excellent—if somewhat eccentric—physician who treated the poor without charge and rescued stray dogs and injured birds, he was in Messina during its ordeal and provided a rare medical doctor's eyewitness account of the torturous hopelessness and travail that people faced.

> I know that I dragged single-handed an old woman from what had been her kitchen but I also know that I abandoned her in the street screaming for help, with her two legs broken. There was indeed nothing else for me to do, until the arrival of the first hospital ship no dressing material and no medicine whatsoever was obtainable...The aqueduct having been broken, there was

no water except for a few stinking wells, polluted by the thousands of putrefied bodies strewn all over the town. No bread,
no meat, hardly any macaroni, no vegetables, no fish, most of
the fishing boats having been swamped or smashed to pieces
by the tidal wave which swept over the beach, carrying away
over a thousand people, huddled there for safety...That robbery
from the living and the dead, assaults, even murders, occurred
frequently before the arrival of troops and the declaration of
martial law is not to be wondered at. I know of no country
where they would not have occurred under similar indescribable
circumstances.[35]

Poor survivors remained without any help and without relief for over
twenty-four hours, as the first ship entered the port of Messina only the
following day, December 29. Many of the injured died from bleeding
or the cold, while other frightened survivors sought their escape across
southern Italy or Sicily. Thus they fled to city after city—including
thousands to Naples and thousands more to other towns and cities along
Italy's coast, swelling their populations and thereby placing significant additional strains on their limited resources. Rome itself took in
many thousands who were put up in army barracks where nuns took
over their nursing. The pope offered the use of the Lazzaretto, which
normally housed pilgrims and where nuns also performed works of corporal mercy. Finding their resources strained to the maximum, munici-
palities soon asked for cessation of the influx. In addition to occupying
all available spaces at the disposal of civic and municipal officials,
monasteries, convents, schools, and churches opened their doors to the
refugees.

RESORT TO EMIGRATION

Earthquake survivors faced the bleakest of realities. Their homes were
destroyed, their family members dead, and the cities around them reduced
to rubble. Although the Italian government tried to relocate many to new
locations within Italy, it was evident that it could not accommodate all.

Under these circumstances, many survivors sought their escape from the tragedy by emigration to America. This was not a novel concept because by 1908 Sicilians had developed such a tradition of emigrating that virtually every family had relatives in either South America or North America, particularly the United States. Because they were important ports of embarkation, Palermo and Naples became the first destination points for large numbers of Sicilians who fled from Messina, where they sought out transportation to the new land. Ironically, for some, this decision once again placed them in peril.

DANGER ANEW

In the face of the desperate plight of survivors completely homeless and totally destitute, an international rescue service was mounted to try to offer some relief to these unfortunate people, including bringing some of the homeless to America. As part of that effort, the cargo ship *Florida* had been commissioned to assist in bringing these displaced people from Sicily to Naples, and thence to New York, the immigration entry point into the United States. Commissioned in 1905, the vessel was a 5,018-gross-ton ship, 381 feet long, with two funnels, two masts, twin screw, and a speed of 14 knots. The *Florida* had been the premier ship of the Lloyd Italiano Line, a steamship company that earmarked the ship for immigrant passenger service across the North Atlantic in a Genoa–Naples–Palermo–New York run. The vessel had accommodations for 25 in first class and 1,600 in steerage. Although bookings were disappointing in 1908, it was expected to benefit from increased trade in 1909. With a crew under the command of twenty-nine-year-old Captain Angelo Ruspini, who had previously led one trans-Atlantic voyage, the *Florida* had on board 14 in first class and 824 refugee-immigrants in steerage as it embarked westward for New York. Earthquake refugees typically were poor people who could only afford to travel steerage class, a daunting form of transport for the masses who were crowded into extremely small spaces below deck, totally bereft of privacy. Families and people who were strangers to one another would now sleep in rudimentary bunks in close proximity and would have to clamor for limited table space to eat the basic food they brought with them, hoping it would last so that they would not have to part with scarce money to purchase ship food. Their belongings were few; they carried virtually everything and anything they owned with them on their backs or in cheap suitcases.

Meanwhile, heading eastward from New York to the warmth of the Mediterranean was the palatial *Republic* from the prestigious White Star Line, a luxury liner as astounding as the *Titanic* would be proclaimed three years later, and also presumably unsinkable. It was renown for a fine-dining saloon furnished in ornamental wood, upholstery of rich texture, and handsome woodcarvings. A large vessel capable of accommodations for 520 in cabin class and 1,000 in steerage in lower decks, it competed for the immigrant passenger trade with Italian liners on the New York-Naples-Genoa run. Indeed, it held the record for the fastest passage between Boston and Queenstown and on January 13, 1909, had just completed a westward voyage from the earthquake-stricken area. Accordingly, the ship's officers, crew, and passengers had observed firsthand the stunning consequences of the earthquake-ravaged area and had carried refugees from the disaster to the United States. It had also recently installed the Marconi "wireless" radio.

Now, as the *Republic* was beginning its eastward journey, it had on board 250 first-class passengers and 211 in steerage, of whom 160 were anxious, homeward-bound Italians whose relatives had been caught in the earthquake and who were understandably worried. Among the passengers were a number who were prepared to offer monetary aid, such as Archbishop Burchese of Montreal, with raised funds from his archdiocese to offer to earthquake victims.[36] The vessel also carried supplies for the Great White Fleet. On January 22, 1909, under the command of forty-nine-year-old Captain William I. Sealby, the *Republic* left New York for the comforting warmer weather in the Mediterranean—it was embarking on a two-month "Thomas Cook" tour.

By a cruel twist of fate, the evening of January 23, 1909, found both ships enveloped in a dense fog near Nantucket Island off the coast of Massachusetts. On January 13, the *Florida* had embarked from Naples carrying hundreds of refugees who were relieved to leave misery and heartache behind, only to encounter, ten days later, another of nature's vexatious problems—ominous dense fog. Searching in vain for Nantucket Lightship, Captain Ruspini was elated to find a thirty-fathom line that he believed placed him in favorable position to enter New York Harbor in the next few hours. Unfortunately, it was also the shipping lane for eastbound ships.

> Around 5:00 A.M. on January 23, this was exactly the situation in which Captain Ruspini found himself. About the same time he began to hear sonorous blasts from the foghorn of a nearby ship, which heralded a potentially deadly situation. The only thing he was sure of was that no one on either ship could see anything as vessels crept through the fog in the dead of the night...
>
> Suddenly Captain Ruspini on the bridge of the Florida heard a whistle blast to starboard and then saw a huge wall appear in front of his ship. In spite of the frantic manuveurs to starboard to avoid a collision, the Florida sank her bow into the side of the other ship just aft of the single tall funnel. On the Republic Captain Sealby heard a whistle at about 5:42 A.M. that appeared very close off the port bow. His reaction was to order full speed astern, and then, when the lights of the oncoming steamer revealed she was on a collision course to hit his ship, he rang full speed ahead in an effort to outrun the disaster. The result was that the Florida rammed the Republic at he most vulnerable place, the main engine room, which soon filled with water.[37]

On the *Republic*, the thunderous crash broke the sleep of radio officer John (Jack) Binns, who immediately ran to the radio shack to contact other ships for help. Binns was a courageous, twenty-six-year-old young man who learned the art of wiretapping when he was only a lad and had become a "Marconi boy"—a reference to young men who dabbled in the new wireless technology and formed a national club in 1909. When the *Republic*'s electricity ran out due to onrushing water that was flooding the ship, he switched to storage batteries that could emit radio signals only sixty miles out, but it was enough to reach the Siasconset Marconi Station, the nearest land station, which had been established only a few years earlier. At the time, the Marconi Company used "CQD" for a distress signal—a general call, "CQ," followed by "D," meaning distress. Because of concern that this could be misinterpreted, SOS subsequently was adopted as a simpler message.

Jack Irwin, the operator on duty at the Marconi Station on nearby Nantucket, picked up the distress signal and relayed it to ships in the area. Soon, two U.S. Revenue Cutter Service cutters, *Seneca* and *Gresham* from Boston, rushed to the scene, as did several other vessels, in answer to the distress call. The Siasconset Station rebroadcast the distress message over a 300-mile range, namely, that the *Republic*, whose location was latitude 40:17, longitude 70, was in distress and in danger of sinking, reaching many ships that could bring aid—this was the first demonstration of Marconi Wireless' ability to aid victims of disasters at sea, and it manifestly validated the worth of the new technology. However, it would be another three years before the United States would require passenger ships to carry wireless. It is interesting to note that the other operator at Nantucket was a recent trainee of Marconi's, named David Sarnoff, who went on to become the president of the Radio Corporation of America (RCA), which later absorbed the American Marconi Company.

The distress signal reached many nearby ships, which proceeded to the collision destination but were similarly impeded by the prevailing fog. Because the *Republic* was listing so dangerously, it was decided to take its passengers off and put them on the intact *Florida*, a laborious task of filling up lifeboats amidst driving rain, fog, and cold. Once it was discovered that the rescued passengers were Americans, in a gesture of gratitude and amity, Italian refugee immigrants from Messina gave up their cabins to accommodate them. There was additional irony in the episode: Americans had come to the help Italians, and it was the wireless invention of Italian Guglielmo Marconi that was vital to the rescue of many Americans. The *Florida–Republic* collision was a point of reference three years later when the *Titanic* met her watery grave. Ironically, the success in saving lives in the 1909 wreck—an early instance in which the wireless technology was used to summon assistance—may have led to some complacency since the only *Florida–Republic* casualties were six people killed on impact, yet all the other passengers were saved. It may have led to thinking that ocean liners could skimp on available lifeboats because the wireless would bring almost instant help. In a further irony, Binns was offered a position as wireless operator on the *Titanic*, an offer he rejected in order to get married. A final postscript revolves around the ongoing rumor, an unconfirmed report, that large sums of money—including millions of dollars in gold bars—were on board the *Republic*, intended for the Italian earthquake sufferers. Further speculation had it that it may have been one of reasons the captain of *Republic* remained on his ship.[38]

Due to the terrible weather conditions, it would take some hours before other rescue vessels could render assistance. The *Florida*, now with a complement of 2,000 passengers, began to move away from the unfortunate *Republic*, which had been abandoned—except for a few hardy souls, including Captain Sealby and Jack Binns, who hoped to keep her afloat until other vessels could help tow her into port. Alas, the *Republic* was so severely damaged that it soon became evident that they too must abandon ship and gain refuge on the *SS Baltic*, which came in response to Binns' distress call. "I looked out the cabin. There was the *Baltic* coming up right alongside of us," recalled Binns, who also described the transfer of 1,600 passengers, "this time from the *Florida* to the *Baltic*. It took eighty-three boat loads in a driving rain and choppy seas to complete the evacuation, and this accomplishment became the largest transfer on the high seas without the loss of a single life."[39] Meanwhile, the overloaded *Florida* was able to transfer over 1,600 people to *SS Baltic*, which had come upon the scene, and on January 24, both ships left for New York with their passengers. There had been no panic by passengers on board the *Florida* until it transferred the rescued *Republic* passengers to the *Baltic*. Believing they had been left behind on a damaged ship that might sink, Italian steerage passengers became agitated. Chaos ensued as the frantic and desperate passengers, fearful for their lives, were on the verge of panic, compelling crew members to display revolvers, marlin spikes, and hard fists to maintain order.[40] In a bold move to stop spreading pandemonium, Captain Ruspini fired gunshots into the air that startled and stopped the hysterical crowd and allowed him to regain control.

Because this was the first occasion when wireless telegraphy was used to summon assistance at sea, it had consequences for the future. Binns became an instantaneous hero. A ticker-tape parade was held in his honor, and he was even offered a $1,000 contract to appear on stage to recreate his role—a proposal he rejected. His heroics were celebrated in song and in a short film. No longer simply "Jack," he was now "CQD Binns." He was besieged by many newspapers, including the *New York Times*, which paid him $250 for his firsthand account of the drama. Binns received a medal for his efforts and testified before Congress about the need for mandatory wireless coverage on ships. Enjoying a celebrity status, Binns wrote the forward for a number of juvenile adventure series of books known as *Radio Boys* and *Tom Swift*, volumes that enjoyed popularity in the 1920s.[41] Many years later, his deed on the *Republic* was acknowledged in a major television documentary.

The battered *Florida*, whose forward tip was so flattened as to be flush with the water, continued in the meantime to sail to New York carrying her Messina refugees and the bodies of three crewmen who had been killed by the maritime accident. Throngs of curious people packed the shores, lined the wharves, and perched on every vantage point as the *Florida* approached the Italian-line pier in Brooklyn accompanied by so many tugs "until her course became a triumphal progress."[42] Count di Massiglia, the Italian consul in New York, greeted Captain Ruspini effusively with a kiss on both cheeks and congratulations for brave and extraordinary seamanship. While the majority on board the *Florida* survived, sadly it did cost the lives of three Italian sailors, including fourteen-year-old cabin boy Salvatore D'Amico. His death was especially pitiful because he was a refugee also—the only survivor of a large family whose home was destroyed due to the Messina Earthquake—who had taken to the sea to escape from that scene of death.

Newspaper accounts of the ship's arrival are revealing not only because of the detailed reports of the episode, but also because of prevailing stereotypical perceptions that were perpetuated about Italians.

"At first it was difficult to make Capt. Ruspini or his officers talk. About them there is nothing of the excited, gesticulatory character that is usually associated with Italians. They walked about the bridge smiling and calm, giving the necessary orders quite like sea dogs of Anglo-Saxon extraction."[43] The *Florida*'s officers then gave accounts of rescuing passengers from the *Republic*, stressing that the transfer of people from one boat to the other over a course of three hours was accomplished without panic. "Everybody behaved admirably, those on the *Republic* as well as those on the *Florida*."[44] It was in this astonishing fashion that Messina refugees on board the *Florida* arrived shaken and unnerved to begin their American adventure. However, in reality, it was not the end of the irony and ordeal since a number of Italians were detained for a time on the Ellis Island Immigration Depot, and two of them were deported to Italy for health reasons.

ENDNOTES

1. Charles Davison, "The Messina Earthquake,"in *The World's Great Events*, vol. 9. AD 1906–1911. ed. Esther Singleton, (New York): P. F. Collier & Sons, 1916), 2809.
2. John Henry Mowbray, **Italy's Great Horror of the Earthquake and tidal Wave,** (G. W. Bertron, 1909), 40–41.
3. John Dickie, John Foot, Frank M. Snowden, "The Smell of Disaster: Scenes of Social Collapse in the Aftermath of the Messina-Reggio Calabria Earthquake, 1908," **Disastro,** (New York), 2002, 235–255, 244.
4. **Corriere della Sera,** January 29, 1909, as quoted in Dickie, **Disastro,** 241.
5. Charles Morris, **Moriss's Story of The Great Earthquake of 1908,** E.M. Sculi, 1909, 74–75.
6. Brooklyn **Eagle,** January 14, 1909. Morris, pp.101–104.
7. **Il Progresso Italo-Americano,** January 14, 1909.
8. New York **Times,** December 31, 1908.
9. **Il Telegrafo,** January 14, 1909.
10. New York **Times,** January 1, 1909.
11. Caroline Moorhead, **Iris Origo :Marchesa of Val D'Orcia,** (Boston, 2002) 15.
12. Morris, Morris's Story of the Great Earthquake, 100.
13. Howe, **Sicily in Shadow,** 53.
14. Morris, **Morris's Story,** 98.
15. Barbara Snell Dohrenwen, Life Events as Stressors: A Methodological Inquiry, **Journal of Health and Social Behavior,** Vol. 14, No. 2 (June 1973), 167–175.
16. Francis Xavier Dercum, **Hysteria and Accident Compensation.** George T. Bisel Co, Philadelphia, 1916, 66.
17. Morris, **Moriss's Story,** 83.
18. Ibid.
19. Ibid., 87.
20. New York **Times,** December 30, 1908.
21. Ibid.
22. Ibid., December 28 and 31, 1908; January 15, 1909.
23. Ibid., December 30, 1908.
24. Giorgio Boatti, **La Terra Trema,** (Milan: Mondadori, 2004, 26.
25. Brooklyn **Eagle,** January 5, 1909.

26. New York **Times**, January 1, 1909.
27. Ibid.
28. Ibid., December 31, 1908, January 2, 1909.
29. William H. Hobbs, "The Messina Earthquake," **Bulletin of the American Geological Society**, Vol. XLI, No. 7, 1909, 409–422.
30. Hobbs, "The Messina Earthquake," 409–422.
31. Frank A. Perret, "The Messina Earthquake," **The Century Magazine**, (April 1909) 921–927. Benjamin R. Southward of Brooklyn was also credited with predicting the earthquake. New York **Herald**, December30, 1908.
32. Perret, "The Messina Earthquake," 921–927.
33. **Il Telegrafo**, January 8, 1909. New York **Herald Tribune**, December 30, 1908.
34. New York **Times**, January 1, 1909.
35. Quoted in R. Snieder and T. van Eck, Earthquake Prediction: a political problem? Geologische Rundschau (**International Journal of Earth Sciences**; 1997, 86:446–463, 447.
36. New York **Sun**, January 24, 1909.
37. William Henry Flayhart III, **Disaster At Sea**, (New York, W. W. Norton Co. 2005), 207.
38. Officials of the White Star Line denied allegation that the *Republic* was transferring the money although they did acknowledge that individual passengers likely were carrying large sums for their relatives. A thorough examination of the "Relief" theory as a possible explanation for a gold cargo indicates the shipment of supplies did occur from the United States to Italy with sums generally wired to overseas banks for disbursement to various relief organizations and settled through the normal process. New York **Sun**, January 25, 1909.
39. Michael J. Tougias, **Ten Hours Until Dawn**, (New York, St. Martins Press, 2006), 175.
40. Brooklyn **Eagle**, January 25, 1909.
41. See foreward by Jack Binns in Allen Chapman, *The Radio Boys At Mountain Pass*, 1922, pages v–vi: In an effort to enthuse young amateur boys tinkering with new ideas the first chapter makes references to Marconi by one of the Radio Boys: "Marconi is one of those fellows that can never rest satisfied with what's been done up to date… . What is true of Marconi is equally true of all the others. [amateurs]."
42. New York **Times**, Jan 26, 1909.
43. Ibid.
44. Ibid.

CHAPTER 3

INITIAL RESPONSE

MORE SHOCKS

In the days immediately after the initial shock, a stunned Italy learned that the disaster had not ended: tremors and dislocations were ongoing and continued to strike terror in the hearts of people throughout the affected area. The Vicentini Seismograph, which was housed in a specially built Messina Earthquake cellar, continued to measure earth movements. It recorded that in Catania, after the initial shock, fifty more shocks were registered that first day, each one less violent than its predecessor, but nevertheless upsetting. The invariable measuring instrument recorded that in that same period, Messina sustained thirty-eight additional shocks. As late as January 2, a heavy shock in Messina caused the collapse of walls that initially had been spared, while the aftershock on January 3 was attended by worrisome volcanic activity at the site of an active volcano. Damaging wave activities that accompanied the earthquake and occurred within minutes of each other tended to vary in height, but all of them negatively impacted coastal communities along the strait. The water, furthermore, was discernible many miles away, almost up to Palermo, Sicily, in the west and measurable also northward near distant Venice. The quay in Messina that previously had been a fish market was under water, while depressions of earth along the shore gave the appearance of terraces.[1] Looming disaster seemed to be in the offing—one that called for immediate response.

THE GIOLITTI GOVERNMENT

Awareness of the acute severity of the earthquake found the government of Italy facing a bewildering undertaking—how to deal with what was the worst calamity in history—a task for which it was unprepared. Indeed, the immensity of the misfortune was so widespread and far reaching that it would be overwhelming for most major nations, let alone a newly unified country still afflicted with internal growing pains of intense regionalism. For heavily taxed poor southern Italy—where poverty was endemic, 80 percent of the people were illiterate, the populace was plagued by an inferior transportation system, and corruption flourished—the problem was simply intimidating for local governments.

Response was necessary on a national level from the government presided over by Prime Minister Giovanni Giolitti—whose skills seemed to be more predisposed to deal with a fragmented political system than such crisis. Italy's economic structure, it must be noted, was weak due to a recent recession, a number of ill-advised steps, and financial manipulations that sought to take advantage of the a precarious banking instability exacerbated by the earthquake. Giolitti did convene the emergency Council of Ministers and called for a special session of Italy's legislative branch, the Chamber of Deputies and the Senate, to deal with the crisis—this resulted, on January 12, in approval of an interim measure to raise taxes to support costs of aiding victims. One scholar argued that "Giolitti responded energetically," citing legislation of January 12, 1909, appropriating 30 million lire—later supplemented by an additional 88 million lire—for the most urgent work of reconstruction and assistance. "In the light of this program, it is clear that Giolitti did not neglect the south in his program of economic intervention, but rather accomplished a great deal to raise the standards in that region."[2] Giolitti also affirmed that speedy support for victims of the distressed area was a solemn obligation of his government. Soon, however, the usual obstacles of bureaucratic delays, confusion, disputes, and finger pointing between local and national government officials lessened the effectiveness of the prospective assistance. Unfortunately, the assistance proffered by Giolitti's administration came to be regarded as so tepid that he was blamed for the high number of deaths that occurred. Infuriated southern Italians, already inclined to believe that his government was partial to the north, now had further proof of his favoritism.[3] Giolitti was chided further when, following the earthquake, his government adopted a strict policy to prevent the return of fugitives for fear of looting, a policy so inflexible that it led to "legitimate complaints that this had prevented the rescue of many people, and even that northern insurance firms bought up individual claims to government compensation so as to gain ownership of the best street sites."[4]

Further criticism revolved around a perception of unfeeling attitudes within government circles whose concerns were prompted primarily by fears of epidemics and looting, thus leading to proposals to raze by fire or bombardment what remained of Messina. Many reached conclusions that Messina had ceased to exist; it was gone forever. Historian Giorgio Boatti cited a January 2, 1909, *La Tribune* account declaring that to prevent an epidemic, what little that was left of the few remaining houses and buildings would need to be totally destroyed as the only way to prevent the spread of infection.[5] The putative plan called for deporting survivors and then bombing the city. To that end, a royal decree of January 4, 1909, asserted that the affected area was in a state of siege and that the military, under the command of General Mazza, had full powers to deal with the emergency. Mazza was depicted as an officious individual whose disdain for victims and survivors was reflected in his assumption of his assignment by remaining aboard a luxury ship while ordering his troops to shoot anyone on the outside near Messina without permit. Even Mazza's surname, "the Sledgehammer," was menacingly suggestive. To force evacuation, military authorities were ordered to suspend food distribution—making it available onboard ships, only to refugees who agreed to leave the city. This step was denounced as a cynical effort to use weapons of hunger and thirst to impose a government determination to deny Messina official approval for habitation. The grieving Messinese protested these government moves as extremely abhorrent and odious steps, especially since some of those buried under the rubble were found alive days after the earthquake and there remained the likelihood of additional people alive in the rubble.

THE ROYAL FAMILY

The response of Italy's monarchs was another story—a much more positive chronicle. Thirty-eight-year-old King Victor Emmanuel III, who was short in stature—hardly more than five feet four inches tall—and who sported sandy, crew-cut hair, was a descendant of the Royal House of (Savoie) Savoy that had ruled Sardinia, Savoy, and Piedmont of Italy for 1,000 years, and had united Italy beginning in 1861. Educated largely along military lines, he was highly cultivated, well informed, and receptive to new ideas. Brisk and vigorous in behavior, he endeared himself to his people by abstaining from pomp and ceremony, and he was ready to act. Upon learning about the horrific earthquake, on December 29, he immediately determined that he and the queen would go to the stricken area to oversee aid efforts and give encouragement to the unfortunate victims. Thirty-four-year-old Queen Elena (Jelena Petrovich Njegosh) was an extraordinary Italian monarch in that she was not of Italian birth but rather was the daughter of the future Montenegrin king who had studied at St. Petersburg, Russia, and had published poetry. Her marriage to Emmanuel was considered a move to further Italian relations with the Slav world. A beautiful woman nearly six feet tall, it was an incongruous sight to see her tower over her diminutive husband. Indeed, the feeling that her height would balance out the unimpressive stature of Victor Emmanuel was one of the motives that prompted Italian officials to make the match. She had innate good sense and, like her husband, preferred simplicity rather than ostentatious ways. An Orthodox Christian, she agreed to abjure her religion in order to marry a Catholic prince in the Church of Santa Maria degli Angeli, Rome. In 1900, upon the assassination of the beloved King Humbert, his son Vittorio Emanuele ascended to the Italian throne and Jelena was made Queen Elena of Italy, Queen of Albania, and Empress of Ethiopia. Despite the arranged marriage, king and queen got along quite well and had five children.

On Wednesday, December 30, the king and queen of Italy sailed through the strait and into the Messina Harbor. As their ship, the *Vittorio Emanuele*, approached the Faro, the gunners of the Russian cruisers, the English men-of-war, and the Italian battleships began to fire the royal salute. Immediately, the king signaled the ships to cease the greeting since this was no time for celebratory royal salvos. Sailing first to Naples, they proceeded to Messina on the battleship *Napoli*; advancing cautiously, they arrived on December 30 carrying medical supplies along with words of comfort. In the face of the menace of pestilence, the king also ordered a supply of the sinister commodity quicklime to cover the enormous numbers of decaying corpses and thereby prevent disease from spreading. Apparently, many soldiers and sailors, who had worked with singular devotion, died from gangrene caused by handling the decomposing bodies. Among government officials accompanying them were the army chief of staff, the maritime minister, Minister of Justice Orlando, and Minister of Public Works Piero Bertolini. These officials began to deploy army units and to direct nearby passenger ships to join in the rescue efforts. Warships and transport vessels now converted their ships into hospitals, loaded the wounded, and then shuttled back and forth to Naples and other coastal cities both to transfer the injured and to transport troops and police to the earthquake site. In what was an eerie sight, vessels that arrived at night used the ongoing fires that illuminated Messina to guide them into port. Representatives from the Italian national government quickly became more aware of the gravity of the situation. Virtually the entire infrastructure of Messina and surrounding towns had disappeared with the death or injury of local administrative officials, community police, and soldiers stationed in the vicinity.

The city lost the custom house, the railway station, the Bank of Italy, and even the local prison, which led to the escape of many desperadoes. "Not a single official or public functionary remains in the streets."[6]

THE ITALIAN MILITARY

Italian naval officers assumed temporary command of the stricken area to conduct rescue efforts, including deploying sailors to establish a field house for the injured and bringing the most seriously hurt onto ships. Sailors likewise teamed up with *bersaglieri* (elite military force) and *carabinieri* (police) in organized patrols to provide public safety. Press reports informed the citizenry of the efforts of the combined forces working in collapsed districts amidst the rubble of houses, destroyed hospitals, and military barracks. Readers learned that entire families, numerous municipal officials, law enforcement officials, and soldiers stationed in Reggio and Messina were missing and presumed dead.

A curious case of telepathy occurred when a crewman on board a rescue vessel, the battleship *Regina Elena*, obtained permission to search in Messina for his fiancée whom he was to marry shortly. Returning in vain after an exhausting search of four days, he fell into a deep sleep in his ship hammock but awoke with a startling dream that his fiancée had called to him that she was still alive and pleaded with him to come and save her. Receiving permission from obliging ship officers, he once again went to the spot designated in the dream—a partially ruined house—and indeed found her alive and uninjured.[7]

QUEEN ELENA

The presence of the king and queen in the middle of the detritus of the earthquake was a tremendous morale booster in southern Italy and beyond. Accustomed to being overlooked by unresponsive governments, the afflicted people could not help but be impressed by the caring royal family. The solicitation and genuineness of the beautiful Queen Elena made an astounding impact. It was indeed a reflection of a woman whose head had not been turned as a result of the luxury of the Italian court. From the outset, she led a quiet and exemplary life and eschewed celebrations and secular matters, preferring instead to immerse herself in humanitarian work. She devoted her whole life to charitable work and maintained an equitable disposition that was brought to bear among the debris and on behalf of the wounded in the devastated city. Her corporal works of mercy elicited such warm praise and gratitude that the Sicilian city built a monument in her honor even during her lifetime.

Survivors were heartened by the visit of their monarchs—who, notwithstanding their royal bearing, hurried to the ghastly sights of the earthquake, coming not merely as ornaments, but to direct and to be of use to their subjects. People saw them distributing food, drink, and clothing to untold numbers of sufferers, and tending the wounded with their own hands. They saw their king join a rescue party, laboring with them unremittingly to personally extricate several people pinned underneath ruins. They likewise deeply appreciated their monarchs who listened sympathetically to their terrible stories of the ordeal. Overcoming her initial fear of the sickening sights, the queen helped to rescue a bleeding three-year-old boy with her own hands, carrying him to the pier where he was turned over to medical personnel. This display of genuine personal concern could not help but win people's hearts. Overcome with emotion at the sight of their beloved monarchs amongst them, they openly wept copious tears of joy and were ready to carry them in their arms.

Queen Elena proved herself to be a compassionate and sensitive woman, one who wholeheartedly sought to succor the victims. Even though she looked far from well and was visibly exhausted, she did not hesitate to become personally involved using her own handkerchiefs to bind up wounds of the victims, and to weep with them when they wept. That her sympathy was genuine was evident in an incident that took place in an impoverished hospital where a wounded and distracted woman she was attending to sprang up and ran into her, causing her mouth to bleed. The next day, the queen returned to the hospital to continue her work. In addition to personal visits, Italy's monarchs set aside a portion of their royal residence, the Quirinal Palace, which they converted into a workshop where the queen supervised making clothes for refugees. Queen Elena's generosity was also manifest in her gesture of donating the very rings on her fingers to sell to raise funds for victims.

The testimony of English Ambassador James Rennell Rodd attests to the bravery of Queen Elena who, in the face of witnessing the terrible condition of the injured and maimed rescued from the ruins, did what she could to alleviate the sufferers. Although unnerved,

> the Queen told me afterwards, very trying to the nerves, but she added, "one does somehow what one has to do." A little episode which was told me by one of the Court ladies impressed me. An unfortunate old woman crushed beyond recovery and evidently dying, was carried in. Her only thought was for a priest to shrive her, and no priest could be found. Her pitiful cries disturbed the other patients, and the Queen came to her and took her hand and said in a quiet voice: "I am the Queen of Italy, and I tell you that you need have no fear." Thus reassured she ceased to cry, and not long after died in peace.[8]

The queen's courageous demeanor helped persuade embassy wives—such as Lady Rodd, wife of the British ambassador—to form committees to join in and help Messina Earthquake victims.

It is not surprising, therefore, to find that Italy's king and queen became much beloved monarchs in Italy and beyond. Newspapers cited them as perhaps the most cherished royal family in the world. The esteem with which the king was held is reflected in the title "Il Galantuomo." By the mid-1920s, the king was so popular worldwide that his picture graced the cover of influential *Time Magazine*. It is indeed ironic to note that attitudes toward them would change a generation later in the face of acquiescence to the emerging Fascist dictatorship of Benito Mussolini and the costly wars that led to the end of the Italian monarchy.

ITALIAN CIVILIANS RESPOND

Towns proximate to the natural disaster were understandably affected within days, if for no other reason than the fact that it was to these locations that many thousands fled the earthquake scene with virtually little or no clothing and with no money. It would take the combined efforts of national and local officials, church leaders, foreigners, and regular Italian citizens to ameliorate conditions of despair, as well as to tend to the physical requirements of the sick and wounded. Between December 31 and the Feast of the Epiphany (January 6), townspeople from all over the Italian peninsula engaged in relief activities on behalf of earthquake victims.

All along the roads of the peninsula could be seen carts full of supplies for the victims. There also were numerous Italian volunteers who flocked to the affected area to administer relief. Of particular interest is the story of one of them, Joseph Micheli, a Catholic deputy from Parma who was entrusted with funds to distribute in Messina. He arrived in Messina a few days after the earthquake and immediately put in place, with the help of Archbishop Letterio D'Arrigo, a Messina rescue committee that was in many ways more efficient than government operations. Dickie portrayed this as "a striking experiment in cohabitation between the central state authorities and Catholic charity."[9] Another figure that emerges is that of the Socialist mayor of Catania, Giuseppe De Felice Giuffrida, whose years of experience in developing collective systems rendered him capable of organizing the political and administrative organs for the distribution of public services.[10] This background proved of great value in the distribution of food to earthquake survivors. The picture that emerges is one of a nation, historically divided over one question or another, now coming together in support of unfortunate Italian victims. It was a unique moment of postdisaster solidarity—a cohesion that contradicts the prevailing view of divergence within the nation. "In other words widespread patriotism is not incompatible with the profound social disunity that is one of the great themes of the historiography of this period," explained Dickie.[11]

KATHARINE DAVIS

Writing in the last days of February and the beginning of March 1909, Katharine Bement Davis left a vivid and informative firsthand account of how the Sicilian city of Syracuse dealt with 4,000 refugees. Davis, a highly educated and well-known figure in the American prison reform movement, happened to be on a six-month leave in Sicily when the earthquake struck, but, unlike most vacationers who packed their bags and fled, Davis did just the opposite. She unpacked all her garments that could be ripped into bandages, rushed with them to the nearest medical facility, and began helping the injured people who were brought in or straggled in from devastated areas. Besides her hospital work, Davis addressed social problems on the streets where hundreds of quake refugees wandered about homeless and shoeless, with little clothing, no work, and less hope. She persuaded Mayor Gaetano D'Arrigo, brother of the archbishop, to open a vacant building and supply sewing machines where homeless women were hired to sew simple clothing for themselves and other refugees. She organized a group of cobblers to make shoes, paying modest salaries out of pocket to seamstresses and shoemakers. She also set up work gangs for adult male refugees, repairing and building roads and simple houses. These activities not only provided emergency items but also gave people something constructive to do. Not only were clothes, shoes, shelter, and roads needed on an emergency basis, but also the enterprise of manufacturing these items gave quake victims a needed purposeful activity to do—important antidotes to counter paralyzing depression and loss of income.

The acquiescence of Messina's mayor D'Arrigo to Davis' direction is a reflection of the pathetic behavior of the city administration in the grave crisis. Overwhelmed, the disappointing mayor virtually turned over his office quarters to her while he and other officials held in awe this little lady who one minute could supervise assembly-line sewing and the next minute direct mixing concrete, who could organize into self-help the people of a land and language other than her own, and who brought them back to life from the listlessness into which disaster had stunned them.

Davis was then asked to represent the American Red Cross and initiate relief efforts. In accepting the assignment, Davis located a small

American flag that she displayed prominently in her office. From this perspective, she was able to describe the impact of so many newcomers upon Ortygia, located within the historic center in Syracuse, where 39,000 people lived within the confines of a hermetically sealed society in which women did not go out unattended and were unused to cooperative activities. Ortygia "had no residents of large wealth and many who are very poor. Until December 28, 1908, probably not a person it the city, from the prefect and the mayor down, had ever had the smallest experience in organized relief work."[12] Traditionally, philanthropy in Italy—as in most European societies—was the preserve of the nobility and the aristocracy; it was understood that they were expected to manifest their benevolence on various occasions and at times of serious danger. Consequently, aside from the church and religious orders, ordinary townspeople had little practical experience in voluntary relief organizations. Both the role of the aristocracy and the few volunteer organizations would now be tested in the face of the huge calamity.

Commencing on December 29, the city was faced with the challenge of how to deal with the influx of thousands of refugees, many of whom were so seriously injured as to require immediate medical attention, a situation rendered all the more serious since all were exposed, hungry, and cold. English and Russians ships, for instance, brought in boatloads of refugees from the ruins of Messina, "the last shipment composed largely of persons who had been under the ruins five days. Death was merciful to most of these."[13] Extant hospital facilities usually were in very old buildings. In one instance, the hospital was a former convent where sisters nursed perhaps a dozen people a year, but was now overflowing with over 200 people. Another makeshift hospital—which was set up in Archbishop D'Arrigo's palace and in the theological study rooms vacated by students who were sent home—accommodated 200 more. A chapel was converted to a supply room, and even an altar was used for serving. Many of those more seriously in need of care went to small, private sickbays or military hospitals. Soldiers' military barracks were transformed into infant care facilities. Compounding the problems was the virtual absence of nurses in Syracuse, although Katharine Davis was able to identify one, an English woman who herself was a Messina refugee. Faced with the seeming hopelessness and despondency in the faces of the survivors, Siracusani, as well as those from small towns nearby, pitched in to do what they could.

> Physicians came in from the little towns of the neighborhood and gentlemen of the town took off their coats, put on aprons and acted as assistants. Every one of them worked day and night and did his very best with a devotion that could not be surpassed. But most of what we at home have learned to think of as essential was lacking and in the first days I said to myself many times: "If any of these patients live I shall always believe septic surgery a fad."[14]

Besides taking care of the grievously wounded, the plight of an unprecedented number of children orphaned by the catastrophe became a priority for private charitable organizations both within and without Italy. The needs of 127 orphans and almost as many half orphans among refugees in Syracuse were met partially by a local committee headed by Marquesa di Rudini, under the aegis of Queen Elena, by housing many of them in a building on the outskirts of town. Davis' positive assessment of this effort notwithstanding, other professionals in the field of charity criticized the steps for paying "too little attention to Italian tastes and customs. But the chief criticism of the extensive field relief activities of Americans in Sicily and Southern Italy was that in maintaining a secular policy in the orphan asylums that were established, Catholic sensibilities were disregarded."[15]

Because American interreligious relations were still adjusting to the influx of large numbers of new Catholic immigrants, it is interesting to speculate whether the charitable-works approach of Davis and her ilk reflected a prevailing Anglo-Saxon attitude that characterized the period—one that subscribed to an enlightened liberal Protestantism vis-à-vis a presumed superstition-laden Catholicism. Be that as it may, Pope Pius X personally thanked Davis for her extraordinary efforts. As the son of a cobbler, the pope could appreciate the wisdom of her decision to include shoemaking among the relief industries she set up with and for the quake victims. Other honors conferred on Davis came from King Victor Emmanuel and the Italian Red Cross.[16] Katherine Davis was truly a remarkable woman, one who was faced with some of the most dreaded consequences normally faced in time of war: grievous wounds, horrible mutilations, and despair—the kinds of tragedies that would crush even the bravest. One of the most heartbreaking cases in which she was involved was that of an Englishwoman who had to have both of her legs amputated. The earthquake had already killed the woman's husband, two children, a brother, and a sister.[17]

When it was time for Davis to leave, she delayed until she had arranged for the relief and recovery operation to continue after her return to the United States. Before Davis left Italy, she was honored with an invitation to a rare private audience in the Vatican. In advance of the audience, she went to a beautician who insisted Katharine's hair be "marcelled"—despite objections from Davis, who never had her hair done in that wavy style. In writing years later about her special interview with Pope Pius X, she recalled the big fuss in the beauty parlor about that once-in-a-lifetime marcel wave that she hoped the pope would notice under her black lace scarf when she knelt down to kiss his ring. Back home, President Taft acknowledged her remarkable earthquake relief labors in a special presentation.

The Messina legacy continued to be associated with Davis, as could be seen in 1914 when she was appointed the first woman corrections commissioner in New York City. Because of the large number of Italian immigrants in the city prisons, her extensive background with Italians—especially Sicilians—apparently figured prominently in her selection for the job. In one instance, an Italian prisoner—a woman whom Davis befriended and helped rehabilitate—returned to Messina to care for children of relatives who had been killed in the earthquake upon completing her sentence.[18]

ALICE FITZGERALD

Alice Fitzgerald, an American nurse who had been educated at Johns Hopkins Hospital School of Nursing, Baltimore, was visiting her parents in Italy when the devastating earthquake struck. When Fitzgerald offered her services to the Italian Red Cross, she was sent to Naples to help care for the victims, where her knowledge of Italian, French, and English made her indispensable to the staff members at the hospital, as well as to the patients. Fitzgerald served with the Italian Red Cross until the need for acute care subsided. She then returned to her parents' home where she received a medal from the Italian Red Cross for her work with the earthquake victims. The next year, Fitzgerald returned to the United States and began working at various times in the Johns Hopkins and Bellevue Hospital, where she reorganized operating nursing service.[19]

AN AMERICAN IN NAPLES

That the enormity of the task before those striving to help the unfortunate refugees was overwhelming is clearly reflected in the following account of Mrs. C. F. Powers, an American in Naples at the time:

> What fearful things have happened here! We are in the midst of such suffering and want. We go daily to the hospital Maria Jesu to wash and comb and feed the poor creatures who are brought here by the hundreds from Messina. All hospitals will soon be full, and most of them are now. The unhurt natives are in the schools, sleeping on straw. This morning we were working over them. The women seem to have suffered the most and have their hair and ears full of mud and stones and blood. Those who are not badly wounded may have their hair combed and we are sent to do this. This hospital, having no English nurse at its head, is a poor, comfortless place. Among the visitors here is one woman who had lain one and a half days in a room under the debris with her two boys, one six and the other ten years old almost dead. She and her husband were saved. She was badly cut and bruised, but remains quiet and uncomplaining.[20]

AN AMERICAN IN TAORMINA

Because it was not too distant from the Messina epicenter, there naturally was concern about the earth's upheaval in Taormina. Providentially, although people experienced the sound and fury of the seismic clash—witnessing a wide circle of whitish-yellow light that stayed in one place in the bay, as well as waves breaking on the shore—basically, they were spared. A perceptive and articulate Bostonian then visiting the city left a vivid description of its impact upon the minds and emotions of townspeople.

> In no time the poor *contadini* were coming out of their houses over on the hills with their lanterns; they looked like Will o' the wisps; they were hurrying over to the town for protection. The big quaking lasted forty seconds, but we had small ones all day. The town was in a panic; men, women, and children ran out into the streets without anything on, or trying to struggle into their clothes. Some of their shirts were upside down; all were screaming with fright.[21]

As in ages past, when confronted with crises of nature that seemed overwhelming, they fell back on their religious foundations. People crowded into the city's many churches from which they formed processions that marched down narrow streets.

> First came the *Misericordia*, dressed in white with red shoulder capes carrying lighted candles. On a *paso* was San Pancrazio dressed as a bishop, with two rows of candles burning before him. As soon as they were in sight of the sea they stopped and cried out a prayer and waved their hands towards the sea; they went on again to the end of the street, waving towards Etna standing against the blue sky like a great white pyramid with a mass of new fallen snow on the summit. It was glorious. The band was playing a slow muffled march, the other instruments stopping while the muffled drum carried on the time with slow steady taps. Before San Pancrazio walked the Archpriest with his two assistants carrying lighted candles, then came the great crowd of men, women and children, the white Carmelite nuns, and the yellow and red handkerchiefs of the peasants were all so terrified and earnest looking! They took San Pancrazio from his own church to the cathedral to wait and protect them for a while until Saint Peter could be brought to join him.[22]

THE ARISTOCRACY

Those who administered corporal works of mercy included many prominent and titled people of means who historically had been expected to render charity to the less fortunate. Madame Bonnano, Marchesa Dora di Rudini (a British woman who was the wife of a former Italian prime minister), and Baronessa del Bosca (the daughter of the Italian ambassador to England) were among those active in this endeavor in Syracuse, as was Mayor Toscano. He was tireless in his efforts to help victims and did not use his office for personal gain in an era and an area where mayors were notorious for their use of nepotism and their enjoyment of personal perquisites. As one historian explained, "[A]fter the Messina Earthquake, some of the relief money disappeared (the ruins were still there in 1940), and accusations were made that too much money was diverted to rebuilding the houses of the rich."[23]

NAPLES

Because all Sicilian hospital facilities were overwhelmed, 50,000 earthquake victims poured into Naples two days after the quake. All social functions in the city were suspended in order to deal with the emergency. Among the first arrivals of 800 brought in by a German steamer were many in pitiful condition with heads or limbs bandaged, while others had not yet received any medical attention. Regular medical facilities in Naples were rapidly overextended, leading to appeals to Neapolitans to give hospitality to the wounded. Public cabs, hotel and railway omnibuses, and other means of public conveyances were requisitioned, while private citizens loaned their automobiles and carriages to move the refugees from the harbor to hospitals and infirmaries. Survivors were dazed, confused, and stupefied. Their world had come to an end, and they were strangers in a strange place. On the pier, they sat in isolated groups, giving signs of mental depressions and, of course, physical exhaustion. Poignancy, emotionalism, and misfortune were characteristic of the stories they told: an old man carrying close to his breast a bleeding child he found on the pavement, the plaintive calls of mothers for missing children, the sole family survivor wishing he had not been spared—then, miraculously, one of the rescued women gave birth to a child on board the rescue boat. Going out to succor and comfort the afflicted were Neapolitan aristocrats like the Duchess of Aosta who took three orphans into her palace.

PALERMO

Interestingly, the sharp shock of Messina's earthquake was hardly felt in Palermo, only 125 miles away, where most inhabitants slept through the morning of December 28. Fourteen years old at the time, Maria Madonia, who lived in a small town bereft of electricity near Palermo, recalled that there was a commotion in village streets, undoubtedly caused by earthquake news that spread by word of mouth. This observation received confirmation from veteran journalists such as Giovanni Ponticelli, of the *Journal of Sicily*, who was in Palermo at the time: "What I considered most remarkable was the fact that the City of Palermo was not aware of the extent of the disaster until twenty-four hours after Messina was destroyed, and this despite the fact that the two cities are only a few hours apart by rail."[24]

It was to Sicily's capital that many had fled either to board ships for America or elsewhere, or to find immediate shelter. One example of the latter was the resolve on the part of Palermo's university professors and teachers to adopt the children orphaned when the earthquake caused the death of most Messina University professors. Although some families were able to take them into their own homes, there were more than sixty others who were cared for in Collegio per Orphani di Maestri in Sicilia, a new orphanage housed in Palermo. Led by Ambassador Griscom who gave $200, other Americans contributed to the cause.

Not infrequently, tragedy is accompanied by additional mockery, as in the case of two families that had left New York on the *SS San Giovanni* and arrived at Messina on December 31, 1908. Giovanna Rizza Argento and her four children, along with Antonia Bertini Sorrentino and her three children, had crossed the ocean to see their families in Sicily only to be frustrated by the ruinous earthquake that had occurred while they were crossing the ocean—authorities refused to allow them to land. Once the travelers learned of the extent of the punishing earthquake, they became frantic in the realization that their relatives at Messina—they very ones they had set out to visit—were likely all killed. Moreover, as poor people, they had come expecting to live with their families, so now their sorrow was compounded because they were destitute and understandably agitated. Fortunately, the steamship owners agreed to return them to New York at their own expense.

Another instance of delayed news involved the *Germania*, a Fabre Line steamer that left Naples on December 23, five days before the earthquake, and after a rough ocean voyage, arrived in New York on January 7 with 194 steerage passengers, many from Sicily. Passengers did not learn of the catastrophe until the ship had docked and was in quarantine. When they became aware of the horror of the land they had just left, they became terrified. Francisco Valesca, who had left his wife and three children in Messina, was so completely distraught and frantic that he lost control and fell to the deck, weeping and calling upon the saints to save his family. Still others crowded about, seeking details of the disaster and becoming increasingly morose—it took some time to quiet sorrowful passengers before they disembarked.

THE CHURCH

In addition to the Italian government, religion was also to play a meaningful part in aid of the Messina Earthquake survivors. Heading the Catholic Church was Giuseppe Sarto who, born of humble circumstances, became Pope Pius X in 1903 and initially maintained his "prisoner in the Vatican" stance, as had his predecessors since 1870. Harboring a personal distaste for politics, his relations with the Italian government remained uneasy as he continued to denounce the government for usurping church lands and interfering with papal authority. His refusal to accept Italy's annexation of the papal territories and his insistence that other nations respect papal sovereignty led to strained relations. The pontificate of Pius X, while noted for its conservative theology, also promoted reforms in liturgy and church law. With the rise of Socialism, Pius X began to relax some church policies and allowed Catholics to vote and thereby participate in Italian electoral politics—a major reversal of earlier policy. Ever mindful of his humble origin, Pius X was embarrassed by much of the pomp of the papal court; he was a pastoral pope primarily concerned with children's communion and liturgy, as well as the reorganization of seminaries. He was canonized a saint in 1954.

Upon hearing the news of the scourge afflicting Messina, the seventy-three-year-old pope became greatly distressed and could hardly believe dispatches describing the enormous devastation. He was deeply affected: he shed many tears thinking about the victims, suspended all audiences, knelt in fervent prayer, and, declaring that his place was amidst his suffering people, gave instructions to begin the journey to the earthquake scene. However, his physician and those who attended him in the Vatican insisted that he not go, owing to certainty of a fatiguing expedition for one his age who was not in the best of health. There was also a suggestion that the self-imposed "prisoner of the Vatican" position would have made such a trip awkward.[25]

Although he did not go in person to the earthquake area, the pope did what he could to ease suffering by providing the use of the Vatican's commodious hospital facilities, offering one of the largest donations for earthquake survivors, pleading with Catholics throughout the world to contribute to fundraising efforts on behalf of the survivors, and personally appealing to priests and bishops to alleviate the victims' suffering. The latter admonition bore fruit remarkably in Catania, where Cardinal Francisca Nava served as archbishop and where a *New York Times* reporter came upon the churchman who was extremely busy directing his diocese's work in caring for survivors. Appearing depressed and obviously overworked, he was nevertheless courteous and understanding as he tearfully answered the queries of anxious Americans who were solicitous about relatives.

Unfortunately I have little comfort for them. There is no exaggeration in the accounts sent from here. From what we know the loss of life at Pompeii and Herculaneum were surpassed by those of this week...All Catholics applaud the initiative of King Victor and Queen Helena, who came to aid us personally. I wish to add my testimony that their presence has had the most beneficent effect in calming the excitement and encouraging the rescuers... Although many of the survivors have come under my personal observation, I have not yet seen an entire family saved. Invariably one or more members were lost.

The Holy Father has been most lavish in his instructions to see that funds were not entirely lacking. The question now is to organize our effort in some way to reach the most needy.[26]

While the interview was underway, an additional influx of refugees from Messina arrived that required Cardinal Nava's personal and immediate attention and effectively terminated the interview.

Pope Pius X sheltered earthquake victims at his own expense in the hospice of Santa Maria, near St. Peter's. The Catholic Knights of Malta order joined the effort by deploying a hospital train that brought dozens of injured to the Vatican Hospital—a work that won warm praise from the pope. The pontiff also sent a relief commission to the devastated region including two Catholic priests who worked indefatigably to help victims. They were Fr. Don Orione, born in Piedmont, northern Italy, and Fr. Annibale Maria Di Francia, born into a family of Sicilian aristocrats. The clergy of eastern Sicily had been decimated and demoralized by the magnitude of the catastrophe, causing the archbishop of Messina to ask the pope to appoint a vicar general from outside the diocese. In response, Pope Pius X named Father Orione the vicar general of the archdiocese of Messina, a step that was fraught with tension given the suspicions and frictions revolving around traditional north–south animosities. However, by his unswerving loyalty to the holy father and by his personal solicitation and extension of charity while visiting the ruins of Avignone, one of the most heavily damaged areas of Messina, Fr. Orione soon won over Sicilian earthquake victims.

Fr. Di Francia had come to that poor neighborhood years before, after meeting a poor blind beggar, Francesco Zancone, who led him to discover a world unknown to him: the world of *le case Avignone* (the Avignone squatters). It was to be his new field of apostolate and the beginning of a long journey of love and sacrifices for the poor, the orphans, and now the earthquake survivors. It was while Fr. Orione worked to help reconstruct the city from rubble and ashes that he met Fr. Annibale and was immediately impressed by the Sicilian priest's personality and holiness.

The plight of the most vulnerable in society—the many who were orphaned by the earthquake—was a major worry of Fr. Orione who became concerned that these young victims who, having already lost their parents, ought not be in danger of losing their historic faith. Given the prevailing atmosphere of delicate, if not strained, relations between the Italian government and the Catholic Church, there was concern that orphan supervision might be placed in the hands of antireligious officials already well represented in Patronato Regina's orphan committee, headed by Countess Gabriella Spalletti, a prominent member of the nobility who, it was incorrectly feared, was anticlerical. Utilizing his contacts, Orione was named to the Villaggio Regina Elena's orphanage committee whereupon he began establishing a good working relationship with the countess that enabled him to start taking care of dozens of parentless children.[27] The queen, furthermore, encouraged him in his work and supplied him with beds for the victims—estimable actions that earned the priest's gratitude. Don Orione then effectively organized relief efforts for orphans and the homeless, a work the Italian government cited in honoring him for his service with a gold medal. In addition, as a token of gratitude, the pope gave Fr. Orione's community a house outside of Rome, the "Colonia Santa Maria," to use as an orphanage. In sum, Fr. Orione's charity toward all—even those who were resentful and hostile—served to endear him to people caught up in the chaotic situation.

While in Messina, the two priests met frequently and often spent nights in the slums where they brought aid to the destitute. Father Di Francia publicly proclaimed his people's appreciation for the "great protection and affection" of the northern Italian priest while also providing him with money to promote his work. For his part, Fr. Orione reminded the Messinese people that in Fr. Di Francia they had a saint in their midst. Both priests led exemplary lives and, in subsequent years, founded religious congregations—the Little Work of Divine Providence (Fr. Orione) and Daughters of Divine Zeal and the Rogationists (Fr. Di Francia)—that became noted for charitable endeavors and vast works of social promotion on behalf of the poor, abandoned, and neglected. Despite Don Orione's enormous efforts to rebuild the city, his presence as a northerner was held against him, leading him to leave a few years later to serve his ministry in another Italian region.[28] The heroic work of these two priests in Messina, and their exemplary lives over the decades that helped bridge solidarity between north and south, led the Catholic Church to canonize them as saints in 2004.

IMMEDIATE PESSIMISTIC ANALYSIS

There were many dire interpretations as to the meaning of the catastrophe. Bologna's newspaper *Resto del Carlino*, preoccupied with the tormenting nature of the catastrophe, described the extraordinary Italian reaction of grief and solidarity that followed almost immediately.

> The anguish of a nightmare bears down on our brains and consternation assaults our fundamental mental faculties. We almost seem to be writhing in the throes of a horrendous dream. A single, identical shudder of pain is crushing the spirits of more than million individuals. It is Italy's soul that is weeping for the loss of two of its most beautiful cities, of so many villages, for the death of so many of her sons.
>
> These extremely widespread manifestations of patriotism in a country that is frequently thought to lack national identity give cause on the way the notion of national identity in the Italian context and beyond.[29]

The Austrian scientist Eduard Suess, president of the Academy of Sciences, analyzed the event as a breakage of the earth along a curved line stretching from Catanzaro toward Mt. Etna, then westward. He predicted that the Lipari Islands in the center of this curve were sinking and that when that happened, it would widen the Strait of Messina, leading eventually to the engulfment under water of that city. He then reached a strange conclusion: "We are witnessing the collapse of the territorial globe that began long ago. The shortness of life of the human race allows us, nevertheless, to be of good cheer."[30] Still another scientist of seismic activities interpreted the earthquake as proof that Italy was sinking.

ENDNOTES

1. Hobbs, "The Messina Earthquake," 409–422; *Il Progresso Italo-Americano*, December 30, 1908.
2. Frank J. Coppa, "Economic and Ethical Liberalism in Conflict: The Extraordinary Liberalism of Giovanni Giolitti," *The Journal of Modern History* 42, no. 2 (June 1970): 191–215.
3. Dennis Mack Smith, *Modern Italy* (Ann Arbor: University of Michigan Press, 1968), 211.
4. Smith, *Modern Italy*, 211.
5. Boatti, *La Terra Trema*, 118–122, is critical of the government plan, maintaining that artillery were not the way to get rid of germs.
6. *New York Times*, December 31, 1908.
7. Ibid., January 7, 1909.
8. James Rennell Rodd, *Social and Diplomatic Memories, 1902–1919* (London: Edward A. Arnold & Co., 1925), 103–104.
9. Dickie, *Disastro*, 25.
10. Boatti, 203–204, 263–268.
11. Dickie, "Timing, Memory and Disaster: Patriotic Narratives in the Aftermath of the Messina-Reggio Calabria Earthquake, 28 December 1908," *Modern Italy* 11, no. 2 (June 2006): 147–166.
12. Katharine Bement Davis, "Relief Work for the Messina Refugees in Syracuse," *The Survey*, April 3, 1909, 37–47. *See esp.* p. 37.
13. Davis, "Relief Work for the Messina Refugees in Syracuse," 38–39.
14. Ibid.; see esp. *39.*
15. Merle Curti, *American Philanthropy Abroad* (New Brunswick: Rutgers University Press, 1963), 221–222. See also Dickie, *Disastro*, 25.
16. Mrs. John A. Logan, *The Part Taken by Women in American History* (Wilmington: The Perry-Nalle Publishing Co., 1912), 538.
17. Mabel T. Boardman, *Under the Red Cross Flag* (Philadelphia: J. B. Lippincott, 1915), 195.
18. *New York Times*, January 11, 1914.
19. Fitzgerald received the Florence Nightingale award for her work in Messina. Alice Fitzgerald, "My Experiences in Naples after the Messina Disaster," *American Journal of Nursing* 9, no. 7 (April 1909): 482–492; "Department of Red Cross Nursing," *The American Journal of Nursing* 27, no. 11 (November 1927): 965–968.

20. Morris, *Morriss's*, 97–98.
21. Howe, *Sicily* in Shadow, 67.
22. Ibid., 67–68.
23. Smith, *Modern Italy*, 212.
24. *New York Times*, January 20, 1909.
25. Ibid., December 29, 1908.
26. Ibid., January 1, 1909.
27. Giuseppe Bertori, *Don Orione e il Novecento* (Roma: Rubbettino, 2003), 85.
28. Paul Burns, ed, *Butler's Lives of the Saints* (London: Burn and Oates, 2005), 35.
29. Quoted in John Dickie, "Timing, Memory and Disaster," 147–166.
30. *New York Times*, January 1, 1909.

CHAPTER 4

ANSWERING THE NEED

HELP ARRIVES

News of the violent earthquake brought about a quick response, one that elicited demonstrations of assistance at the global level to help alleviate the situation and bring relief to survivors. It resulted in a kind of friendly naval rivalry in humanitarian deeds and in the recording of many remarkable instances of persons sheathed in vaults and passages, blocked by the fall of upper stories, and liberated alive after almost a week's confinement. Altogether, over forty nations participated in bringing assistance of some kind; however, the help rendered by several major nations was truly remarkable and deserving of comment.

RUSSIAN AID

The enormity of the great disaster that rocked Messina—its scope and magnitude, and the horrendous toll on human life—elicited urgent and noteworthy activity on the part of Italian and non-Italian neighbors in Europe and beyond. Owing to the fact that Russian ships were in Augusta, Sicily—not too distant from Messina—when the earthquake struck, the resources of the Russian navy were the first to swing into action. A case in point was the *Admiral Makaroff* and two other Russian ships that were in the waters off Italy on that fateful December day. Ensign Paul Alexeyevich Voronov, born into a family of the hereditary nobility, and the officer on the deck of *Admiral Makaroff* when the terrible Messina Earthquake occurred, led the rescue of more than 1,800 homeless people. For his valor, Ensign Voronov was awarded a medal by the Italian government. Among other Russian ships that rescued survivors was the battleship *Slava*, which transported 500 injured survivors from Messina to Naples, and the steamer *Semito* which also brought from Messina to Naples 400 injured, of whom 100 were soldiers. The crews of the Russian ships *Bogatyr* and *Slava* were equally prompt and efficient, with their crews displaying so much courage and daring in rescuing victims among the unsafe ruins that they won the highest commendation. Other Russian ships that assisted at the time were the *Guilak*, the *Korietz*, and the *Cesarevitc*.

That the Russians empathized profoundly with the plight of Sicilians in their misfortune is illustrated by their absolute intolerance of acts of desecration perpetrated by some Italian escaped prisoners—they did not hesitate to shoot the vandals. Nor did the Russians waver in exposing themselves to danger as they dug under tottering walls or entered unsafe buildings; in one instance, they responded to the plea of a frantic woman whose husband or child was under piles of debris. On another occasion, a party of Russian sailors came upon a wall of a four-storey house, still standing precariously in the center of the town. Only a foot or two of the third and fourth floors remained, and upon these narrow ledges, two women and three children were clinging and crying for help. With no ladders available, rescue seemed impossible; however, the sailors showed their mettle: while one stood on another's shoulders against the outside of the wall, a third, carrying a pick, climbed over them, and using his implement as an ice pick, drove it into the mortar high above his head. By this means, he pulled himself up to a window sill, released his pick, and used it again in the same way to go higher. Finally, he reached the terror-stricken refugees and lowered them with a rope to his comrades. On the ground, as one of the sailors was wrapping his jacket around one of the almost naked children, the tottering wall fell upon them and killed both the victims so perilously saved, as well as the brave rescuers. The peculiarity of finding so many survivors in a state of nakedness was attributed to a then prevalent Sicilian mode: the old habit of sleeping without nightwear. It was based on a widespread prejudice against nightclothes—namely, that it was unwholesome to sleep dressed. This absolute nakedness, both of the living and of the dead, seemed to the rescuers the last touch of horror.

When three babies were born among the refugee survivors that the Russian warship *Tsarevitch* was taking to Naples, the Russian officers drank champagne to the health of each newcomer. A Russian sailor even offered to adopt one of them born to a mother whose husband had perished. The Russian warships performed great humanitarian work as they became laden with the injured and the homeless refugees whom they transported to safety. Onlookers were profoundly impressed by still another rescue effort in which Russian sailors were involved. They witnessed a group of sailors who had gathered around a hole amidst the debris of what used to be a house in response to a baby's plaintive cries. A young, red-faced Russian sailor with a trowel in one hand and a rag soaked with condensed milk in the other was lowered headfirst to barely reach the infant who sucked on the rag until it stopped crying. Alas, the next day the same sailors were brokenhearted to learn the baby had died.

Russia's participation in helping unfortunate Italian victims made a deep impact on the Russian psyche. It soon entered into the realm of Russian literature as exemplified by Valentin Katayev's novel *The Cottage in the Steppe*, which traces the voyage of Petya who arrives in Messina filled with anticipation of imbibing in the glorious and historic atmosphere.

> What a wonderful change it was! Here was the picturesque Italy of world-famous water-colours and oleographs: a blue sky, a still

bluer sea, white sails, cliffs, and shores covered by orange and olive groves.

From the harbour, Messina looked enticing and beautiful, but Petya suddenly felt there was something wrong in the number of houses and the way they were spaced. There seemed to be fewer than there should have been. And there were sinister dead spaces between them, hidden amongst the scraggy underbrush. Then, suddenly, he recalled the words the whole world had uttered in terror three years before: the Messina earthquake. He himself had often repeated those words, without really understanding them. He had seen the ruins of Byzantium, of ancient Greece, and of early Roman settlements, but these had been magnificent stones, historical monuments, and no more; they had fallen into a state of decay over thousands of centuries. They were truly astounding, but they did not wring the heart. Now, however, Petya was looking at heaps of recent debris, which, not so very long ago, had been streets of houses. The city had been destroyed and tens of thousands of people had perished in a matter of minutes, and neither fortress towers, nor marble columns, nor anything else remained as a reminder of the catastrophe. A pitiful heap of rubbish, bits of walls with shreds of cheap wallpaper still clinging to them, stucco laths, broken glass and twisted iron beds, overgrown with pea-trees and nightshade, was all that met the eye. It was the first destroyed city that Petya had ever seen; and it was not a famous ancient one from his history book-no, this was a very ordinary, rather small modern Italian city, inhabited by very ordinary Italians.[1]

For famed Russian playwright Maxim Gorki, who was in exile in Capri during the earthquake, the cataclysm was so shocking that it raised fundamental questions about mankind and government mismanagement. The earthquake forced a reexamination of man and society—that is, before the forces of nature, all were equal: rich and poor, social classes, and national boundaries. His was a sober but optimistic appraisal. "Italy is seriously wounded, but his soul is alive: in the national day of pain it has shown the world the power of courage and love, and burned brightly in those days the torch of noble democratic spirit of the Italians."[2]

Italy's gratitude to Russia has been manifest over the years. In 1923 a Russian, anti-Boshevik sailor named Biagovesechensky, seeking eventual admission to the United States, sought and received political asylum in Italy. He had been, in fact, decorated by Italy for saving several lives in the Messina Earthquake. In explanation for its action, the Italian government maintained that it was "in recognition of his services during the Messina disaster."[3] The latest example occurred on February 11, 2006, when the Italian government hosted a ceremony to commemorate the contribution of the Russian Navy to relief efforts after the 1908 Messina Earthquake. The commemoration took place at an informal meeting that came at the end of a meeting of NATO in Taormina, which was joined in by high-ranking Italian Navy representatives, including Italian Defense Minister Antonio Martino and his Russian counterpart, Sergey Ivanov.

English Assistance

British sailors aboard warships in the vicinity likewise came to the rescue, even at the risk of their lives. On the fateful December 28, 1908, the steamship SS *Afonwen* that had arrived in Messina four days earlier was lying at her moorings. Captain William Owen's first intimation of the disaster was on being awakened in that early morning by the noise of the upheaval and the commotion caused by the tidal wave. However, the full extent of the disaster could not be ascertained for some time owing to the darkness and dense clouds of dust. Having satisfied himself as to the safety of his vessel, Captain Owen proceeded ashore with his crew, as the dawn broke, to render assistance. They came across a five-storey building where they noticed children at a great height crying for help. Although the building's interior had for the most part collapsed, and one of the walls had disappeared, rendering the structure in a very dangerous condition, valorous British sailors proceeded to extricate the victims.[4]

King Victor Emmanuel called for assistance from British ships stationed at the British naval base in Malta that also had experienced both the earth tremor and a tidal wave. The Malta-based British responded quickly by assigning a field ambulance section of the Royal Army

Medical Corps with two members of the Queen's Military Nursing Service, as well as a stationary hospital, which were transported to Messina by the Royal Navy, taking with them ten days' supplies and rations. Once in Sicily, they cared for survivors on board *HMS Minerva* and *HMS Duncan*, which set up dressing stations on board for victims. Other British vessels on the scene included warships *Sutley*, *Lancaster*, *Exmouth*, and *Euryalus*. The stationary hospital was created on January 2 in nearby Catona in what was a market place, and it remained on the scene until January 15, 1909. The twenty-five crew members of the English cargo vessel *Stork*, which belonged to the Steam Navigation Company, having just entered the harbor after the earthquake struck, also were among the first to throw themselves into the work of rescue, a deed that earned the gratitude of the stricken townsmen.

British sailors were unflagging in their hunt to reach British citizens living or stationed in Messina, as in, for example, searching out the home of the British chaplain Charles V. Huleatt and his family. Huleatt enjoyed an estimable reputation beginning in 1901 when he acquired three pieces of a manuscript on the murky antiquities market of Luxor, Egypt. He donated the papyrus fragments to his alma mater, Magdalen College in Oxford, England, and it was subsequently realized that he had stumbled on the oldest known fragments of the New Testament. Huleatt then went with his family and a number of British football players to Messina where he helped put together a football club called "Caulifield." He took over as Messina player-manager and led the team to victories over its archenemy Palermo in 1904—an achievement that helped instill a sense of pride in Messina.

It took several days before this rescue party from the Lancashire Cruiser arrived at the site of Huleatt home that was now in complete ruins—they finally reached it on Saturday. Discouragement turned to optimism when, amidst the remains, they heard some groans, an indication that members of the Huleatt family were still alive. Infused with fresh vigor, the rescuers worked heroically late into night in desperate efforts to rescue them—but without success. The English began digging once again on Sunday morning, but by now only one voice was heard;

still the sailors persevered. At night, rescuers were shaken by another distinct tremor that tumbled more walls and made their endeavor more dangerous. The sailors, joined at one point by the bishop of Malta, continued digging until they finally found the severely crushed bodies of the chaplain and one of his sons. Several English football players also perished. Undeterred by this gruesome find, the men kept hard at work, constantly calling out, "Is anyone there?"—until finally, the groans beneath the twisted ruins ceased, and they were convinced that the entire family had perished. Only then did the men quit work.

Although dispirited, sailors and soldiers continued to be optimistic, responding vigorously to a voice or a groan under debris. For the most part, they found few alive—those they lifted from the wreckage were covered with a mantle of white dust that gave the corpses the ghostly appearance of living images in plaster. It was surmised that those victims who had not been immediately crushed by the walls and ceilings were probably smothered beneath the choking weight of the dust. Forgetful of the danger, the sailors continued their task, and their persistency was occasionally rewarded—as in the instance when they found, under some wreckage in a small cubbyhole that was protected by two heavy beams, two little babies who were safe and uninjured and seemingly oblivious to the danger surrounding them, playing with the buttons on their clothes. No trace could be found of their parents, who undoubtedly lost their lives. Several other children who were taken from the ruins cried and kicked until their favorite dolls or toys were found, and one youngster was found still clasping a teddy bear in his arms. A sailor who rushed in to rescue survivors at Reggio was attracted by a sound of infant voices. Looking under a fallen beam, he found twins about a year old in a basket and uninjured. Although their clothing indicated the babies were from a well-to-do family, no one came to claim them.

J. Rennell Rodd, English ambassador in Rome, dispatched his military attaché—the famous animal hunter Colonel Delmé-Radcliffe—to Messina to offer the assistance of his nation. Delmé-Radcliffe was also very knowledgeable about volcanic eruptions, having personally witnessed the highly destructive eruption of Mount Vesuvius in Italy in 1906 and written a detailed and extremely valuable report. Rodd then ordered crews from English vessels to land and cooperate in rescuing survivors pinned in the basements—an assignment continually fraught with danger of subsequent masonry collapse, but performed with devotion and resourcefulness: "It was gratifying to receive as I did letters from many parts of Italy expressing appreciation of their splendid service."[5]

British officials within English cities, dominions, and colonies started fundraising campaigns that met with a magnificent response. Realizing that after food, the most urgent need in the stricken area was for clothing and boots, Delmé Radcliffe telegraphed wholesale orders for blankets and shoes to be sent to Naples. The ambassador's wife instituted workrooms in the embassy and there assembled all the British ladies in Rome to cut out and make clothing. Hundreds of suits were completed and dispatched with remarkable promptitude.

Other British officials became involved in the Mansion House Fund, which raised some £160,000 that was turned over to Ambassador Rodd, who in turn passed some £65,000 on to the central Italian Relief Committee during the first weeks of emergency. This was followed by the creation of a British committee operating in Rome, and local committees were organized in Sicily and Calabria to assist the marshaling together of rescue resources, with the military attaché acting as the intermediary and controlling agent. Rodd related an account of how his nephew and the British Lord Granby went to Calabria to establish a camp and a depot on the shore. He likewise cited other relief activities that he kept in constant contact with, as well as the devoted services of officers of the Salvation Army. The latter organization made it their special duty to carry supplies into remoter mountain centers that might have easily been overlooked.

After dealing with urgent need for food and clothing, England concentrated on reconstruction. It supplied a number of wooden houses that, with the cooperation of the archbishop and Calabria's local authorities, rebuilt the village of San Giovanni, where not a house had remained standing. The English also constructed a number of wooden houses for the survivors among the British colony in Messina that continued to be occupied years afterwards.

FRENCH AID

The news that several French families had perished in the catastrophe added to France's zeal in aiding its neighbor. France now began to take a great part in coming to the relief of Messina Earthquake sufferers, raising money to send to Italy by sponsoring several benefit opera performances in Paris, such as *Carmen*, and asking for donations from various private groups. That the appeal was being heeded is reflected in, for example, reports that groups like the Protestant Federation of France addressed a letter to all its churches asking that collections be made specifically for earthquake victims. The French Red Cross Society was exceptionally conspicuous for its meritorious efforts—its workers overcame fatigue after a long railroad journey to Naples where its members went to work immediately in the city's hospitals where they tended the wounded brought in from Messina and Reggio. Along with other nations, France dispatched five ships of the French fleet to Messina where sailors quickly joined in the arduous and dangerous rescue effort of digging survivors from the ruins. Other French vessels laden with provisions also brought vital aid.

French media became a valuable source through which the world became better informed about the Great Earthquake. One example was that of the *Le Petit Journal/Parisien*—a leading, illustrated news journal published in France at the time and noted for its brightly colored prints that graphically depicted news events around the world in addition to happenings in France. Accordingly, Messina Earthquake events were prominently featured in the publication—including handsome, front-cover illustrations in startling, pastel colors showing collapsed buildings and rubble in the devastated streets of Messina, and French sailors in blue uniforms going through the detritus in hopes of pulling out survivors. The back caption of the publication read, "French Navy is helping."

Among the French who won renown for extraordinary efforts in bringing help was the Duchess of Aosta of Naples who was, in fact, born a member of French nobility. In Naples at the time of the earthquake, the duchess's aid "has taken every form, from pecuniary practical help or actual nursing to the kindest demonstration of affection. Children robbed of their parents and relatives have been taken in her motor car to her place in Capodimonte."[6] Together with her husband, the Duke of Aosta, she also personally visited the city of Palmi and surrounding villages that were among the most devastated, where she continued to give solace.[7]

ITALIAN ARMY

In the light of recent poorly executed operations, disparagement of Italy's military accomplishment was a commonly held view in the late nineteenth and early twentieth century. The Italian Army, while not always enjoying respect as a military unit in comparison with other major powers, nevertheless, performed most notably during the earthquake crisis. The thousands of troops who were brought in from other parts of Italy to become engaged in rescue operations would soon win acclaim from the international community. On January 17, 1909, the correspondent on the scene from the *New York Sun* rendered what was considered one of the finest pieces of newspaper reportage of the event as he graphically portrayed the Italian troop rescue operation.

> I stopped for half an hour on Monday afternoon to watch the dramatic climax of a rescue operation that had been going on for forty-eight hours. It was in the ruins piled forty feet high adjoining the principal theater in Garibaldi street. On Saturday morning a faint response was heard deep down in the debris to the constant cry of the rescue parties, "Is anyone there?" The original building had been a very solid one of six stories of stones and mortar. Its destruction had been as complete as if a rock the size of a house had been dropped upon it from the sky and rolled away. It seemed impossible that anything could remain alive beneath that apparently solid mass of pulverized walls, blocks of granite, and a few splinters of wood.

But the cry was human and fifty men set out to work. They dug valiantly for hours above where the voice came. They seemed to get nearer and night came. Searchlights were brought and the work went on. On Sunday morning the location of the sufferer was fixed more definitely. They could talk with him, and he told them he was not hurt, there were a few inches of space above his head, and his hands were free. He pleaded not so much for release as for drink and food. The dust was suffocating and he feared he would choke if they came closer. The soldiers forced a pipe down through the debris and the imprisoned man succeeded in reaching the end of it. Beef tea and brandy were poured down in succession.

The correspondent continued to describe the consideration, care, and intrepidity shown by Italian soldiers in the process of extricating the imprisoned man.

The gratitude that came in response was as heartfelt as if the poor fellow was already in the free light and air instead of crushed down beneath twenty feet of ruins. That additional twenty feet amid material impossible to excavate by ordinary methods required another thirty hours to conquer. The impalpable powder which filled every crevice of the more solid material slipped back almost as fast as it was taken out. Besides it was necessary to proceed with utmost caution for the victim's sake. It was just as the rescuers had come in sight of the poor fellow that I happened to climb over that section of debris. A few moments apparently would effect his release, and a stretcher was hastily brought to the entrance of the little tunnel which had been driven through the side of the excavation. And then, when safety was in sight, the treacherous sides of the great hole began to slip, and in a few seconds the man was buried anew. There was a cry of horror on all sides. A dozen soldiers buried their faces in their hands and wept. The downpour of powdered lime and stones stopped for a moment. Suddenly the officer in charge cried: "Who will go in with this rope and fasten it beneath his arms underneath the dirt? It may mean death, for if the dust comes down again it will mean suffocation for whoever goes?"

"Let me go! Let me go! I don't mind what happens to me!" were the cries from almost every man in the detachment.

> A noose was quickly made in a stout rope and a lithe young private went quickly into the bottom of the suffocating tunnel. He dug away with his hands around the head of the victim. He found, fortunately, that small arch had protected him from the worst of the last dust slide. In a few moments the rope was fixed and a dozen men dragged the poor creature into freedom.[8]

Robert Rives LaMonte, in his fascinating debate with Henry Louis Mencken, alluded to the praiseworthy performance by Italian soldiers during this distressful period. LaMonte was a Socialist intellectual exponent of equality among people, while Mencken—an essayist, editor, and prolific author of biting satire—was an advocate of individualism. LaMonte rebuked Mencken's division of society into "high caste" and "low caste" by citing the heroism and sacrifice of lowly Italian soldiers in the aftermath of the Messina Earthquake.

Upon arrival in Messina, rescuers were confronted with a sunken marina, great yawning cracks in the solid ground, and a railroad station with the cars heaped together—a locomotive lay overturned on its side. They saw also an endless procession of soldiers and sailors with stretchers bearing the wounded file past, and they heard the rattle of the characteristically gay, little, painted Sicilian carts heaped with the dead ceaselessly moving towards the huge funeral pyre. The fumes of the burning bodies reached them on board the rescue ships, where despite inhaling the revolting and sickening stenches, they nevertheless persevered.

The heroism demonstrated by rank-and-file Italian soldiers lives on in the hearts of their descendents. A case in point is that of Renato Sciumbata whose grandfather was an Italian soldier—a member of the Reggimento Genio Telegrafisti, a specialized communications army unit stationed in the Messina vicinity at the time of the disaster.

> The story my grandfather told me about the Messina earthquake did not have anything to do with wireless telegraph; it was more of the surprise and scary moments he had when the barracks he was in as a military soldier started to shake and break apart.

He was in bed and grabbed his boots to run down the stairs which collapsed as he was running down with just one boot on. The most vivid memory he had of the city after the quake was that of a woman holding on to a baby while on a balcony of a building that had just collapsed behind her, and just the façade with the balcony stood up. The woman was in a state of complete hysteria, and her screams were so intense that my grandfather thought she had gone crazy! All the Italian military were involved in search and rescue during that time, and he participated in the effort; however he never told me any other details that I can remember now—he died in 1971, and he was just 22 in 1908. Anyway that is pretty much all the information I got from him about Messina earthquake, I think he did not want to go in gory details since at the time I was young, and I think he had what is now known as PTSD (post traumatic stress syndrome). I still have his Italian certificate of telegraph operator he received in 1909.[9]

The valor of Italian sailors is also remembered by descendants as illustrated in the Web site of Gregg Patruno who cites his mother's grandfather Giovanni Nardone. Twenty-one years old at the time, Nardone was in the Italian Navy on board a ship deployed to Messina to engage in the harrowing work of assisting victims of the disaster. Likewise, in 2008 Rose DeCarmine still proudly displays the diploma issued to her father, Leonardo LaRocca, an Italian sailor who was given the award for his role in bringing aid to victims of the devastation.

AMERICANS IN ROME

For some prominent Americans in Rome in the Christmas season, during which they enjoyed the company of friends within their familiar international group, December 28 was recalled as one of the coldest in memory as they warmed themselves near the grand fireplace of their hostess Vera. Although the *Tribuna*, an evening newspaper in Rome, provided them with their first news of the earthquake, it did not initially strike them as being particularly awful, as Maud Howe Elliot remembered. Initial inquiries about the earthquake elicited from an alert English journalist a factual response about a tremor in Calabria that was otherwise regarded as unremarkable. The newspaperman further assured the group that newspapers generally sensationalized events like this but that not much damage had been done. "Poor people, how they have suffered!," Vera sighed comfortably. After a few more comments, the subject was dropped. After drifting on to other subjects, the evening ended and the company went to their respective homes. On the next day, they learned more of the appalling nature of the disaster that grieved them so deeply and was expressed so sympathetically and sincerely by Maud Howe.

> Nothing but a death in the house has ever made so sharp a difference as I knew between the evening of the 28th of December and the morning of the 29th, for it was only on Tuesday, the day after the earthquake, that we in Rome began to understand—but only began to understand—that the greatest disaster of European history had stricken Italy, our Italy, the world's beloved. To each of us our own country is really dearest; we hope to die and lay our bones in the land where we were born. But Italy, like a lover, for a time makes us forget home, kin, native land, in an infatuation heady and unreasonable as lover's love.[10]

As news of the calamity deepened, the effect upon foreigners in Rome and Roman society in general became more obvious. The usual, *Buon Anno* cards with best wishes for the New Year seemed a mockery as, for the most part, normal conventions and civilities of Rome were dropped. People eschewed customary social duties or pleasures, even those whose normal routine consisted of worrying over the proper number of cards, appropriate visits, exchange of banquets, and other formal courtesies. Celebrations during this mournful time seemed too strong a travesty against such a mass of death of humanity and destruction of glorious buildings.

ROMAN GENEROSITY

The realization that a major part of Italy had been grievously wounded saw Romans responding to calls for help. On Wednesday, December 30, groups of students from the University of Rome traversed city streets in carts pulled by donkeys and accompanied by Italian troops, asking for donations from citizens and visitors. As the bugler in each cart sounded his trumpet, the carts navigated various sections of Rome—the Corso, the Old Flamian Way, the Piazza del Popolo, and so on—while clusters of students implored people for donations for victims in Calabria and Messina. The perceptive Maud Howe followed their journey and was impressed by the outpouring of generosity.

> From every window fell an *obolo*. A hail-storm of coppers rattled on the pavement, white envelopes with money folded in them came fluttering down like so many white birds. Outside the Palazzo Fiano, where the Italian flag tied with crape hung at half mast, the forage cart halted. At an open window on the top floor two sturdy men servants appeared and threw down a red striped bundle of pillows, another of blankets, a third a great packet of clothes. From every house, rich or poor (there are many poor houses in the Corso), came some offering. Two good beds were carried out from a narrow door. The cart was now filling fast, the money boxes were growing heavy. From a shabby window a pair of black pantaloons came hurtling through the air and the crowd, strung up and nervous with the tension of a night of mourning for Rome mourned as I had never believed it could mourn for anything—laughed from pure nervousness.
>
> At the shop of A. Pavia, the furrier, on the second floor, two people came to the window, an elderly woman with a face swollen with weeping, and a dark man who looked as if he had not slept. The cart stopped again, and from that modest shop there hailed down no less than twenty warm new fur coats and tippets—and this in Rome, the heart of thrift. If I had not seen it with my eyes I should not have believed it. At Olivieri's, the grocer's, a great quantity of canned meats, vegetables and groceries were handed out. From a hosier's near by came two great packages of men's shirts, some of cotton, and dozens of brand new flannel shirts. At a tailor's bale after bale of stout cloth was brought out and thrown into the cart. Another bed with pillows was given by a very poor looking woman; at the sight of this a man of the middle class took the overcoat off his back—it was a cold morning, too, with a good nip in the air—and threw it into the cart.[11]

Because of the emergency, by January 2, refuges were established usually in the poorer areas of Rome. It was to these locations that many who were able to escape from Messina came frequently—separated from families, and strangers to one another. Rallying to help their fellow countrymen was seen elsewhere in Italy. In the city of Bergamo, for example, children were given money collection boxes in which to save coins on behalf of the earthquake survivors.[12]

GRISCOM

Lloyd C. Griscom, scion of a prosperous Quaker American family and heir to a great shipping fortune, was a member of the diplomatic corps.[13] During the Progressive Era, service in the diplomatic corps held a special attraction for well-to-do, young, American men of proper lineage, who subscribed to the belief in a liberal, democratic, free-enterprise political and economic system, convinced that this formula under United States leadership would promote human development. In 1899, at age twenty and after earning a law degree from the University of Pennsylvania, Griscom began his diplomatic career in subordinate positions in England, Turkey, Persia, Japan, and Brazil where he served as ambassador until 1907—when, at thirty-four years old, he became a full ambassador to Italy, where he would remain until 1909. "I was the youngest of a sophisticated Corps, trained by years of experience at home and abroad in concealing their own minds and confusing those of others."[14]

Griscom's early impressions of Italians found many of their customs unwieldy and mediocre, but he also confessed that he could not be angry with them "because they were so like children—simple, good-natured, and incredibly superstitious." Griscom also developed an extraordinarily close relationship with King Victor Emmanuel, on occasion being invited to shoot and hunt boar on the royal estate. He regarded the king as a "regular guy" and at the same time "being the single really learned monarch in Europe."[15] He was likewise favorably impressed by Queen Elena's preference for unfussy, unadorned ways.

Expecting the year 1908 to ring out on a prosaic note, at breakfast on December 29, Griscom gleaned from the meager newspaper headlines that an earthquake had struck at Sicily and Calabria, knocking out communications. He soon learned that the sparse headlines failed to convey the gravity of the situation and that he would now have to give serious attention to the status of Americans in Sicily. Griscom immediately contacted the Italian foreign minister requesting the assistance of Italy's army and navy to ascertain the status of Americans in Messina, especially the ninety Americans registered in the Trinacria Hotel. He was also concerned about the safety of American Consul Cheney who had not been heard from. Alarmed American relatives of visitors in Italy at that time besieged the State Department, mainly because they had not heard from them since the earthquake struck

Going out into the streets of Rome, Griscom heard wild rumors of the devastation—that the Lipari Islands had been swallowed up by the sea, all of Messina had been engulfed by a tidal wave, and so on. Information was, of course, incomplete; however, government officials were clearly worried—a concern that intensified as refugees from the earthquake area began to arrive in the capital. These panic-stricken survivors related the horrors they experienced when they were hurled out of their beds in the still blackness of the night, heard the shrieks of agony of those caught under heavy beams and falling roofs, saw the wild scenes on the streets where under low-hanging clouds there glowed an angry red reflecting copious fires, and tried to cope with great cracks yawing in front of them. Griscom was certain that no disaster in history matched this one—up to 150,000 dead, a half-million homeless, and untold numbers of wounded and missing.

> Who was to help them? Apparently the Italians were too bewildered to know how to deal with this misfortune, and furthermore Italy was a poor nation. No organized international relief then existed, but American response was immediate. Dozens of my countrymen in Rome came to the Embassy repeating, "Can't we do something?" and I was certain that their feeling would be reflected at home.[16]

On December 30, Griscom sent a telegram to the American secretary of state Elihu Root stating, "I think it would be highly appreciated if we sent one or two warships at earliest possible moment."[17] Acting Secretary of State Bacon responded that although no warships could reach the scene until about January 14, the *Scorpion*, stationed in Constantinople, was on the way.[18]

PHILATELY AND COLLECTIBLES

The Great Earthquake made a deep impact on the philatelic world as evidenced in the productions of series of stamps and commemorations that were to be used for fundraising purposes. From Austria to Spain, an assortment of stamps in an assortment of colors were issued depicting activities that revolved around the earthquake. Emil Dopler, Italian ambassador to Berlin, convened an international committee to coordinate issuances of stamps and seals of various sizes and shapes. In Italy these stamps feature historic architectural remains and institutions like Salvemini's Library (in honor of Salvemini's wife who died in the earthquake) and the reconstructed steeple of Messina's cathedral.

Other countries concentrated on other types of memorabilia to raise funds. For example, Denmark produced a collector plate with a Viking ship with the Danish coat of arms and the word "CARITAS" in the sail. On the stone with an agave plant, the inscription read "MESSINA 1908." Countries such as Austria, with a series of stamps of four values, and the United States, through a Red Cross series, appealed to the conscience of citizens of their respective countries. In Berlin the Italian ambassador promoted the creation of an international committee that, among other initiatives, prompted the issuance of stamps about charitable fundraising efforts to cope with the consequences of the disaster. Austria, Denmark, France, Great Britain, Holland, Hungary, Italy, and Russia joined in the initiative with the issuance of eleven bullets, the same for all countries with the exception of the coin sales. Germany also used the same designs to deliver an alternative—something bigger and in two colors. Ten of them with images of Sicily were printed on the same sheet and arranged in five rows.

ENDNOTES

1. Valentin Katayev, *The Cottage in the Steppe* (Moscow: Foreign Languages Publishing House, 195[6?]),
2. Peter Zveteremich, "La Sicilia," March 23, 1989, RussianEcho.net.
3. *New York Times*, February 3, 1923.
4. James Vivian, Reed British War Medals, The Messina Earthquake Medals, relaces original, www.northeastmedals.co.uk/britishguide/colonial/messina_earthquake_medal_1908.
5. Rodd, *Social and Diplomatic Memories, 1902–1919*, chapter 5.
6. *New York Times*, January 2, 1909.
7. Ibid.
8. Robert Rives LaMonte and H. L. Mencken, *Man Versus the Man: A Correspondence Between Robert Rives LaMonte, Socialist and H. L. Mencken, Individualist* (New York: Arno Press, 1972), 99–101.
9. Renato Sciumbata, letter to author. January 5, 2008.
10. Howe, *Sicily* in Shadow, 6.
11. Ibid., 15–16.
12. Dickie, "Timing, Memory and Disaster," 148.
13. At one time, the shipping firm was associated with John P. Morgan in the formation of the International Mercantile Marine Company that acquired the White Star Line, the Atlantic Transport Line, the Leyland Line, and the Dominion Line—regarded as the new "Shipping Trust."
14. Lloyd C. Griscom, *Diplomatically Speaking* (New York: The Literary Guild of America, Inc., 1940), 284. For more on Griscom's diplomatic career, see Salvatore Prisco, "Griscom and Trade Expansion," *Diplomacy & Statecraft* 18, no. 3 (September 2007): 539–549.
15. Griscom, *Diplomatically Speaking*, 296.
16. Ibid., 308.
17. *Telegram*, December 30, 1908; Griscom to Sec State, *International Cases Arbitrations and Incidents Illustrative Peace*, vol. 1, ed. Ellery C. Stowell and Henry F. Munro (Boston: Houghton Miflin Company, 1916), 447.
18. Bacon to Griscom, telegram, 31 December 1908, in *International Cases Arbitrations and Incidents Illustrative Peace*, Vol. 11, 447.

CHAPTER 5

AMERICA'S HISTORIC ROLE

As an up-and-coming world power, the United States was destined to play a vital and historic role in aiding distressed and homeless earthquake victims, thereby demonstrating a refreshing sympathetic humanitarian dimension to its ascending military prowess. The needs of survivors were many, complex, and immediate; requiring extensive planning, organization, and implementation regarding the specific type of aid needed in the areas of food, shelter, transportation, clothing, financing, medical assistance; assembling of personnel; acquiescence and cooperation with the host Italian government.

Organizing relief in a foreign country was a major challenge given the usual restraining protocols of the diplomatic world in which the host sovereign nation could not appear to be incompetent or subservient to other powers. Saving face was part of the equation. Griscom sent a telegram to President Roosevelt on December 29, 1908, describing the earthquake as "terribly disastrous" and further reporting that Messina was completely destroyed and that while no official figures were available, it was estimated that over 50,000 perished in that city alone.

"I saw the king this morning before he left for the scene and expressed to him the heartfelt sympathy of the President and the American people."[1] On December 31, Griscom telegrammed the secretary of state, saying, "The prime minister has invited me to proceed to Messina and offered steamship accommodations from Naples. I have accepted the offer, in order to avail of the exceptional opportunity of getting transportation for two consular officers and to profit by special opportunities which are offered me…I leave Rome January 1."[2]

The American ambassador did not leave for Messina on January 1, however.

Although Griscom at first had been invited to go on an Italian warship to the stricken area to oversee rescue work, he delayed his departure from Rome for a couple of days, obviously aware that King Victor Emmanuel was disinclined to have a foreigner play so large a role in the enterprise. "It is altogether likely that Ambassador Griscom may have received a hint that the invitation to take charge of the work was premature."[3] Fortuitously, overwhelmed Italian officials—realizing the enormity of the task that lay before them—readily and enthusiastically welcomed assistance offers. From king to premier on down, Italian officials expressed gratefulness for American generosity. When King Victor Emmanuel learned that the Americans were preparing to organize relief, his reaction was one of genuine gratitude. "Our people will be delighted to hear of this mark of international humanitarianism, and will follow with the keenest interest the work of mercy which will be performed by the *Bayern*." Premier Giolitti's words were equally expressions of appreciation. "What the United States has done on this occasion is magnificent and shall not be forgotten. The United States stands first, outdistancing all others in sympathy and generosity."[4]

AMERICAN RELIEF COMMITTEE

One of the first things to be done was the formation of the American Relief Committee, made up of five capable volunteers: William Hooper of Boston who served as treasurer, historian and writer Nelson Gay,

Winthrop Chanler (once married to beautiful opera singer Lina Cavalieri), lawyer Samuel Parrish, and George Page. In addition, Griscom would make efficient use of the talents of artists John Elliot and Robert Hale, as well as naval attaché Commander Reginald Belknap. Under the leadership of Griscom, the committee oversaw issues of transportation, finance, basic needs of food, clothing, and shelter, assembling medical help, and so on. An auxiliary women's committee of American wives of consul members and others—part of the American colony in Rome—was also formed to begin the work of bringing succor to afflicted survivors. A participant described the group's activity amid the business and confusion in the American Embassy—crowded with packing cases piled halfway to the ceiling, bales of goods, and boxes of clothing, boots, food, medicines, and various relief supplies. Virtually every able-bodied American in Rome who volunteered to work on behalf of sufferers in Sicily and Calabria convened at the ambassador's residence because it was

> not only the nerve-center of the relief work but a warehouse, a base of supplies. From the ballroom came the sound of women's voices, the snip-snip of shears, the click of sewing machines. Here was another transformation; the sumptuous ballroom with the smooth polished floor had become a busy workroom. Under the gilt chandelier stood a long table, heaped with bales of flannel and cloth, over which leaned four or five ladies, scissors in hand, cutting out skirts, blouses and jackets. On the satin-covered benches sat a bevy of young women and girls, basting, sewing, planning, and chatting as they worked. "I have nothing left but red flannel," said the chief cutter-out, "what shall I do with it?" "Petticoats and under jackets," said the Doctor's wife. "We must put all the colored goods into under-clothing. The poor things beg so for black dresses. You wouldn't want to wear red or blue if you had lost twenty-five members of your family, as my *profughi* have."[5]

However well intentioned the move, it also became embroiled in what was called "a state of revolution" within the American colony because the said committee failed to include certain traditional leaders among the group in Rome such as Mrs. Lee and Mrs. Berdan, F. Marion Crawford's mother-in-law. Because feelings of resentment at exclusion by the older group was somehow linked with their lengthier residence in Italy and their closer ties with Italians, to cast aspersions against them was interpreted as casting aspersions on Italians as unreliable and dishonest. "The Italians as a whole resented the imputation that the funds contributed will in some part be lost, strayed, or stolen before they reach the refugees."[6]

Despite the furor, Ambassador Griscom proved equal to the subtle task that required complicated coordination of all the elements for a successful response. He immediately set about conferring for many arduous hours with his committee of American volunteers. "We made a list of the foods, tools, clothes, and medicines we thought would be most needed, and every member of the committee was assigned a single category, such as shoes canned goods, macaroni with tomato sauce (I was warned the Italians would not eat it without relish)."[7] Committee members were to ascertain how much of the commodity that was his responsibility could be procured in Rome, and the cost involved. When it became evident that the demands were beyond Rome's resources, other Italian locations were found.

Having previously received consent from the grateful Italian government, Griscom was apprised that the pressing priority need was transportation. Since the single-track railroad to Naples was overloaded with military units rushing to the scene, as was the Italian water transport system, Griscom had to find independent transportation. Accordingly, by January 4, 1909, he used his authority as a representative of the United States to charter the *Bayern*, a North German Lloyd Company cargo ship then laid up for the winter in Genoa. The rental arrangement was for two weeks, with the only costs being the expenses of the ship's operation. When the American Relief Committee learned that, although the American Red Cross had agreed to finance the undertaking estimated at $100,000, the money was not immediately available, individual committee members Parrish, Hooper, and Griscom—convinced that speed was essential—personally guaranteed covering the costs until the Red Cross had time to accumulate funds. The subject of which flag the ship should sail under posed another potentially contentious problem that could lead to delay given the usual slow pace of Italian bureaucracy. Obfuscation threatened the proposal that the *Bayern* should fly the Red Cross flag; however, Griscom cut another strand of the red tape that normally strangled quick action in Italy by obtaining permission to fly the Red Cross standard.

Thus, flying the Red Cross pennant, on January 7, the *Bayern* set sail for the Messina Harbor, thereby enabling the American Relief Committee to bring many tons of supplies to the stricken people including $58,000 worth of clothes and necessaries for survivors; it also brought on board three surgeons and fifty nurses, three of whom were American and three English.[8] The committee also provided $15,000 in cash for distribution through the proper authorities in the incapacitated district, and $10,000 for the vice consul at Messina, William Bayard Cutting, for distribution as agent of the Red Cross Society.[9]

WILLIAM BAYARD CUTTING

With the scale of the task confronting him, Griscom needed all the competent and experienced help he could find. One of the men he chose was William Bayard Cutting (1878–1910), who was from an immensely wealthy family which made its fortune in real estate and sugar beet refining, and who also happened to be his wife's cousin.[10] Married to the daughter of an Anglo-Saxon peer, the fifth Earl of Desart, Cutting was desirous of working in the diplomatic corps and served for a time as secretary to the United States Embassy to the Court of St. James, and as American vice consul in Milan. Plagued by a severe terminal tuberculosis condition from which he would die at age thirty-one in 1910, Cutting sought to cope with his deteriorating health in Italy where he, his family, and his retinue were spending the winter of 1908. Given the grave status of Cutting's health, Griscom was hesitant to engage him; however, he relented when the ailing man pleaded that he wanted to do something worthwhile in the short time remaining to him—a plea supported by his wife.

As the newly designated United States vice consul in Messina, Cutting and other American diplomats went to the suffering city where he established a small headquarters on January 2—he pitched a tent from which he flew the American flag, and recorded insightful and critical observations as he prepared to participate in rescue and rebuilding activity personally and officially. His first message indicated how grim the onsite situation was, providing scenes of destroyed and open houses "with corpses in every room." He also described the policy adopted by authorities to search exclusively for the living, namely, that "officers have orders to pay no attention to dead bodies...Officers are lowered in ruins head first, with a rope tied to their feet, and in this way they rescued many...Up to today all the work has been done by foreigners, the Italians have seemed more or less dazed."[11] Bayard asked for sterilized milk for children.

Bayard was also very critical of the manner in which Italians handled matters, accusing them of mostly idly talking while leaving the real work to foreigners. He labeled the local mayor incompetent and corrupt; frustrated and concluding that his role was futile, Bayard decided to go to other areas. For example, he also traveled to Taormina to superintend the care of the wounded and ascertain the status of Americans there at the time of the earthquake, to thereby relieve anxious Americans who sought news of their relatives who had traveled to the area—some were reported dead and some survived. Cutting's dedication while in the stricken area impressed Red Cross representatives. They were struck by the fact that in spite of his delicate health, he took no thought for himself in his devotion to the work in the midst of pitiful misery. They acclaimed him for laboring day after day and journeying from one place to another, accomplishing much with his fine ability and his sympathetic nature.[12]

FUNDRAISING IN THE UNITED STATES

In the United States, the American Red Cross—especially the New York County subdivision—assumed the major responsibility for raising the enormous amount of funds needed to assist earthquake survivors. Accordingly, it advertised in popular newspapers the advantages of making contributions through that body, that is, that no matter how the contributions were made—either individually, through societies, or through the Red Cross directly—the latter, as the regular auxiliary emergency relief organization of the American people, would provide assurances that monies would be directed to the purposes for which they were collected. The organization further emphasized that it was under the governmental supervision (as in other instances) of the president of the United States and chief executives of states and cities, as the proper depository of such funds. William Howard Taft, the president-elect, who was then president of the American Red Cross, lost no time in communicating with Count Taverna, president of the Italian Red Cross, that the United States was offering assistance. "The American Red Cross desires to express to the Italian Red Cross its profound sympathy because of the terrible earthquake in Sicily and Calabria. An appeal has been issued by the American Red Cross for contributions for the benefit of the sufferers."[13]

While the Red Cross did not itself raise and collect money for relief purposes, it issued appeals and received the money contributed, which it transmitted to its Washington headquarters, where it then was sent expeditiously to places in need. The agency stressed its experience and efficiency and assured people that they would receive receipts for contributions and that regular audits would be made public by a government accounting department. It was explained that money could be sent to the national Red Cross of a foreign country that was skilled in dealing with emergencies and commands the confidence of the people. Financier and philanthropist Jacob H. Schiff was treasurer of the New York State and County Red Cross.[14] That the Italian Americans appreciated the help being organized was evident in front page coverage it received in the Italian-language press as well as the formal thanks extended by Baron des Planches, the Italian ambassador to the United States, who confessed he could not have imagined how much real sympathy there was in American for Italy's plight.[15]

The American Red Cross was regarded as the best medium for the distribution of the fund, a fact that was readily acknowledged because it possessed facilities for the work that could not be easily duplicated and because of its reputation for promptness and discrimination. Given the huge amount of money most likely needed by Italians from Americans, it was the optimum organ. It was the opinion of the *New York Times* that "[a] people who raised $20,000,000 for the victims of the California earthquake [1906] may be relied upon to give that much, or more, to the homeless and starving of Calabria and Sicily."[16]

Although the *Bayern* was financed and under the auspices of the American Red Cross, much of the work of actually dispensing supplies and providing medical assistance was undertaken by members of the Italian Red Cross. The latter was respected as a well-organized operation that immediately established sixteen temporary hospitals to provide assistance to the stricken coastal towns. The German Red Cross of Berlin was also active in this effort. There were, in addition, some unusual but effective actions Italy resorted to in order to raise funds—including that of selling off part of its patrimony to raise funds for survivors. One involved putting up for sale a collection of rare Roman antiquities that included, among others, objects with inscriptions on stone in Latin and Greek that most likely came from the columbarium tablets uncovered for the first time around the turn of the century. In this instance, the University of Kansas purchased the assortment of items in 1909 to strengthen significantly its rare Roman museum collection.

DISMAY IN LITTLE ITALY

"Yesterday was a dismal feast day for Italians around Mulberry Bend," wrote a keen reporter regarding the muted New Year's Day that normally is one of joy and festivity.[17] Preoccupied with news about the earthquake, people gave what they had to collections of various societies. There was apprehension also about thousands of Italian laborers in America who were employed in seasonal work and regularly returned to their homes and families in Italy during the winter. Nativists had for years denounced those who participated in this practice as "birds of passage"—a negative epithet that likened them to parasites who used America as a place in which to earn money but then spent it in Italy. Because there was little work for them with the coming of winter, and because their families were abroad, those 5,000 New York Italian laborers who lived near Lafayette Street and who had recently left America for their homes in Italy became a source of anxiety to their friends and relatives in New York. They were in a state of frenzy. "They went about wildly yesterday to any place where they thought they could learn something—to Italian newspaper offices, the consulate, and to the homes of those they recognized as leaders. What little news they got was discouraging."[18]

Churches in Little Italy held masses for the dead that were crowded with worshippers, especially at Old St. Patrick's and the Church of the Transfiguration on Mott Street. Other Italian parishes that were part of the effort were the Church of the Holy Blood and Our Lady of Pompei in Brooklyn. Catholic Archbishop Farley of New York asked for extraordinary collections for those destitute through the earthquake. "A great many Italians who cannot afford to cable or do not know what a cable is, are crowding the parish houses to have letters written to their people in Italy by the priests. This, according to Father Ernest Coppa, is because the people are giving to funds all they can spare."[19] Since so many immigrants were illiterate, they relied on the better educated to write on their behalf. At one point, Antonio Sabatini went to see Fr. Coppa of the Church of Transfiguration on Mott Street, pleading with him to write a letter to his mother—for although he had her cabled three times, there was no answer and he had spent all his money.

An estimated 150,000 Italian immigrants in New York, becoming despondent over their failure to get firm, accurate information, stormed the offices of cable companies, the Italian consul general, Italian banks in Mulberry bend, and Italian-language newspapers. Besieged by worried Italian Americans fretful to ascertain the status of close relatives, newspapers like *Il Telegrafo* published extra special editions in an effort to keep their nervous readers informed. Even people with regular business communications with Italy had problems. Italian American Chamber of Commerce President Salari, for instance, received a cable from a friend in Rome informing him that it was impossible to get more than rumors, although all indications pointed to excessive damage.

In many a tenement house in Little Italy and around the Five Points District in lower Manhattan, the children of the immigrants who had learned English in the public schools were enlisted to translate to their families accounts of the disaster in the American language press. In other instances, anxious immigrants approached religious and social institutions to obtain more information about the calamity. Social centers within Italian immigrant centers, in some instances, provided useful information about the Great Earthquake.

ITALIAN SETTLEMENT HOUSE

The Italian Settlement House in Brooklyn, founded in 1901 by Rev. William E. Davenport (who was also its director), was a case in point. Servicing a community of immigrants largely from Naples, Calabria, and Sicily, the center was especially distressed at the news of the horrendous devastation of their ancestral homes where they had many relatives from whom no word had been received nor telegrams answered since December 28. Anxious immigrants appealed to the center for help in obtaining information. Feeling helpless to calm their fears, settlement house authorities decided to grant a leave of absence to the head worker in order for him to visit the stricken region and to ascertain the status of relatives. The resultant trip provided an early and rare insight regarding the destiny and dislocation of dozens of earthquake victims whose relatives were in New York.

Accordingly, the head worker arrived in Messina on January 30, where he served as a connection between neighborhood Italian Americans and earthquake survivors. His efforts to contact relatives of immigrants were complicated by the fact that some Brooklyn correspondents merely provided names without addresses. Staying until March 13, 1909, the head worker visited many towns and cities, as well as forty chief asylums such as Red Cross stations, army barracks, monasteries, public schools, and main clinics in Naples, Palermo, and Catania. The fruits of his investigation were very enlightening in imparting important details as to what happened to a number of people, which most likely mirrored the experience of the populace as a whole.

> Of 160 persons names in the lists first received, sixty-seven were found to be living and of these many were personally seen and aided either in Messina or other cities to which they had been taken.
>
> In nearly every case where letters arrived on time, and the names were accompanied by address, the house of the family sought for was visited and where this proved to be a ruin and a sepulcher the fact was reported to the inquirer. Where the house was found intact, or but partly damaged and empty, we tried to learn the whereabouts of its late occupants and whether or not they were in communication with relatives. This involved the study of the registered names of refugees issued by the "Central Committee of Aid for the Sufferers" and the Card Catalogue compiled in towns where the sick were cared for...
>
> In various hospitals patients were found who were either the sole survivors of whole families or sole survivors with the exception of relatives in America whose addresses were lost.
>
> The names of these last with those of their relatives here were sent, as previously arranged, to the editor of the *Bolletino della Sera* of New York. This work was steadily prosecuted throughout our stay in Italy: for the effort to relieve the loneliness and the mental depression of patients without from single relative seemed imperative.[20]

A typical pithy newspaper reference illustrated the pathetic situation survivors and relatives faced. "Giovanni P., Hospital 'Conceszione,' Palermo. 16 years old, back broken: all in family in Messina dead. A brother, Colangelo, in New York: address lost." Cooperation with the Italian newspaper *Bolletino dello Sera* apparently was quite constructive and elicited an editorial comment stating it was pleased "that by means of our work many Italians have been put in communication with their relatives and wish to thank us for our efforts."[21]

The head worker made other pertinent observations. He explained, for example, that uncertainties about names and addresses of relatives was undoubtedly due to the fact that "the nervous shock suffered by many, pinioned for hours or days in the ruins, was such that for weeks after their rescue the name of wife or husband was unrecalled." He also stated that although he was able to extend sympathy to a number of people he visited or whom he came across, nevertheless, "the effort to learn of the fate of those whose friends wrote to us for news of them, was in a majority of cases, futile." He confessed that although much of the work in trying to locate relatives of Brooklyn Italian immigrants was disappointing, it nevertheless needed to be done and was appreciated. Above all, his esteem for Italians increased. "Let us add that our experience with south Italians in this time of crisis but deepens our sense of their good natural qualities and their promise of their value as citizens among us."[22]

REFUGEES

Tales of woe from newly arrived refugees further underscored the scale of tragedy. Having arrived on Hamburg-American liner *Moltke*, Mrs. Isabella Silifini, of East Fourteenth Street, with husband Domenico, a broker in Italian products, was visiting and staying at her parents' house in Messina at the time of the earthquake. She was the only one to survive— her mother, father, two sisters, four brothers, and many nephews and nieces perished. She saw her husband crushed to death before her eyes.

> On the morning of the earthquake my husband and I were asleep on the second floor of my father's home, at 27 Santa Pelegia, in the very heart of the city…When I woke immediately after the first great shock it seemed as if we were being swallowed up by the earth. We could see the walls of our house crumbling before out eyes and could hear the crash of those that were falling. Above the noise of falling houses we could hear the shrieks of the people.
>   Domenico got out of the house with me, but when we reached the street we lost each other for a moment or two and in that little space of time he was killed. I was looking for him and found him when the wall of a house near him fell with a crash burying him.[23]

Sympathetic friends, moved by her mournful ordeal, helped her to return to New York.

It was a doleful time for the 500 Italians—more than half of whom were Sicilians—who had left Italy on the steamer *Germania* a few days before the disaster. They were steerage passengers coming to their new homes in America, completely ignorant of the earthquake because the ship did not have wireless equipment. The ship's officers learned of the disaster from tugboat operators as they approached the harbor, but the captain enforced strict silence until the ship actually docked, fearful that the concerned passengers would become uncontrollable upon learning about it since so many came from the afflicted area. "The natural and easily excitable nature of his steerage passengers forced him to maintain strict silence until morning." When the ship docked and passengers were made aware of the earthquake, "fully two hundred of the passengers were weeping and gesticulating wildly."[24]

There were indeed countless examples that the Messina Earthquake had become the basis for profound anxiety and extreme grief in many an Italian American community, especially where Italian immigrants from the devastated area resided. In one instance, the utter despondency experienced by the wife of a prominent druggist in the Bronx, New York, led to her demise.

> She was found dead from gas fumes in the bathroom by her husband when he returned home late at night. She came from Messina, where the quake claimed its great sacrifice of lives…Friends of the Italian woman told the police that she read constantly of the disaster abroad and brooded over the news. Dr. Quagliata declared that he could attribute no other cause for his wife's suicide than despondency over the earthquake.[25]

For Dr. Nicola Gigliotti of Erie, Pennsylvania, who had earlier received an uncanny prophesy of the city's demise from his archbishop friend, it was especially mournful to learn that his brother, who was mayor of Reggio, perished in the earthquake along with most townspeople. The poignant news prompted Gigliotti and several others to return to Italy to bring assistance. For opera singer Mme. Blanche Marchesi, then in Chicago, but with dozens of relatives in Palermo and Messina, news of the tragedy was especially stressful. Having lived and survived earlier earthquakes, she knew well the terror that these natural disasters could bring. "The tremors of the earth are so frequent that the people have become used to them...In Sicily people are taught to rush to an archway or a window as soon as the slightest shock is felt."[26]

Many Italian Americans lost no time in rushing to Italy. On December 30, two ocean liners, the *Adriatic* and the *Lucania*, left New York for European ports taking back large numbers of Italians who feared their relatives were among the earthquake victims. Among them was Frank Rando, owner of a New York importing firm who had returned only two weeks previously from Naples where he left his wife and children to spend the winter.[27] The disturbing earthquake news also led to extreme apprehension and anxiety within Sicilian and other southern Italian enclaves, including among immigrants who lived and worked in Inwood, Long Island. As one newspaper account described it,

> Along the Rockaway branch there are several colonies of Sicilians and Albanazians [Albanians] who are greatly excited over the terrible catastrophe which had befallen their home country. These are located in Lawrence and Inwood, and there is a small contingent of them in Far Rockaway near the Nassau County line. When the first news of the earthquake was received there, these people became greatly excited and as later and more terrible news arrived, the conditions bordered on insanity, some of the foreigners going so far as to pack their belongings and make preparations to leave for the earthquake zone. Many of the Sicilians and Albanazians [Albanians], together with Calabrians, emigrated to America, leaving their families in Italy, and these are the more frantic. Many believe their whole families have been wiped out and have implored the Italian consul to aid them in securing news from their home country...In the belief that they might be able to locate some of their relatives, there are some who are on the verge of leaving this land and go to the stricken country. Their countrymen who have families here with them are doing all they can to

console their bereaved friends and subscriptions are being taken
to forward to the sufferers of the disaster.[28]

Notwithstanding lack of specificity, there were indications that a substantial number of Sicilians did, indeed, return to their homeland.

ITALIAN AMERICANS RESPOND

Staggered by the weight of the devastating news from the land of their
birth, New York City's Italian Americans, stirred by the example of sacrifice demonstrated by Italy's monarchs, were profuse in their praise.
They were especially affected by the genuiness of grief and concern
exhibited by the Italian monarchs who immersed themselves in a dangerous mission. On January 1, three days after the Great Earthquake
struck, a group of Calabrians living in New York "flashed this message across the Atlantic to their mother country: 'Do not forget Scylla!'
Scylla, how the old name thrills! Scylla had suffered severely, though its
gray castle, perched high on the cliff that rises sheer from the shore, was
spared. Scylla, the ancient village at the foot of the purple Calabrian
mountains."[29] Perhaps the poorest of the recent immigrants to the United
States, they were, nevertheless, determined to do what they could within
their means to help their fellow Italians—including in many instances
their own immediate relatives. No matter how modest their incomes, they
contributed. For example, most of the $1,500 donated by the staff in New
York City's Knickerbocker Hotel to the Italian Red Cross came from
Italian employees, while the proprietor also gave $500. A New York
merchant advertised in Italian ethnic newspapers that it would donate
18.5 percent of sales for the week to fundraising for earthquake victims,
while several Italian American newspapers sold earthquake postcards to
benefit the victims.[30]

Two days after the disaster, an *Il Progresso Italo-Americano* editorial
abundantly reflected the empathy of New York Italian Americans. "Our
poor brothers—blood of our blood—condemned to cry for mercy to
God…You know our hearts are with you in this hour of tears, you are not

abandoned. Know that your brothers in America will prove once again our affection for you...No we will not abandon you."[31] The New York ethnic newspaper *Il Telegrafo*, citing the optimism of Italian officials with cries of "Vive Messina," proclaimed that just like San Francisco's determination to recover after its 1906 earthquake, there was hope for Italy because it too had the will and the power to recover.[32]

ORGANIZATION HELP

In New York City, where the largest concentration of Italian Americans lived and had formed various organizations and societies, virtually all joined in the effort. By January 1, 1909, it was reported that the Italian American Red Cross had already accumulated $10,000 while the Italian Chamber of Commerce had totaled $7,000 in subscriptions—the latter organization also cancelled its annual dinner scheduled for February 21 and contributed to the Italian Red Cross approximately $6,000 that it normally spent for the event. The newly organized Italian American General Relief Fund reported $8,000 in donations only two days after it had been organized by Patrick F. McGowan, president of the New York City Board of Alderman, the city government's legislative branch. With John J. Freschi—who had offices in the prestigious World Building—as treasurer, the committee set as its goal raising $50,000 in the next couple of days to send to Italy without delay. The son of Sicilian-born parents, Freschi—who was destined to achieve some prominence within his ethnic group by becoming a magistrate—concentrated on rallying businessmen in downtown New York to contribute to the McGowan/Freschi Committee. To this end, he mailed out 10,000 circulars urgently appealing for contributions.

The Italian American Trust Co. quickly collected $3,000 while the Italian Consulate in New York City reported that $1,023 had been turned in to the Italian Red Cross offices in the city. In an era when Italian immigrants tended to deposit savings in institutions run by members of the their own nationality, "Little Italy" bankers such as Lionello Perera carved out for themselves an important niche in the financial world of the

United States. They accordingly played a helpful function in fundraising for earthquake survivors. Thus, Perera, who represented the Italian Red Cross in the city and "probably is the largest and most influential Italian private banker in the city," was entrusted with the task of coordinating local fundraising on behalf of the Italian Red Cross.[33]

The Italian American press played a consequential role both collectively and individually with regard to fundraising for earthquake sufferers. Media people energetically pressed for the creation of a relief committee of one hundred members of the best-known Italians in New York to organize under the auspices of the Italian consul and to meet at the Italian National Club on Sixteenth Street in order to devise the best means of raising relief funds. The committee included all the Italian-language editors, the directorate of the Italian Chamber of Commerce, prominent bankers and businessmen, and heads of societies. It elected Luigi Solari of the Italian Chamber of Commerce as its president, and Dr. Antonio Stella, "doubtless the best known and most efficient Italian physician in the country," as vice president.[34] This activity on the part of these men inspired Italian American women to form another like committee representing the one hundred best-known Italian women. This committee, led by Countess Rayboudi Massiglia, wife of the Italian consul, planned a fundraiser on February 1 beginning with an afternoon "dramatic" tea and evening musical entertainment at the Waldorf-Astoria. The committee also sponsored a "tag sale" and bridge tournament at the Plaza Hotel with proceeds earmarked for the relief fund.

POLITICAL ORGANIZATION

The Italian American Democratic Union focused on a direct appeal to "Little Italy" residents and to the district leaders of Tammany Hall in these neighborhoods. Tammany Hall was the major political club within the Democratic Party in New York City with such gigantic political clout that it was judged indispensable in attaining major elective offices locally and even nationally. Fully aware of changing demographics that saw an increase in the Italian population in the city, local Tammany Hall leaders, anxious to curry their support, looked for ways to accommodate them—a vigorous espousal of subscriptions to relief funds or to the victims was such an opportunity. Accordingly, they joined with Italian American local leaders like James March in asking people to contribute. Born in Italy in 1873, Antonio Michelino Maggio earned his initial success when he became *padrone* (labor boss) of fellow ethnic railroad workers in upstate New York. Maggio then changed his name to James March and in 1894 came to New York City where he attracted the attention of "Big" Tim Sullivan, Tammany Hall chief, who, seeing him as an important factor in organizing Italians, appointed him a Manhattan Democratic district leader.

As a member of the New York State Legislature, Sullivan had introduced a bill together with Alfred E. Smith to establish Columbus Day as a state holiday—a move that served to highlight Irish leadership eagerness in currying favor with Italians. That the designation of Columbus Day (a long sought-after prize by Italian Americans) as a state holiday came to fruition on March 23, 1909, may have been a coincidence. However, in elevating attention to the Italian contribution to America's discovery, it also represented an opportunity to expand the appeal for more help for earthquake victims. The Italian-language press vigorously emphasized the view that genuine concern for Italians must manifest itself by works of charity on behalf of the 3,000 children orphaned by the disaster. As *Il Progresso Italo-Americano* put it, "We have sent much money to Italy, but it is not enough to help the unfortunate orphans."[35]

James March followed the Irish political model, becoming a boss on a local, ethnic neighborhood level. As an influential East Side boss, March, meeting with other Italian American leaders on January 1, 1909, raised $1,000 on the spot for earthquake survivors and simultaneously sent out appeals in circulars that were expected to raise much more. Another Italian immigrant who had become successful economically was Rocco Marasco who earned his livelihood as a humble bootblack owner of a small operation that began to thrive when he obtained the privilege for polishing shoes on Pennsylvania ferryboats. He invested wisely in the lucrative real estate business and became the purported owner of twenty-five apartment houses. A vice president of the Italian Savings Bank, a founder of the Italian Hospital, and an active participant in Democratic city politics, he sent one of largest checks to aid Messina Earthquake victims.[36] Marasco was a close friend of the aforementioned influential state senator "Big Tim" Sullivan, a member of the political clan that had developed a strong relationship with the emerging Italian bloc in the city. It was not surprising to learn that "Little Tim" Sullivan—another member of the Sullivan clan—as chairman of the Board of Alderman, proceeded to call on the city legislative body to appropriate $100,000 for Italian survivors.

ITALIAN-LANGUAGE NEWSPAPER DRIVE

At the urging of Carlo Barsotti, editor of the largest Italian American daily, *Il Progresso Italo-Americano*, direct appeals were made in the heart of Italian American neighborhoods, many of whose inhabitants were from the devastated regions. On the second Sunday in January, the newspaper-sponsored fundraising committee traversed Italian enclaves in Manhattan, Brooklyn, and the Bronx to collect funds and material for earthquake victims. It was recognized that Italian immigrants were hard working and poor and that their offerings would be modest but given with great moral fiber.[37] In Manhattan, the drive took the form of processions in which four carriages—decorated with Italian and American flags and manned by Italian military veterans and prominent ethnic leaders—and ten trucks made available by the Nanziante Forlenza of the Italian Express Company trekked through neighborhood streets of the famous Mulberry Street of Little Italy, as well as its emerging counterpart near First Avenue and 125th Street in Harlem. The carriages carried large boxes for money donations and other items such as clothing, medicine, and other supplies. Lively girls in carriages wended their way through crowds of rough men "who have the reputation of cutting throat without a second thought, and the men gave every penny they had."[38] It was truly remarkable demonstration of response to human need by people of all nationalities, races, and religions in the neighborhoods. By the time the day was over, the tin boxes with pennies and other coins totaling $2,500 were so heavy they required the strongest men to lift them.

> Rarely has New York seen so extraordinary a display of human sympathy and generous as yesterday furnished on the east side among people who have nothing to spare. Many of them weeping, many blessing the men and women in the two caravans, they crowded around the carriages and trucks, throwing into them the very clothes from their backs.
>
> The Jews gave eagerly what they could and even the Chinamen ran stolidly into the street to drop coins into the big iron boxes carried by people in the vehicles. The policemen on their beats contributed.[39]

Italian steamship lines agreed to carry, free of charge, freight of supplies to Messina directly. For months, the earthquake disaster and fund-raising efforts on behalf of victims became front page news in Barsotti's newspaper, as well as the consequent publication of names of small donor contributions—whose denominations of from $1.00 to as little as $0.10 collectively accumulated over $85,000.[40]

ITALIAN AMERICAN BUSINESS LEADERS

When Salvatore Di Giorgio, manager of the Atlantic Fruit Co., made an appeal for funds that raised $1,500, the happy entrepreneur was prompted to write a letter to the *New York Times* in which he confessed his gratitude.

> I have been so deeply touched by the generosity shown by my business associates and friends. Who so liberally responded to my petition for a contribution for the poor sufferers of the recent earthquake in Southern Italy, that I wish to take this means of sincerely thanking the following for having subscribed to the amount of $1,500, which sum I am today forwarding to the Red Cross Society at Rome.[41]

The amount Di Giorgio forwarded to the Italian Red Cross delegate was the result of inducing 300 people to donate $5 each. Leaders of the

New York Stock Exchange passed a resolution calling upon members to answer the urgent need for help for the stricken people of Italy and Sicily; it also created a committee of prominent stock exchange members to spearhead a special appeal to its members. Fundraising in the New York Cotton Exchange took the form of publishing a subscription list beginning with the first seven subscribers of $50 each.

COUNTESS MASSIGLIA, WIFE OF THE ITALIAN CONSUL

Countess Massiglia, wife of the Italian consul, organized a bridge tournament in a large ballroom at the Plaza Hotel, with the management's cooperation. On her committee were wives of prominent New Yorkers—such as Mrs. Joseph Pulitzer and Mrs. Cornelius Vanderbilt—who sold tickets at $5 each with assurances that proceeds would be sent directly to the queen of Italy. With the support of President Roosevelt and his wife, the countess also organized a fundraising bazaar at the Waldorf-Astoria that offered a charitable musicale in which Geraldine Farrar, Enrico Caruso, and Antonio Scotti performed. The committee for this event, which included Mrs. Archibald Alexander, Mrs. C. Vanderbilt, Mrs. Fabbri, and Mrs. N. M. Butler, presented many of the seasons' debutantes in Italian costumes. In addition, Caruso drew caricatures and Scotti sold pictures and photographs to raise money for earthquake sufferers.

OPERA FUNDRAISING

To raise funds for earthquake survivors, Metropolitan Opera director Guilio Gatti-Casazza organized two stellar concerts featuring performances by luminaries of the opera world such as peerless composers Arturo Toscanini and Gustav Mahler—along with singers like Enrico Caruso, the opera worlds' greatest tenor, Geraldine Farrar, the reigning diva, and the elegant baritone Antonio Scotti, all of whom performed gratis. The Metropolitan Opera House management asked the unionized musicians to provide an orchestra, and chorus girls were assigned to implore help from members of the Wall Street Stock Exchange as they were leaving their offices, in an effort to auction off seats to the highest bidders. In addition, souvenir books were available for sale, and proceeds were earmarked to benefit earthquake sufferers. At the first concert on January 10, 1909, all the stars of the Metropolitan Opera House—accompanied by the full orchestra and led by renowned conductors—devoted their legendary talents on behalf of the benefit. Regular patrons paid full prices to hear the concert: $100 per seat from box holders, which garnered $1,000 per box, as purchasers then turned them back for sale. Special programs were sold for $1,000, and a silver snuffbox was auctioned twice, netting $600, while a program signed by all the artists who appeared sold for $160.

> The public was as generous as the artists themselves, and an audience outnumbering any that has been in the Opera House since the memorable Prince Henry performance.
>
> So many singers from the Met volunteered their services not possible to have solo numbers the programme was made up of the greatest and most popular operatic duets, trio, quartets, quintets, and sextets. There probably never has been an occasion when so many leading singers have been heard on one stage by one audience, and not only heard, but seen without costumes, so that their admirers could gaze upon them as themselves and not as the characters in which they have become familiar. The result was an evening of the keenest interest and enjoyment marked by applause and personal tribute to the artists that must have been wonderfully gratifying to them. There were, of course, no encores permitted.[42]

Among the outstanding operatic arias was the sextet from Donizetti's *Lucia di Lammermoor*, conducted by Francesco Spetrino and sung by Marcella Sembrich, Enrico Caruso, Marie Marttfeld, Giuseppi Campanari, Giulio F. Rossi, and Angelo Bada; Verdi's quartet from *Rigoletto*, sung by Frances Aida, Marie Gay, Alessandro Bonci, and Pasquale Amato, and conducted by Arturo Toscanini; and duet from Mozart's *Don Giovanni*, featuring diva Geraldine Farrar and Antonio Scotti with Gustave Mahler conducting.[43] The concert raised $14,000 to aid the earthquake victims.

The second Metropolitan Opera House benefit was held on January 13, highlighted by a performance of *Aida*—there was an interruption following the second act to sing the American and Italian national anthems. The event attracted leaders of New York's Italian community including Dr. Antonio Stella and his wife. With the red, white, and blue, as well as the red, white, and green colors of the American and Italian flags flying over a sold-out performance that also included crowds of standees, the opera house presented a vibrant and colorful spectacle. The Italian Society for Immigrants and the Italian Benevolent Institute sponsored the benefit in which their presidents Ernest G. Fabbri and Celestino Piva, respectively, presented a solid gold Lincoln medal to Enrico Caruso for his generosity. The Naples-born, world-famous tenor contributed a week's salary—which, at $2,000 a performance, four times a week, was equivalent to $8,000 for the relief fund. This event raised $8,000.

The Manhattan Opera House was another center of serious music that participated in fundraising for earthquake sufferers. This was the venue of Oscar Hammerstein I, a confrontational promoter, showman, and impresario dedicated to revitalizing opera in America. Perhaps to counter a negative perception over his unwillingness to cooperate in Brooklyn's abortive fundraising effort, this time he did allow use of his Manhattan location for the purpose. This change of heart became apparent after the Manhattan Opera Company appointed Italian American Helen Santoro as press representative. She was also able to get Hammerstein to acquiesce as well to additional benefit performances in Paterson, New Jersey. Not only was every seat at the Manhattan Opera House sold, but also up to 500 patrons paid to stand during the January 17, 1909, concert. This performance featured acclaimed coloratura soprano Mme. Luisa Tetrazzini and prima donna Miss Mary Garden who appeared in solo performances while souvenir programs were auctioned. Although the orchestra and stage band were paid, members returned part of their pay to the relief fund that reached a total of $10,000.

MADISON SQUARE GARDEN

The Italian American Relief Committee sponsored a mammoth fund-raising benefit for Madison Square Garden scheduled for January 7, to which they invited President-elect Taft who sent his regrets while encouraging the effort. One hundred Italian marching clubs striding down the streets of New York to Madison Square Garden participated in a major relief benefit drive; however, due to extremely cold weather, many people who had purchased tickets did not show up. Nevertheless, some 2,000—many of whom had friends or relatives in the stricken district—did attend the benefit where they heard addresses by Vice President Charles Fairbanks who, in pleading for aid, reminded the audience, "We are bound to Italy by so many ties, so many of her sons and have become incorporated into our citizenship, that the calamity seems almost as if it had visited our own National household. One touch of sorrow makes all men kin." Mayor George B. McClelland also urged New Yorkers to help, especially in view "of the large percentage of Italians in this city and of the keen interest New York feels in the situation in the stricken districts because of the large Italian population here."[44] Representing Italy was Consul General Count Massiglia who expressed his country's gratitude in glowing terms. A flag-decked platform had been raised on the north side of the garden. "Above the speakers and in one of the galleries stood a number of Italians bearing the colors of the United States and of Italy draped in mourning."[45] A one hundred-piece National Royal Italian Band played music for the event.

Over 2,000 East Side residents—about half of them residents of Little Italy, and many with relatives and friends among the earthquake victims—attended the benefit at the Bowery's Atlantic Garden. Among the leaders of the ethnic community who assisted in planning the event was Coroner Acritella. Tickets at fifty cents and seventy-five cents were sold in every East Side factory, and handbills were distributed all over the neighborhood. Regular cast members at the garden such as Elizabeth Savarese, Frances Ragano, and Virginia Novelli gave their services gratis.

PROBLEMS IN BROOKLYN

Notwithstanding all the goodwill voiced in favor of supporting fund-raising for relief of the earthquake victims, there also was some controversy. Feeling rebuffed that the aforementioned Italian General Relief Committee did not include leaders from Brooklyn's Italian American community, members of the ethnic group led by Assistant District Attorney Francis L. Corrao formed the Brooklyn Italian Earthquake Relief Fund Committee. It proposed to sponsor a massive fund-raising benefit to be held at the Grand Opera House in Brooklyn that would feature renowned celebrities from the Metropolitan Opera Company and a leading Italian orchestra. A similar event was also planned for Brooklyn's Bijou Theater. Alas, the entire enterprise collapsed when Corrao was unable to obtain either the singers or the musicians. Corrao blamed the failure on a contretemps between Oscar Hammerstein and directors of the Brooklyn Academy of Music, which caused Hammerstein to refuse to permit any of his singers to perform in that borough. Even more disturbing was the refusal of Italian musicians to perform unless they were paid. Brooklyn's Italian American leaders were chagrined and disappointed by the apparent failure of Italian Americans to contribute to the fundraising effort. Consequently, Corrao resigned as chairman of the group and was succeeded by Dr. Peter Virdone.

BROOKLYN CONTRIBUTES

Notwithstanding this setback, Brooklyn's emerging Italian American community did play a substantial role in helping the land of its ancestors during this critical period, much of it evident in the county's Catholic churches.[46] At the behest of Bishop McDonnell, special collections were taken in all the Catholic churches within the Brooklyn Diocese. It was reported that each pastor and assistant made such earnest pleas for generosity on behalf of the earthquake survivors that they generated gratifying results—146 parishes gave $16,608. Efforts were especially emphatic in Italian parishes that were so crowded that people filled the aisles, and many local Italian societies with traditional banners and sashes were in attendance. In each of these churches, a catafalque was placed in the center aisle as a visible symbolic coffin for the dead. One of the most impressive services was held at the Church of the Sacred Hearts of Jesus and Mary in South Brooklyn where Fr. Ferrara, a Capuchin priest and a noted Italian orator, preached so eloquently about the glories of Italy and the misfortune that now faced them that it elicited sobbing and weeping, sometimes unrestrained, and virtually everyone in the congregation was seen wiping tears from their eyes. The otherwise modest sum of $107, collected at another Italian Brooklyn parish, St. Lucy's, was considered "remarkable considering the humble circumstances of the majority of the parishioners."[47]

Help for earthquake survivors also came from other Brooklyn sources. Brooklyn's principal newspaper promoted fundraising via cartoons featuring Uncle Sam holding his hat upside down, upon which was written, "For The earthquake Sufferers." Above the hat were several hands pouring in coins and dollars. The *Brooklyn Eagle* contributed $1,000 and began to receive donations from businesses and individuals, which it transferred to the Brooklyn Red Cross. Other religious groups like the South Congregation Church and the First Church of Christ Scientist held special collections. Donations also came from political organizations like the United Italian American Republican Club and the Patrick F. Lynch Regular Democratic Association.

OTHER ITALIAN ORGANIZATIONS

By January 3, 1909, other Italian American organizations in New York were reporting their contribution totals in fundraising for survivors. The Societa Musicalo and Italian American residents of Lefferts Park donated $231.25, the Democratic General Committee of the Twenty-Sixth Assembly (an uptown New York Italian election district headed by Nicholas J. Hayes) collected $1,200, *Il Progresso Italo-Americano* sent in $4,100, the Italian League of Masons sent in $1,000, *Bolletino della Sera* $700, the Piccirilli brothers (the renowned stone sculptors)

$100, and John Rofrano $300.48. The Calabria American Citizens' Society raised $500, La Lega $250, the Calabria and United Societies donated altogether $1,000, and each of thirty societies agreed to give one-third of the net profits of their annual balls—this was expected to raise $10,000. The Calabria society, moreover, committed itself to aid the Italian regions of their birth well into the future.

ITALIAN AMERICANS BEYOND NEW YORK

News about the calamity in Messina and Calabria was of paramount interest in all Italian American enclaves throughout the nation. They read about the event in dozens of small Italian-language weeklies, as well as in the daily English-language press. The feature story on the front page of the *Syracuse Herald*, for instance, informed readers about the huge death toll and the magnitude of the disaster, even though an adequate casualty-number total was impossible to arrive at that early after the quake.

> Rome, Dec. 29—South Italy and the Island of Sicily have been visited by an appalling calamity, the extent of which cannot yet be grasped. An earthquake yesterday morning wrecked city after city and obliterated smaller towns and villages without number. Then a tidal wave swept along the Strait of Messina and added to the horror, drowning the people in their helplessness and panic. Fire came to complete the work of destruction. Flames broke out in the devastated cities and countless numbers of the wounded men, women and children were burned to death.[49]

Coverage of the event penetrated the unlikeliest of places as, for example, a December 30, 1908, item in *The Ogden Standard* of Utah that provided an account of the disaster along with information about sending donations for the relief of refugees to the Italian Chamber of Commerce in New York City, where it would then be transferred to the Italian Red Cross. Readers in Nebraska read about big warships "which are transformed into great floating hospitals. It is imperative that the dead be removed from the ruins to avoid a pestilence."[50] The Manitoba

Morning Free Press reported that the relatives of some local residents
might have been in the earthquake region.

> Italians in Winnipeg are horror-stricken as the news of the awful
> extent of the earthquake devastation in Calabria and Sicily is made
> known. Few of the Italian-Canadians in the city have relatives in
> the old country however, an exception is Frank Cancilia, of the
> Venice restaurant, whose sister and brother-in-law, both of India-
> napolis went to Italy for the winter.[51]

Although most within the ethnic group lacked the financial resources
of society's more affluent, within their ability, they responded promptly.
The seemingly modest sum of $114.60 sent by Middletown, Connecti-
cut, in early January represented the sacrifice on the part of a small but
emerging population of Middletown Italians who emanated from eastern
Sicily. The Italian American colony of West Hoboken, New Jersey, sponsored a night of singing with all the proceeds going for earthquake victims. In Buffalo, New York, home to another large Sicilian enclave, the
Italian-language newspaper regularly "printed subscription lists—usually small individual donations of less than a dollar, and club donations
of twenty-five or fifty dollars—from local Italians and their organizations."[52] Help came also from many Italian American Catholic parishes
such as St. Ann's in Providence, Rhode Island. Its pastor, Italian-born
Fr. Antonio Bove—whose commitment to his Italianita was reflected in
his building St. Ann School, the first Italian American school in the diocese—never forgot the land of his birth and saw it as his duty to raise
funds on behalf of earthquake victims.

A UBIQUITOUS RESPONSE

It was not only Americans of Italian ancestry who responded to the needs
of survivors—for, indeed, it was a generally widespread answer. The
governors of New Jersey and Connecticut asked the public to support
fund drives on behalf of the Red Cross, while the San Francisco, Cali-

fornia, Relief Committee approved resolutions to turn over tens of thousands of dollars left over from the funds that were collected to deal with the Great San Francisco Earthquake of 1906. Similar appeals came from the president of the Daughters of the American Revolution. Contributions came from wealthy business leaders like banker J. P. Morgan, who was a fervent admirer of Italy, where he was popular and where he spent considerable time. He was the first to notify Ambassador Griscom that he put $10,000 to aid victims at his disposal. His was a genuine interest, even to the extent of planning to visit earthquake-stricken Messina. Beer magnate Adolphus Busch donated $25,000, as did the United States Steel Corporation, while the Standard Oil Company offered $10,000 and H. C. Frick bestowed $2,500.

New York City newspapers like the *Herald* provided very extensive coverage for several days, including dramatic front page headlines, plus several additional pages of the disaster, replete with vivid photographs of the ruins. It also performed a singular and extraordinary service to the Italian American community by covering the episode via columns of articles written in the Italian language. That this was unique is evident in that it was the only major American newspaper to accommodate Italian-language readers. Accordingly, it elicited genuine praise and gratitude from a number of letter writers within the ethnic community. One correspondent wrote "to express my admiration of your magnificent account of the awful disaster to Southern Italy. The Italian page is worthy of all praise." Another congratulated

> the Herald on this splendid enterprise and humanity in printing in its columns details of the horrible catastrophe in Sicily and Southern Italy. While there are Italian newspapers in New York that inform our people in their language of this terrible disaster, we cannot fail to appreciate very deeply the humane spirit which animates the Herald in laying before the Italian people of the city in their language the complete news of the cataclysm.[53]

The newspaper also began a fundraising drive to aid earthquake sufferers.

NEW YORK THEATER

With employees volunteering their services, New York City's Savoy Theater held two special performances of "The Man from Home" for the benefit of the Italian earthquake victims fund. Over 2,000 tickets were sold and presented to Leonello Perera to promote the event among Italian Americans. The Metropolis and Yorkville Theaters also made free tickets available to Perera's committee to sell tickets within the "Latin quarters"—a revealing appellation then used to describe Italian immigrants' lodgings.[54]

AMERICAN RELIGIOUS GROUPS

Given the earth's stupendous 1908 eruption in a Catholic nation and the further fact that virtually all of the victims were Catholics, the Messina Earthquake was of momentous meaning to the American Catholic Church. Although still a minority religion, it was a growing institution whose followers included a huge number of Italians immigrants. A manifestation of the church's solicitation for survivors was evident in religious activity to honor and extend mercy to survivors in the Pontifical Requiem Mass for the dead held at St. Patrick's Cathedral on January 7, attended by Mayor McClelland, President McGowan of the Board of Alderman, and the Italian and British consuls. The appeal for the distressed Italian nation was demonstrated also in the establishment of a fund for survivors sponsored by Archbishop Farley—followed by immediate contributions of $2,000 by J. E. Schwab and $1,000 by James Butler. Soon the total would run into many thousands. Bishop Charles McDonnell of the Brooklyn Diocese ordered a special collection in all the Catholic churches in Brooklyn for earthquake victims. Once again, it was a remarkable response that was estimated to have stimulated collections of from $10,000 to $15,000.

Archbishop John Ireland of St. Paul, Minnesota, emerged as the most prominent cleric in raising funds within American Catholic circles. The influence of his personality rendered him a commanding figure in many important movements, a recognized civic and religious leader, and a friend of presidents. Such was his influence in the church that when he visited Rome shortly after the earthquake, he met with Pope Pius X, Vatican Secretary of State Cardinal Merry del Val, and Archbishop D'Arrigo of Messina, all of whom asked him to lead the American petition for relief funds. He proceeded to do this by petitions for help not only throughout his diocese but also by writing to many friends throughout the country. Ireland was full of praise over the generous support. "If there could be any compensation for such terrible miseries," he proclaimed, "these are to be found in the marvelous uprising of universal charity toward Italy." He further stated that by extending its generosity, America showed "itself also to be a great world power by the munificence of its charity."[55]

Pope Pius X technically broke precedent when he left the Vatican to cross the bridge to St. Peter's Papal Hospital in order to visit and console the injured. The gesture elicited the observation of him as a tender and generous pontiff whose action thereby lessened the exclusiveness of the Vatican. It was also noted that the antagonistic anticlerical Rome mayor Ernesto Nathan also broke precedent by cordially welcoming the pontiff when he entered the hospital. "The incident illustrates the tremendous effect of the earthquake in Italy...more than destroy cities...It has brought Church and State perceptibly nearer each other. They must work together and in harmony to relieve suffering and restore order."[56] By January 5, it was estimated that Italy suffered losses of $400 million in Messina alone and $200 million in Reggio. Although no large industrial plants were destroyed, the silk and citrus industries suffered damage, although probably not permanent. Analysts expected that the soil and sea would retain their fertility and would infallibly stimulate recovery, just as was witnessed in the recent Galveston, Texas, and San Francisco calamities. Losses, it was observed, were, in fact, localized with limited harm to the insurance industry, which was largely foreign owned. The heavy burden was to be borne by Italy: "We doubt if there be a single American who disapproves what has been done in his name by President and Congress."[57]

New York Episcopal Bishop David H. Greer asked Episcopalians to
help men, women, and children made helpless by contributing money to
the New York branch of the American Red Cross that would then be forwarded to the Italian Red Cross for allocation to sufferers. He cited the
Italian Red Cross as "one of the best Red Cross agencies in the world,
and all the money intrusted to it will be wisely and effectively used."
Under the leadership of Dr. Louis Klopsch, the fundraising efforts of
the *Protestant Christian Herald* newspaper proved to be one of the most
noteworthy.[58] It was regarded to be so generous an assistance that it led
to an audience before King Victor Emmanuel in which the monarch
expressed his deep gratitude.

> What a beautiful work you are doing! Come sit down...He said
> that the princely generosity of America had deeply touched his
> heart, and that he was glad of the opportunity for expressing
> his sincere gratitude for the practical shape the sympathy of the
> American people had assumed...America is a rich country, very
> rich: and its people know how to use the bounties of a kind Provi-
> dence in a way that must be pleasing to the giver of every good
> gift...How do you raise such vast sums? Do the millionaires of
> your country give you large sums?[59]

When he learned that money was donated by people in modest circumstances, he responded, "Then they must be very good people." Bishop
Goodsell of the Methodist Episcopal Church sent a message to ministers
in his jurisdiction, making a similar plea for funds, while American Jews
also were generous in support of fundraising for earthquake sufferers. For
example, Samuel Untermeyer and Jacob Schiff played prominent roles,
as did the great philanthropist Nathan Straus who made important donations of food, clothing, and medical supplies for the Messina victims. The
American Jewish Committee also made a strong appeal to its members.

> In common with other organizations of its kind, your Commit-
> tee viewed with profound sorrow the disaster, which befell Italy
> due to the earthquake in Sicily and Calabria in December 1908.
> The question of rendering assistance to the Italian people who

were made homeless and destitute by the disaster was discussed at some length. It was determined that, as the collecting of funds was in the hands of a capable organization, the American Red Cross Association, the following appeal be issued to the Jewish people: "The American Jewish Committee, in executive session assembled, expresses its deep sympathy with the Italian people in their distress. On behalf of American Jewry, it sends the Italian people messages of encouragement and brotherhood, with the prayer that they may be strong and hopeful of the future." We call upon the Jews of America to open wide their purses and to contribute what they can to the funds now being gathered by the American Red Cross Association. Let every Jew do his "Contributions should be sent to the nearest local Red Cross treasurer, or to the National Red Cross treasurer at Washington."[60]

FUNDING THE RESCUE EFFORT

It would soon become apparent that a rescue and rebuilding enterprise as vast as that which the Messina Earthquake required was to be extremely costly. Indeed, it would be beyond the capability of all but a few nations. Once again, the United States came through. On January 5, 1909, the United States Congress approved an expenditure of $800,000 for the relief of sufferers of the earthquake in Italy. The bill originated as H. R. 24832 and was enacted into law, Public No. 184. Thirteen days later, the Treasury Department issued Appropriation Warrant No. 16 for $800,000 in favor of the Navy Department, the agency designated by the president to expend the relief funds. The Treasury Department was to credit its General Account of Advances, Navy Department, for $800,000 with adjustments effected through the auditor for the Navy Department in the same manner as for other naval disbursements. The proposal called for assigning $300,000 for stores and supplies to be shipped on one of two steamships, the *Celtic* or the *Culgoa*, or other vessels en route to Italian waters, while $500,000 was earmarked for the purchase of building supplies and related expenses in the shipment and construction of shelters.

THE BATCHELDER PERSPECTIVE

America's generous spirit evoked favorable comments from many keen observers. One was Tryphosa Bates Batchelder—an American of upper-class comportment and a woman of letters whose travels to Italy suggested special admiration for the beauty of the ancient land and its history—mentioned the catastrophe in her reminiscence. Her approbation extended to peasant Italian immigrants who, in the early 1900s, experienced blatant discrimination in America.

> There are those who form their judgments of that great and glorious land from some poor peasant only a short time after his arrival in what seems to him a harsh, cold country, for he shrinks more from the jeering tones of those who call him "dago" or "guiney" than because he understands the meaning of these rude terms.[61]

Although Batchelder's volume on Italy was written before the terrible earthquake, significantly, she did refer to the event in an appendix, registering her opinion that the disaster helped bring about "a bond of friendship which I think has grown out of the sympathy of the American people for their suffering fellowmen in Calabria and Sicily." Batchelder took some satisfaction in the nearly $1 million expended by the American Red Cross and congressional appropriations of $800,000 for earthquake sufferers as "substantial proofs indeed of American sympathy and generosity toward Italy, that country which all men honor, admire and love."[62]

SYMPATHETIC AMERICANS

The American public responded sympathetically to earthquake victims as very many cities in the United States—especially those centers that housed large Italian American populations—raised funds. Thus, along with a sum of $100,000, Massachusetts dispatched to Sicily a Bostonian with rescue expertise having previously been in charge of assistance efforts in the wake of a devastating fire. The large Italian

American population of Chicago did its share of fundraising. Catholic churches, along with religious institutions of various denominations, instituted special collections for earthquake victims—appeals that elicited a sympathetic response in Italian parishes. Utilizing their talent in benefit performances to raise funds all over the country, the theatrical profession provided vaudeville actors who passed their hats among audiences to collect funds, while in Chicago, small theatrical establishments known as "The Five-Cent Theatres" tried to match large theaters in fundraising. The Italian Relief Committee in Chicago sponsored a "tag sale," while big-city newspapers hired chorus girls to stand in front of large downtown office buildings where they sold newspapers and simultaneously asked for donations for the earthquake victims.

There were numerous examples of cooperation from the private sector including the Hamburg-American line, which on January 5, 1909, publicized the sailing of one of its steamers from Hoboken, New Jersey, to Naples, laden with relief cargoes. The corporation further "announced that it would transport without charge a limited number of passengers who are desirous of reaching the scene of the horror with a view of learning the whereabouts of relatives and friends."[63]

ENDNOTES

1. Lloyd C. Griscom to Theodore Roosevelt, telegram, 29 December, 1908;House of Representatives, 80th Congress, 2nd sess., Doc. no. 1040; Papers relating to the foreign relations of the United States with the annual message of the president transmitted to Congress, December 8, 1908 (Washington, DC: Government Printing Office, 1912).
2. Griscom to Secretary of State, telegram, 31 December 1908; House of Representatives, 80th Congress, 2nd sess., House of Representatives, Doc. no. 1040; Papers relating to foreign relations.
3. *New York Times*, January 3, 1909.
4. Ibid., January 7, 1909.
5. Howe, *Sicily in Shadow,* 80–81.
6. *New York Times*, January 24, 1909.
7. Griscom, *Diplomatically Speaking*, 309.
8. Mabel T. Boardman, *Under the Red Cross Flag*, 194; Griscom, Diplomatically Speaking, 309–310.
9. Felicia Buttz Clark, "American Aid to Messina," *Colliers* 23 (February 6, 1909): 2; *New York Herald*, January 22, 1909.
10. The Cutting family donated the famous Cutting Arboretum in Great River, Long Island, in memory of the father who started the sugar beet industry.
11. Caroline Moorehead, *Iris Origo: Marchesa of Val D'Orcia*, 14.
12. Boardman, *Under the Red Cross Flag*, 196.
13. Bacon to Griscom, telegram, 31 December 1908; House of Representatives, 80th Congress, 2nd sess., Doc. no. 1040; Papers relating to the foreign relations.
14. *New York Tribune*, January 1, 1909.
15. *Il Movimento*, January 2, 1909.
16. *New York Times*, January 3, 1909.
17. Ibid., December 31, 1908.
18. Ibid.
19. Ibid.
20. William E. Davenport, *Errand to Messina*, March 31, 1909, 1–2.
21. Davenport, *Errand* to Messina, 3.
22. Ibid., 4.
23. *New York Times*, January 20, 1909.
24. *Brooklyn Eagle*, January 7, 1909.

25. J. Martin Miller, *The Complete Story of the Italian Earthquake Horror* (N.p.: J. T. Moss, 1909), 149–150.
26. *New York Times*, December 30, 1908.
27. *New York Herald*, December 31, 2008.
28. *Rockaway News*, January 6, 1909. Salvatore J. LaGumina, *From Steerage to Suburb, Long Island Italians* (New York: Center for Migration Studies, 1988), 16–17.
29. Howe, *Sicily* in Shadow, 77.
30. *Il Telegrafo*, January 19, 1909.
31. *Il Progresso Italo-Americano* December 30, 1908.
32. *Il Telegrafo*, January 13, 1909.
33. John Mariani, *The Italian American Contribution to Democracy* (Boston: The Christopher Publishing House, 1921), 55.
34. Antonio Mangano, *Sons of Italy* (New York: The Methodist Book Concern, 1917), 115.
35. *Il Progresso Italo-Americano*, April 4, 1909.
36. *New York Times*, January 16, 1913.
37. *Il Progresso Italo-Americano*, January 8, 1909.
38. *New York Times*, January 4, 1909.
39. Ibid.
40. Ibid., January 5, 1909. See *Il Progresso-Italo Americano*, December 28–31, 1908, January 1–20, 1909.
41. New York Times, January 1, 1909.
42. Ibid., January 9, 1909.
43. Ibid., January 11, 1909.
44. Ibid., January 8, 1909.
45. Ibid., January 8, 1909.
46. A January 1909 appeal for young Italian Americans to unite in an organization was an indication of an emerging Italian ethnic consciousness, *Brooklyn Eagle*, January 9, 1909.
47. *Brooklyn Eagle*, January 4–5, 1909.
48. *New York Times*, January 3, 1909.
49. *Syracuse Herald*, December 29, 1908.
50. *Nebraska State Journal*, December 30, 1908.
51. *Manitoba Morning Free Press*, December 31, 1908.
52. Virginia Yans McLaughlin, *Family and Community, Italian Immigrants in Buffalo, 1880–1930* (Urbana: University of Illinois Press, 1982), 155; *Il Progresso Italo-Americano*, January 14, 1909.
53. *New York Herald* December 30, 1908.
54. *New York Times*, January 5, 1909.

55. Ibid., January 17, 1909.
56. Ibid., January 6, 1909.
57. Ibid., January 5–6, 1909.
58. United States Department of State/Papers relating to the foreign relations of the United States with the annual message of the president transmitted to Congress December 8, 1908, File no. 1719271; Telegram from Acting Secretary of State Bacon to Griscom December 31, 1908, refers to $20,000 submitted by Klopsch to the State Department for earthquake relief, 501.
59. Louis Klopsch, *Romance of a Modern Knight of Mercy* (Whitefish, MT: Kessinger Publishing, 2007), 238.
60. "Third Annual Report of American Jewish Committee," *American Jewish Year Book* www.ajcarchive.org/AJC_DATA/Files/1910_1911_8_AJCAnnualReport (Washington, DC), 352–353.
61. Tryphosa Bates Batchelder, *Italian Castles Country Seats* (New York: Longmans and Co., 1911), viii.
62. Batchelder, *Italian Castles Country Seats*, 512.
63. *Il Progresso Italo-Americano*, January 7, 1909.

CHAPTER 6

THE UNITED STATES IN ACTION

With astonishing alacrity—only a few days after the catastrophe—the United States government undertook to respond with generous humanitarian assistance. After conferring with congressional leaders—Republican Senator Eugene Hale and Senate Head and House Speaker James Cannon—on January 1, 1909, President Roosevelt announced that a request would be made to appropriate $300,000 in the form of supplies, not cash, for earthquake relief needs. This would render it the largest sum ever expended up to that time by the United States on behalf of another country in distress because of natural disaster. Roosevelt met with Secretary of the Navy Truman Handy Newberry and Assistant Secretary of State Robert Bacon to ascertain the probable amount of supplies that had already been dispatched on the cargo ship *Celtic* and the supply ship *Culgoa*, as well as the probable amount needed for other shipments of aid.

CONGRESSIONAL APPROPRIATIONS

Upon reviewing the relief needs, President Roosevelt asked Congress to increase aid to $500,000 and then further to $800,000. Although his call for aid was concise, it touched on salient points and was listened to attentively.

> The appalling calamity which has befallen the people of Italy is followed by distress and suffering throughout a wide region among many thousands who have escaped with life, but whose shelter and food and means of living are destroyed. The ordinary machinery for supplying the wants of civilized communities is paralyzed; and an exceptional emergency exists which demands that the obligations of humanity shall regard no limits of nationality.
>
> The immense debt of civilization to Italy, the warm and steadfast friendship between that country and our own, the affection for their native land felt great numbers of good American citizens who are immigrants from Italy; the abundance which God blessed us in our safety; all these should prompt us to immediate and effective relief.[1]

On January 5, 1909, with only one dissent, Congress approved the expenditure of $800,000 as stipulated in H. R. 248832 that was enacted into law, Public No. 184. The Treasury Department issued the appropriations to the Navy Department, the designated agency to expend funds for purchasing all materials needed for rebuilding devastated areas of Italy, and Pay Inspector Mudd of the Naval Department in New York was charged with overseeing the loading supplies on vessels.[2] This included $300,000 worth of supplies already on its way on board the *Celtic* and additional supplies to be delivered on the *Culgoa*, *Illinois*, *Yankton*, and *Connecticut*. While these developments were transpiring, newspaper reports on January 28, 1909, a month after the earthquake, continued to describe the situation as very grave—part of the population in Reggio and Messina being "yet only half-clothed and scantily fed."[3]

USS *Culgoa*

The USS *Culgoa*, a refrigerated supply ship built in 1889 and one of four auxiliaries accompanying the sixteen battleships on the cruise of the Great White Fleet, was among the first American ships to enter the distressed area. On January 3, 1909, she broke off from the fleet to bring emergency supplies to the ravaged area. Contrary to earlier claims, Lieutenant Commander J. B. Patton, the *Culgoa* chief officer, maintained that the Messina coastline remained unchanged physically and that few lighthouses were permanently destroyed. He reported that relief supplies were left not only in Messina but also in a number of small towns, such as Sant Agata, Canziri, Reggio di Calabria, and San Giovanni. He confirmed that inquiries of Italian authorities he encountered indicated the greatest immediate need was "for medicines, clothing for women and children, and food suitable for the sick and the children, such as milk etc." Patton further reported that Captain Cagni, representing the Italian government, "requested me to deliver directly to the inhabitants when possible, as he wished them to understand what country was aiding them"—a remarkable and revealing act of selflessness and appreciation by Italian officers eschewing credit for themselves.[4]

USS *Celtic*

"Good Things for Sailors Go to Earthquake Sufferers" was the newspaper headline explaining the guideline the U.S. Navy was ready to follow as its humanitarian deed. Specifically, items loaded on the *Celtic* originally destined as holiday cheer for sailors of the Great White Fleet sailed out of New York with the same cargo but on an entirely different mission. Messina would now be the *Celtic*'s destination, where it would dispense one and a half-million navy rations to earthquake sufferers. In a rather bold step and anticipating congressional approval, a newspaper report stated that the navy vessel subsequently would make an account to Congress.

The idea of changing the Celtic into a relief ship came to her commander, Harry McL. P. Hust, last night. It met with the immediate approval of Rear Admiral Casper F. Goodrich, commandant of the navy yard, who promptly communicated with the department, at Washington. Red tape was cut out in a jiffy on the ground of humanity, necessary preparations were hurried at the yard, and the Celtic, with Christmas trees still lashed to the mast-heads—it had been designed to make the Celtic the Christmas ship for the fleet—sailed late today. Her supplies will not be eaten by American sailors, but by suffering survivors of the Calabrian and Sicilian disaster.

Will Account to Congress Later

In the face of the overwhelming need of the Italian, the department is considering its own men second; how they will be provided with food is something that will be considered later. The Navy Department takes full responsibility for this sudden gift of supplies belonging to the United States government to the Italians without warrant or law. It probably relies upon Congress to approve of its action, but the expectation is that Congress will be only too well pleased at this evidence of American pluck and of the "get there" qualities of the American navy.

Just as its ships were the first to reach Kingston after the West Indian earthquake disaster, so the American naval flag on the Celtic may be the first to bring actual food supplies to Messina from any country, even though we are 3,000 miles away. Certainly the ship has been dispatched to sea in record time—in less than eighteen hours after her captain conceived his humane plea.[5]

The recently recommissioned *Celtic* crossed the Atlantic with relief supplies for earthquake-damaged Sicily; crewmen set up a tent city at Messina and also made runs to various ports in the earthquake area, delivering supplies originally intended for the homeward-bound Great White Fleet. Its reentrance on February 12 into the Messina Harbor with three large American flags at her masthead was indeed colorful and somewhat baffling to Italian officials, until it was explained that it was Washington's birthday. Upon receiving that information, the Italian vessels in the Messina port immediately hoisted their masthead flags, sharing in the celebration.

United States naval officers exercised exceptional ambassadorial skill in rendering aid, realizing that positive interaction with officials of other nations was an essential ingredient of American diplomacy. This expertise is clearly reflected in the report submitted by Commander Harry P. Huse of the *Celtic*. After delivering vital supplies to Messina, he reported to Naples where he met and interacted with officials of both the Italian and Spanish navies.

> On arrival, an invitation was received to a reception on the 4th given by the Syndaco [mayor] and municipality to the Italian, Spanish and American officers. I attended with four commissioned officers. An address was made by an official of the city thanking the three navies for the services rendered in the earthquake district. I replied in French. The Naples papers of the next day commented very favorable on the reply, and dwelt on the fact that our officers fraternized with the Spanish officers present. The last fact seemed to create considerable interest and, I believe was given considerable publicity through the Italian newspapers generally. The same evening, boxes at the San Carlo were placed at the disposal of the officers and a large number of tickets were sent to the ship for the men. The national airs of the three countries represented were played amidst great enthusiasm. Of course, the proper formalities were observed and the proper acknowledgements were made from the American box.
>
> The lady at the head of the relief committee here, the Duchess d'Andria, requested that I visit her box in order that she might return thanks personally for the relief stores from the *Celtic*. I mention this to show how the leading Italians are quick to express their appreciation of the assistance received from America.[6]

Commander Huse then went to Rome, where he conversed at length with Italian Minister Vice Admiral Mirabello and where he commented positively on the performance of Italian soldiers and sailors assigned to relieve earthquake sufferers. His observations demonstrated an uncommon depth of understanding.

He was particularly interested in what I said of the excellent and efficient work done in the earthquake district by the Italian army and navy. I was able to refute the attacks that have been made on the two services from irresponsible sources, and explained how natural it was that individuals should feel bitterly because of the utter inability of the authorities to give individual assistance and aid.[7]

In his report to the Navy Department, Huse registered the opinion that Italian soldiers had been unfairly maligned by widely circulated reports that they merely stood around idly in the midst of the rubble. "I feel sure these were exhausted men who were resting while off duty" was his emphathetic explanation that was especially welcome to the Italian admiral.[8]

THE GREAT WHITE FLEET

It was determined that the U.S. Navy would be the best instrument through which American aid was to be delivered—a calculation based on practicality and fortuitousness. Ever since his tenure as assistant secretary of the navy, Roosevelt proved to be a firm advocate of an immense naval presence. He subscribed to the hypothesis of Albert Thayer Mahan, naval officer and historian, who energetically espoused sea power as fundamental for any nation aspiring to wield global influence. Because of the inactivity of Navy Secretary John Long, Roosevelt, as undersecretary, was able to play a key role in beefing up the navy—a position that intensified during his presidential years. Upon entering the White House, his deep conviction that only through a strong navy could the nation project its power and prestige abroad was strengthened. Sensing that the world was becoming more dangerous for the country because of military buildups, and notwithstanding its emergence as an economic power, he concluded that it would be unwise to appear to be a second-rate military power. Accordingly, he called for a major increase in the strength of the navy—in reality, there had been pressures in this direction since the 1880s. Democrats in Congress balked at his appropriations request, preferring to finance only a purely defensive naval arm—a view Roosevelt rejected. He proposed increasing the number of warships (battleships, cruisers, destroyers, etc.) and, with solid Republican support and some Democrats behind him, won a big victory in modernizing and strengthening the navy. From 1904 to 1907, the United States constructed eleven new battleships—"[l]ike so many other Roosevelt initiatives, the naval program and the strategic thinking behind it were ahead of their time."[9]

And thus it transpired that on a warm and cloudy morning in December 1907, President Roosevelt proudly stood on the deck of the presidential yacht *Mayflower*—then in the waters off Hampton Roads, Virginia—to witness a mighty armada of American battleships passing in review before him. Roosevelt and throngs of onlookers on shore felt a great sense of pride as sixteen battleships all painted white instead of the customary gray, for gilded bows, steamed in a long majestic column out of Hampton Roads to the open sea, flanked by their attending auxiliary ships. (Only when the navy realized that the dazzling white warships made fine targets were they painted battleship gray and remembered as the Great White Fleet.)

ROOSEVELT IN COMMAND

When in 1907 Congress refused to appropriate funds for fuel for the fleet to circumnavigate the world, Roosevelt simply used available funds on hand and ordered the fleet to sail halfway around the world; he then informed Congress that it would have to supply funds for fuel if it wanted the navy to return, forcing its compliance. The vessels of the Great White Fleet were divided into four squadrons of warships manned by 14,000 sailors and marines under the command of Rear Admiral Robley "Fighting Bob" Evans, who was later succeeded by Admiral Charles S. Sperry. The armada was embarking upon something unprecedented—the first circumnavigation of the world by a fleet of steam-powered, steel battleships. Over a period of fourteen months, the ships would travel 43,000 miles and include twenty port calls on six continents. Given concern and strain in relations with Japan, which had demonstrated naval superiority in the Pacific after brilliantly defeating Russia in the 1904–1905 war, the Great White Fleet's visits to Yokohama and Tokyo Harbors and target practices in the Pacific were designed to impress the Japanese—by comparison to the sixteen United States battleships, Japan had thirteen.

The Great White Fleet was steaming through the Suez Canal where it then stopped to take coal in Port Said, Egypt, when Fleet Commander Admiral Sperry received word of a terrible earthquake that had struck Messina, Sicily. After coaling up, Sperry assigned some of the fleet's ships to set a course for Messina at top speed. The Italian calamity presented an opportunity for the United States to show its friendship to Italy by offering aid to the sufferers via an immediate dispatch of rescue ships—the *Connecticut, the Illinois, the Culgoa, and the Yankton*—to Messina. Because America's recent foray into world affairs was proffered through naval power, the matter of American aid administered in a foreign country through American naval forces had to be undertaken with great delicacy. Specifically, would her warships be welcome or would Italy be reluctant to open its country to such a powerful nation? The USS *Scorpion*, the Fleet's station ship at Constantinople, and the USS *Celtic*, a refrigerator ship fitted out in New York, were then hurried to Messina to relieve the *Connecticut* and the *Illinois* so that they could continue on the world cruise. The *Scorpion* left Messina for Turkey on January 9 and returned to Naples on February 2. On February 24, thirty-four sailors from the ship were temporarily transferred to the *Celtic* to aid relief operations. In mid-March, forty-one of its crew—including two Italian Americans, A. Desio and Frank Tortorelli—were transferred to a camp in Messina to help naval officers assigned to aid Assistant Surgeon Martin Donelson and Lt. Allen Buchanan. Meanwhile, the Great White Fleet completed its tour, arriving at Hampton Roads, Virginia, on February 22, 1909, where it was reviewed by outgoing President Roosevelt. The global nautical demonstration confirmed in Roosevelt's mind the significance of American strength vis-à-vis other powers.

> Nothing better for the Navy from every standpoint has ever
> occurred than the cruise of the battle fleet around the world...
> The American people have cause for profound gratification, both
> in view of the excellent condition of the fleet as shown by this
> cruise, and in view of the improvement the cruise has worked in
> this already high condition.[10]

Linking naval strength with humanitarian deeds as illustrated in his
account of the Messina operation, Roosevelt wrote laconically,

> I first directed the fleet, of sixteen battleships, to go round through
> the Straits of Magellan to San Francisco. From thence I ordered
> them to New Zealand and Australia, then to the Philippines, China
> and Japan, and home through Suez—they stopped in the Medi-
> terranean to help the sufferers from the earthquake at Messina,
> by the way, and did this work as effectively as they had done all
> their other work.[11]

In more prosaic but effective language, a machinist crewmember on
board a ship en route to Messina expressed the events from a sailor's
viewpoint.

> We was to Suez on the "Culgoa" long about the end of Decem-
> ber, when we got a message from Roosevelt to get up steam and
> push through to Messina, and give them all the food and clothing
> we could spare. We had a thousand loaves ready when we sailed
> into that Lord-forsaken place! We let it down to 'em in nets.
> We been hanging around these parts ever since...Sure! Didn't
> you know? Roosevelt is sending out wood to build three thou-
> sand houses for these Eyetalians, and we're the Johnnies that's
> with going to build 'em. Did you ever hear the likes o' that? Ain't
> he a wonder![12]

CONSUL ARTHUR S. CHENEY

Arthur S. Cheney, of New Haven, Connecticut, was the highest-ranking
American diplomat to perish in the Messina Earthquake. A graduate of
Yale School of Medicine, Cheney was in Messina celebrating Christmas

with his wife when the deadly upheaval of the earth took place. In the midst of the most damaged area of the city, the consulate was so completely and utterly demolished that, by December 30, it was concluded that it would be extremely unlikely that he had made his escape—especially since his lame leg impeded quick movement. After Stuart K. Lupton, vice consul and an Italian official, tried in vain to locate the Cheneys, Lupton opined that it would take 200 men two weeks to clear the mass of ruins and find the Cheneys—an estimate that was not an exaggeration. With the arrival of the supply ship USS *Yankton*, more sailors were assigned the task of recovering the bodies of Consul Cheney and his wife. Even though soldiers already at work at the site under Major Landis had removed the broken walls of the adjoining building that had fallen on top of the consulate, more work needed to be done. A personal visit to the consulate by Ambassador Griscom confirmed the difficulty as he saw rescuers facing dangers themselves in dealing with crevices five feet wide, solid lumps of stone, and twisted and bent steel girders.[13]

The USS *Illinois*, under the command of Captain John M. Bowyer, was in Port Said, Egypt, and on its way to Malta when it received orders to steam to Messina. It arrived and anchored at 2:30 p.m. in Messina Harbor on January 14, where officers of the Italian flagship *Regina* and Lt. Commander R. R. Belknap, U.S. naval attaché, greeted it. Its arrival added more needed personnel—hundreds of marines in blue. The next day, Bowyers sent 300 men and officers to shore under the command of Lt. Commander C. R. Millis to commence evacuating the U.S. Consulate. On this same day, Bowyers made an official call upon Lt. General Mazza at the Italian Headquarters in Messina.

Altogether, no fewer than 400 men engaged in working at the remains of the American Consulate, digging through tons of rubble thirty-five feet high. Forming human chains, they used hundreds of recently delivered wicker baskets to remove debris, which were passed hand to hand to be dumped on side. It was tedious, knuckle-scraping work with little time to rest. Finally, after nineteen days, sailors from the USS *Illinois* found the bodies of Cheney and his wife buried deep in the debris—they evidently were asleep in their bedroom when they lost their lives. Their bodies were so disfigured that identification could only be positively confirmed by recognizing Cheney's slight physical deformity and his wife's locket and wedding ring. The sailors removed the corpses with much reverence, and as they "bore them through the ruined streets to the water front, Italian soldiers and sailors saluted, the people took off their hats, and the eyes of many of the spectators filled with tears."[14] They were then placed on a ship to be brought to the United States.

The arrival of the coffins containing the Cheneys in New York was the occasion for another manifestation in which Italians, by demonstrating genuine mourning and deep respect, rendered gratitude to the United States. Significantly, save the port collector, there were no officials of the United States government or contingents of the marines or the army on hand to greet their remains on board the steamer *Venezia* when it arrived. However, there were multitudes of Italians—4,000 of them, representing twenty-eight societies—to offer their respects. Italian Ambassador Massiglia and Luigi Solari, president of the Italian Chamber of Commerce, led various Italian groups in New York. The Italian representatives were present at the Fabre Line Pier in Brooklyn where the coffins were deposited, and they followed the bodies of the Cheneys to Grand Central Station. Italian bands played the dirges while flags of Italian societies were draped in black, and their escorts wore mourning badges. The whole atmosphere of the affair was suggestive of an Italian funeral, and as the procession passed, many persons asked, "What prominent Italian is dead?" Thousands lined the streets and men bared their heads as the procession moved through Manhattan and a band played "Nearer, My God, to Thee." The sight was even more impressive because "so many in the waiting band wept for the loss of friends or relatives in the earthquake."[15] In expressing its regrets over Cheney's death, one New York Italian-language newspaper used the occasion to point out that the 10,000 Italians who had turned out to do him homage had paid their debt to America "through the tears of its unlettered people, through the tears of the workers, through the tears of the unlucky, but these were sincere tears."[16] The bodies of the Cheneys were then taken to New Haven, Connecticut, for final burial, and once again, grateful Italian Americans were present to acknowledge their debt—a delegation from Boston that was unable to be in New York. They marched in procession under a large red, white, and green banner on which were inscribed the following words: "Sympathy of the Italians of Boston."[17]

AMERICAN SHIPS IN MESSINA

The *Scorpion* received orders on December 31, 1908, to proceed for Messina. Since it was low on fuel, it was necessary to load one hundred tons of coal—a task that was completed on the same day, allowing for the vessel to start sailing at 11:30 p.m., whereupon it encountered severe gale-type weather that caused the ship to roll and forced it to seek shelter. On January 3, 1909, six days after the earthquake struck, the USS *Scorpion*, a converted yacht under the command of Commander G. W. Logan, arrived in Messina—it was the first vessel to fly the American flag in the harbor following the eruption. It was believed that the *Scorpion* would be of value in possibly picking up American tourists in the stricken area, and "it is also desirable that the American flag should be represented in Italian waters during these trying times."[18] Strangely, local Italian officials at first did not seem enthusiastic about the offer of help—deeming Italian personnel sufficient. "It was evident that there was no disposition on their part to take advantage of the offer."[19] After conferring with the American vice consul, it was determined that the best deployment for the *Scorpion* was to proceed to Naples. The *Scorpion* left a day later for Naples where the ship discharged some passengers and amassed some stores. It also picked up some supplies at Reggio and returned to Messina on January 6 where it distributed supplies to Italian medical officers.[20] Although sailors on board the ship continued to feel shocks and heard buildings fall, they continued their duties as the ship placed a searchlight on shore to assist recovery efforts.

In addition to sending soldiers to work in the rubble of the American Consulate, the *Scorpion* constructed an Anglo-American station adjoining the consulate ruins as a temporary hospital; these were basically tents under the supervision of the ship's chief surgeon, Assistant

G. C. Rhodes, who planned to confine his work largely to redressing wounds of considerable numbers of Italians who had been to America or who had relatives who lived there. This priority consideration apparently was in response to pressure from those who came to the attention of the authorities when they besieged the consulate to send word to relatives or to obtain permission to recover personal property. After conferring with the American military attaché and an Italian admiral, Commander Logan, along with Lieutenant Commander John B. Patton of the supply ship *Culgoa*, delivered the latter's supplies ashore and distributed them from that point. They also engaged many women refugees—even the injured—to work making garments on the theory that the activity would not only speed up convalescence but also distract their minds from the disaster. American ship crews also buried hundreds of dead.

INDICATION OF HOPE RETURNING

While the American ships were performing these somber tasks, there were indications of an initial return of some hope illustrated by a religious procession of Messina survivors passing through the devastated waterfront area. Priests walked through the group carrying sacred relics, and people prostrated themselves as they passed by. There were additional early signs of a return to a semblance of reality. On January 16, it was estimated that some 10,000 people still resided in Messina, and when it was reported that seven newly born babies were baptized, it was regarded as another indication of the city's return of life—although the archbishop of Messina officiated in the baptism service in a wooden hut transformed as much as possible into a church. For the first time since the debacle, Messina's provincial council met and among other things offered expressions of gratitude to the king and queen and to foreign nations, especially the United States, for their help.

Other American ships that were dispatched to Messina included the previously mentioned USS *Connecticut*, the flagship under Captain Hugo Osterhaus's command, and the USS *Illinois*. They were instructed to do everything they could to assist the beleaguered city and were given the sad task of recovering the bodies of the American Consul. Crewmen from the *Illinois*, accordingly, would receive medals from the Italian government for their role in retrieving the bodies.

Italy's appreciation of the assistance rendered by the presence of American ships was palpable in an invitation that King Victor Emmanuel extended to Admiral Sperry that led to a lengthy audience in which the monarch expressed gratefulness about American help. It was of particular interest to the admiral that, speaking at length in English, the king demonstrated extraordinary familiarity with the world cruise of the Great White Fleet. The king, whose affinity with sailing was longstanding—prior to ascending the throne, he made two trips near the Arctic Circle—likewise made a deep impression on the admiral with his striking knowledge about technical naval matters and his equally unusual familiarity with colloquial naval expressions. In his report, Sperry made sensible observations regarding Italy's acceptance of relief from outside powers.

> There is every reason to believe that while very willing to receive actual practical assistance in giving immediate relief, the Italian officials are extremely sensitive about any procedure which looks like ostentatious charity, or could be construed as a reflection upon their ability to administer the situation properly and effectively. The greatest care is being exercised by the commander-in-chief and the officers of the fleet to avoid any remarks which by sounding natural and proper feeling might have the effect of in any way hindering or dealing the relief of suffering.[21]

COMMANDER REGINALD BELKNAP

Among American navy officers at the earthquake site, few played so vital a role as did Commander Reginald Belknap. He was Ambassador Griscom's invaluable right-hand man and arguably the U.S. Navy's most resourceful representative in Italy during its recovery from the destruction. Born in Malden, Massachusetts, in 1871, the son of a rear admiral whose footsteps he followed, he graduated from the United States Naval Academy and had a rich naval experience, including service in the Spanish-American War, the Chinese Boxer Campaign, and the Philippine Insurrection. He served as naval attaché in Berlin in 1907, and then in Rome. Before his career was over, he too became a rear admiral. Belknap's value lay not only in representing the American ambassador but also in his naval background; he was in a unique and ideal position to integrate and amalgamate the immense, multifaceted assistance that was to come from the U.S. Navy. He impressed perceptive observers as uncommonly assiduous and extremely hardworking. "By ten all lights are out except Belknap's, always the last. Every night he knots up the business of the past day; each record, answers all letters, plans out the next morning's work."[22] His daily routine was one of being available in his office where he steadfastly communicated letters and reports with United States and Italian officials. Those who corresponded with him were convinced that he read their communications with care and responded promptly in minute detail, thereby demonstrating

> the will of iron, the heart of a child, the training of a sailor who, in order to command, learned first to obey. Nowhere in all this mass of letters and reports will you find Belknap "posing" before his correspondent or that imaginary audience.
>
> Belknap is one of those natural leaders of men, who seem providentially to arise in great emergencies. His tireless energy, his cheerful courage are positively infectious; his example and influence are felt in every phase of the enterprise of which he was the leader Just what was his work? To bring order out of chaos. Men are the instruments of mankind; the race chooses the individual to carry out its desires, as the sculptor his tools. The nation, torn by a sister's anguish, acted first with the heart of Roosevelt, second with the mind of Griscom, third with the will of Belknap; these three men were the triumvirate who put through the imperial thing America desired.[23]

SHELTER A PRIORITY

Heeding the Italian government's request, the American Relief Committee agreed that one form of assistance that was desperately needed was shelter for tens of thousands of homeless in the stricken region. The issue was succinctly summed up in a New York newspaper reporting from Rome: "The gravest problem which Italy now faces is that of providing for the 200,000 made homeless by the recent earthquake, who were scattered throughout Sicily and Calabria and congregated in Naples. Their support is costing approximately $100,000 a day; an enormous sum, which neither charity nor the resources of the state can bear for any length of time."[24]

Griscom reacted speedily by delegating essential administrative tasks to Belknap, including locating the site, organizing work crews, and planning the overall operation. In consultation with Italian civil engineers, the conscientious Belknap proceeded to designate for development in the area of Messina proper a former lemon grove lying on fairly high ground with an unsurpassed view of the strait—the property's owner, along with his entire family, had perished in the earthquake. Called the "American Village," it was commonly known as Mosella, and together with "Villaggio Regina Elena" on the other side of Messina, would become the sites for 1,500 American-style cottages. Another group of 500 cottages were planned for the outskirts of Reggio and Palmi, several hundred in small locations along the coast from Messina and Taormina, for a total of 3,000 homes. There were, in addition, thousands of homes to be constructed by other nations, the Italian government, and private parties.

The model house designed by Italian contractors was a long, wooden building showing eight doors on the street, each pair having an interior door, leading to two connected rooms that constituted one dwelling. In the rear, there were small (Kitchen-Ls) kitchens with brick walls, floors, and fireplaces. Each group of houses included two large four-family houses and two shorter dwellings accommodating one family each that were grouped around a central court for ten families. From this section, one could cross a newly constructed bridge built by Italian contractors who had much experience in similar work in the United States at the Naval Academy in Annapolis.

On the other side of the bridge was the section characterized by American-designed homes, one that saw "a marked change in the street scenes, the appearance of some of the cottages nestling under the big Mulberry trees in some corners suggesting a New England village."[25] These cottages were painted white with green doors and window trimmings. House fronts were sixteen feet long facing the street and twenty feet in back, with a partition dividing the interior into two rooms. Kitchen-Ls resembled the Italian design. Windows were on either end, as well as in the kitchen. The American section had a group of larger buildings: a church built in the form of a Greek cross, two schoolhouses, and a hotel that could accommodate one hundred. Five hundred American-designed houses were also erected across the strait in Reggio, and hundreds more in smaller villages—altogether some 3,000 houses. The house building enterprise required considerable cooperation between American personnel such as Chief Carpenter Howard Freer and Italian Chief Engineer Cavalieri Simonetti. For Americans involved in the house-building project, motivation revolved around pride in building shelter for the destitute and in spreading international goodwill.

> [It] was not merely to build the houses, but to do all in such a way that the good feeling between the nations would be promoted. How we succeeded in the latter endeavor may be inferred from the cordiality of our relations, official and personal, with every one, throughout our stay in the earthquake region.[26]

JOHN ELLIOTT

John Elliott brought to his important role not only the fame of an accomplished artist but also an uncommon lineage. Born on Good Friday in 1859, he was the son of famous Scottish ancestors and related to author Robert Louis Stevenson, who in 1887 married Maud Howe, daughter of celebrated Julia Ward Howe. The Elliotts had been living in Rome for years. With unfailing good humor, John readily agreed to Ambassador

Griscom's request that the American artist lend his talents to the recovery of the earthquake-damaged district. Commander Belknap, who was at the head of the American relief forces, put Elliott to work as architect for the erection of the American Village in the lemon groves on the outskirts of the stricken city. Recognizing that construction of shelters for untold numbers of homeless was a dire need, Elliott shared in every deprivation as he devoted himself wholeheartedly to the project, working up to sixteen hours a day for four months. Elliott confessed that although he had not been trained as an architect, and that his only experience was that of building a house in Cornish, New Hampshire, he nevertheless would do what he could.

The scope of the project presented many challenges since most of the available lumber had been cut for the erection of small houses, and the door and window frames were similarly small stock pieces. Under these circumstances, Elliott put his mind to designing and building as rapidly as possible not only houses offering some comfort but also a church, a hotel, three schools, and a hospital—all out of these undersized lumber units. The entire project in which the Americans were engaged was of immense interest to the queen of Italy—especially in the section that acquired the name: "Villagio Regina Elena." Elliott frequently consulted with Queen Elena, who was so deeply involved in promoting the construction of an attractive, sanitary, and yet practical village that she personally reviewed Elliott's plans. Therefore, Queen Elena was very specific about the requirements for the hospital: three wards, dining room, pantry, bath, office, dispensary, linen closet, operating room, sterilizing room, doctors' room, nurses' room, and so on. Elliott consequently designed a building sixty feet by forty feet for the main hospital, with smaller buildings nearby for the kitchen, servants, and so on. He dealt with the need for some large buildings by combining small-sized, precut lumber units into groupings and arranged small stock windows in a pattern so as to give an agreeable effect. He also laid out plans for the streets in such a way as to preserve as many trees as possible and designed a rose window for the church.

ALFREDO BROFFERIO

Belknap went about his vital supervisory task exercising great perspicacity in seeking out individuals who not only were competent in their fields, but also were Italian-speaking people who respected Italian customs and mores. Realizing the need for cooperation and integration of efforts, he lost no time in establishing cordial relations with Tenente di Vascello Alfredo Brofferio, an Italian naval officer assigned by the Italian government to be his colleague. The American and Italian naval officers worked well together as they analyzed conflicting reports about the extent of damaged areas, especially in the early period. Belknap and Brofferio studied many details that had to be made, such as which supplies could be purchased in Naples, the number of Italian carpenters and workers required, the distribution of timber, the mix of Italian and American workers, pay scales, and so on. All of these aspects and more had to be coordinated with the U.S. Navy Department through Pay Inspector John A. Mudd, U.S.N. in New York. Mudd ventured to charter four vessels in New York and one in New Orleans to ship 11 million feet of lumber, doors, windows, sash, tools, nails, hardware, glass, roofing paper, wheelbarrows, shovels, picks, axes, fire extinguishers, stationery, and so on.[27]

Brofferio proved a fine choice because of his intelligence and astuteness and because he was well acquainted with Messina, having been stationed there previously. The house in which he had lived and that could now be spied from the poop deck of the *Celtic* was in utter ruins. Indeed, he had been transferred from Messina only days before the catastrophe—fortuitously, because of his wife's premonition, he and his family left.

> I lived there with my Signora and our children for two years. On the 22nd of December, six days before the earthquake, I was ordered away to sea. My wife decided to remain in Messina. "We are so comfortable here," she said, "the climate suits the children." So it was agreed. The night before I was to leave, there was a slight earthquake shock, but a mere nothing; we had often felt worse. I thought nothing of it. Women, however, feel things that

we cannot—my wife said to me: "This is a warning; tomorrow morning the children and I will depart with thee for Naples."[28]

Arrangements were made for Belknap and his party to enter Messina on board the *Celtic*, commanded by Captain Huse who graciously accepted them even though space was at a premium. With its own complement of 149 men and bow and stern guns, and limited officers' quarters, the ship could accommodate the Belknap contingent only by having men sleep in bunk beds in the sick bay. Belknap's party included officers Lieutenant Allen Buchanan, Ensigns Wilcox and Spofford, and Dr. Martin Donelson, as well as thirty-four petty officers and enlisted men from the USS *Scorpion* who were stowed in different parts of the ship. These navy personnel, Italian workers, and various officials arrived in Messina fifty-six days after the earthquake, February 22, and already saw signs of life returning to the city in the form of tradesmen and foot and cart traffic; they also saw half a dozen steamers unloading lumber and other building material. However, at 5:30 p.m., all signs of life melted away as the night curfew took effect.

Brofferio served as an indispensable intermediary with local officials in Messina, translating and explaining the proposed American Village project to Messina's prefect, chief engineer, and Italian naval officials. On February 23, the *Eva*, a British ship flying the American flag and a broad pennant inscribed "U.S. Carpenters," arrived—it was the first American ship bearing building material.

HIRING WORKERS

The early phase of the American house-building project consisted of unloading huge amounts of lumber and other material from the ships and stacking them in sites where they could be readily accessed. Although sailors from the *Scorpion* performed some of the actual labor, it was native Messinese, supervised by Americans, who were the primary employees for these tasks. Dozens of native, skilled carpenters were engaged in construction, some of them like a man named Grandy who was American born but of Italian parentage. There was also Tortorella, from Messina, who years before had enlisted to work on an American ship, but who now obtained permission to come to Messina to search for his family, which he happily found alive. Because he was familiar with language, people, and locality, Grandy proved to be invaluable. Soon other interpreters were found. Workmen in the rebuilding project were given white armbands marked "U.S." and a number, and were taught American ways of stacking lumber, as well as various other chores and work habits.

Similar work on preparing housing in Reggio was under way. A Norwegian steamer, the *Herm*, brought carpenters and equipment into Reggio. Generally, the American and native workers followed the model set in Messina, with occasional supervision from Belknap and Brofferio. Although Reggio did not receive as much publicity as Messina, it was just as severely damaged. Nevertheless, evidence of revival was manifest within a few weeks in the form of the reopening of a comfortable hotel, electric light for the first time ever, cleared streets, and rebuilding of houses. Wooden houses were also features of Reggio's rebirth as the emerging residential sections took on the names of Italian regions, organizations, and donor countries. The most significant of the latter was the Tremulini district, the location of the American villages that featured street names of American states like Pennsylvania, California, Arizona, and Florida.

For work to proceed efficiently and rapidly, it was deemed vital that the Americans establish a headquarters camp for Belknap and other Americans near the work site in Messina. This was a delicate undertaking since it was, on the one hand, tantamount to establishing a foreign physical presence within a sovereign nation, a move most nations were ordinarily reluctant to authorize. Ever the careful diplomat, Belknap wrote a formal letter to Commendatore Dottore A. Trinchieri, prefect of Messina, requesting his permission to approve the request for the camp. Trinchieri's reply effectively elaborated the satisfactory accord.

It is with great pleasure that I inform you that my Government, highly and fully appreciating the most noble work of Charity that you are doing in the name of that great Nation, the United States, in the cause of the sufferers from the earthquake in Calabria and Sicily, entrusts me with the honor of according you the right, in the valley of the Mosella, to occupy the camp for your personal shelter and for your officers and men.

As this camp will be considered as the official residence of the authorized representatives of the Embassy of the United States of America, His Excellency, the President of the Council, acknowledges the justice of the desire you express, that the national Flag of the United States of American should fly during the day above the place.[29]

Belknap's men then proceeded to locate a safe water-supply source and constructed a kitchen, icehouse, and a group of houses for American personnel. At noon on March 15, 1909, Belknap, Commander Huse of the USS *Celtic*, John Elliott, and a few other Americans, as well as Tenente Brofferio and other Italian officials, were present at a flag raising ceremony.

Given differences in cultures, Americans working in Sicily and Calabria perforce made adjustments to mores and customs, as well as to food traditions. For instance, although money had been provided and was entrusted to Dr. Donelson to purchase food familiar to Americans engaged in house building, the doctor was so preoccupied with a heavy stream of patients that he had no time to shop. Dr. Donelson was, in fact, one of the most sought out in the American camp, as Sicilians lined up before his small office to be treated for various injuries and illnesses. In addition, he did not hesitate to go into small hovels, even where scarlet fever raged, to minister to the sick. Consequently, American workers were left with a continous diet of Sicilian dishes including a hefty consuption of spaghetti. This prompted Belknap to observe, "Had it not been for the family dishes of spaghetti, they might have been in a bad way."[30] However, in time, they found the Sicilian chef's repertoire limited and welcomed the cook from their ship who prepared meals with which they were more familiar. Sporadically, workers were confronted with stomach or bowel trouble attributed to spoiled meat or flies. However, even though these problems eased once fly screens were installed in the houses, meat was virtually eliminated as a food source as a precaution.

As in many important undertakings that shaped final outcomes involving creative choices, improvisation and adjustment guided the construction of American-built homes in Messina. Thus, although the original plans called for ceilings nine feet high, the plans were altered to construct them seven and a half feet high, thereby saving 15 percent of siding material and resulting in a better-proportioned outcome. Changes in original plans concerning the sizes of frames to be cut were especially welcome because of the considerable amount of lumber saved and greater efficiency. Likewise, after visiting the houses constructed by Engineer Giovanni Pella, an Italian builder, John Elliott recommended construction of a semibrick kitchen that was safer and more suitable to Italian habits of living. Pella now came to be regarded as a valuable addition to the project. Elliott also drew up plans for a hotel—a two-storey structure of seventy rooms of various sizes, averaging twelve feet, each large enough to accommodate two, was the result.

DISTRIBUTION

From the outset, many of those who were made homeless eagerly sought shelter in the new American Village, beseeching American authorities for priority designation to move in. They were clamoring emphatically for new American-built homes rather than those built by Italians—a situation that led to jealousy. The awkward matter caused distress for Ambassador Griscom who opined that "in the following weeks we began to learn how impossible it was to administer charity without treading on somebody's toes. I made up my mind that we ought to finish quickly and get out."[31] Exercising great tact and discretion, Belknap prudently referred all petitions for houses to Italian authorities who soon came to regard this as one of their most onerous tasks. Griscom likewise rejected entreaties from individual Italians who asked him to build houses for them. Simply put, this was inadvisable—something that could not be done. It was imperative that Americans not be sidetracked and remain faithful to original commitments. Such resoluteness required strong willpower to resist humane pleadings enveloped in eloquence, pathos, flattery, tears, and every kind of appeal. The scarcity of lumber and other building materials in the vicinity also meant a great deal of attention was necessary to provide adequate security over their lumber stacks and stores. Americans relented only when native Sicilians carried away short ends for firewood, providing they were less than one foot long.

EARTHQUAKE REMINDERS

As if to bring home the earthquake's ruthlessness to American naval personnel constructing the American Village, the ongoing discovery of bodies caused by the calamity was a constant reminder of the enormity of the catastrophe. Because the cemetery was right below the village site, American workers witnessed, almost on a daily basis, the grim activity of workers bearing the remains of the unearthed bodies for interment. The somber burial activity continued for two months after the arrival of the Belknap party. Excavation for bodies followed a pattern: "Diggers and boys wore sacks over head and neck; and on dry days a cloud of dust hung over the spot, which must have made it stifling for the workers. Ten francs a day was their wage."[32]

Endnotes

1. *New York Times*, January 5, 1909.
2. *New York Commercial*, January 18, 1909.
3. *New York Sun*, January 29, 1909.
4. Letter by Lieutenant Commander John B. Patton to Navy Department, January 15, 1909, Naval Records, Area file M 625, *National Archives*.
5. *Philadelphia Inquirer*, January 1, 1909.
6. Letter from Harry P. Huse, February 21, 1909, Naval Records, Area file M 625, *National Archives*.
7. Ibid.
8. Ibid.
9. Aida D. Donald, *Lion in the White House* (New York: Basic Books, 2007), 201.
10. *Compilation of the Papers and Messages of the Presidents*, vol. 14 (New York: Bureau of National Literatures, 1917), 7237.
11. Theodore Roosevelt, *Theodore Roosevelt: An Autobiography*, part 10 out of 11. (New York: The Macmillan Company, 1913).
12. Howe, *Sicily*, 220.
13. Griscom, *Diplomatically Speaking*, 312.
14. *New York Times*, January 17, 1909.
15. Ibid., January 30, 1909.
16. *L'Araldo*, January 30, 1909. *New York Times*, January 30, 1909.
17. *La Gazzetta del Massachusetts*, February 6, 1909.
18. *New York Times*, January 1, 1909.
19. Letter from Commander Logan to Navy Department, January 13, 1909, Navy records, *National Archives*.
20. Ibid.
21. Letter Admiral Charles Sperry to Navy Department, January 17, 1909, Navy records, *National Archives*.
22. Howe, *Sicily*, 260.
23. Ibid., 260–261.
24. *New York Post*, January 21, 1909.
25. Belknap, *House Building*, 6.
26. Ibid., 13–14.
27. Ibid., 18–19.

28. Ibid., 224.
29. Ibid., 56.
30. Ibid., 209.
31. Griscom, *Diplomatically Speaking*, 317.
32. Belknap, *House Building*, 92, 95.

CHAPTER 7

RECOVERY ON THE HORIZON

RECOVERY SIGNS

By late March 1909, Messina evinced small signs of recovery: the opening up of some forty "salone" barbershops, then a number of restaurants, followed by various vendors. These commercial establishments opened in temporary quarters provided by the municipality. The times also encouraged a new and unsavory industry in the form of unscrupulous people who "sold" misinformation regarding the earthquake and the availability of relief work. They also spread malicious tales about official wrongdoing.

By April, Messina's streetlights had been restored, leading to a termination of night restrictions and affording residents an opportunity to go out for dinner. One enterprising restaurateur brought in a portable cinematograph, thus offering entertainment along with food. Soon labor on Sundays was no longer needed, and the Messinese could now promenade down the streets in their best clothes, enjoying strolling serenaders playing their mandolins and guitars. American sailors could now spend

Sunday afternoons playing baseball in their camps. In the meantime, houses for the homeless were constructed in other earthquake-destroyed areas. Steamers transported house-construction material to Naples that was then sent by railroad to Palmi and other designated areas. Americans erected a sample house in Palmi and other locations, then local contractors built groups of thirty to sixty houses in approximately eleven towns.

AID FROM MASSACHUSETTS

Through the Massachusetts Relief Committee, which raised $100,000, Massachusetts came to play a significant role in supporting recovery efforts in the Messina area. Appointed by Governor Ebenezer Draper, banker Edmund Billings—who was placed in charge of dispensing the large sum—went to Sicily in January 1909 to personally oversee fund distribution of the largesse among the earthquake victims. Former Governor Curtis Guild made a heartfelt plea for funds, calling upon men of means such as members of the Boston Chamber of Commerce to lead in fundraising "for our brothers across the Atlantic."[1] For some Massachusetts residents, collecting funds was more than a simple act of good works. In their understandable anxiety about the fate of relatives in Messina, they provided Billings with money to relay to 200 relations in the stricken area—a gesture, in many instances, of futility since so many for whom the money was intended were either dead or orphaned and surviving in various locations. The Massachusetts Relief Committee raised $250,000, a sum that enabled Billings to remain in Sicily for an extended stay in order to visit small, outlying villages, which led him to a determination that something needed to be done for these neglected communities. The outcome was that the Massachusetts Relief Committee financed the dispatch of a steamer to Catania loaded with material for 300 homes to be built in small villages between Taormina and Messina. In the belief that reconstruction could be accelerated by prefabrication—that is, erecting house parts in the United States and assembling them in Sicily—the committee also transported forty-nine portable houses. Nonetheless, the results were less than satisfactory because of weather impairment to joints, as well as numerous damaged parts because of poor handling. The munificence of the funds administered by Billings, however, did make it possible for Messina to construct its first postdisaster boulevard—appropriately named Via Billings.[2]

Italian Americans in Massachusetts became very alarmed upon learning about the earthquake in Sicily and Calabria, especially since it was from those very regions that most of the Italian migrants to Massachusetts came. As a reporter for *La Gazzetta del Massachusetts* who went to the stricken area shortly afterwards wrote, "Our brothers in Italy—can it be—rush to help—is it possible to see, to know." He imploringly continued as he described the paralyzing powerlessness of the region. "There was an upsurge of sorrow to realize the suffering and need that we are asked to fulfill, to embrace the injured and those unable to move. It is the heart of mother Italy whose blood lies under tremendous ruins. They are our elderly, our wives, our sisters, our brothers, our children and our parents, our friends, our race."[3]

On December 29, 1908, the Italian-language newspaper circulated thousands of copies of an appeal to ethnic group members in Massachusetts to contribute to a fund drive on behalf of earthquake victims. The paper announced that it had collected over $6,400 that was turned over to a local bank and earmarked for the Italian Red Cross, and also printed the names of thousands who donated—usually small amounts. Heading the drive was Antonio G. Tomasello, president, and Giuseppe Pistorino, treasurer. Even while the latter was sincerely dedicated to the fundraising, he was preoccupied over the fate of his family—father, three brothers, and five sisters—who lived in the stricken region. From the beginning of January 1909, *La Gazzetta del Massachusetts* cited contributions from various ethnic organizations such as Italian mutual aid societies and Italian national parishes—even a sum of $4.75 from the Roma Barber Shop. Numerous musical benefits were held in various locations including famed Faneuil Hall. Even as it named the organizations involved, *La Gazzetta del Massachusetts* was critical of those that did not come through, stating that although there were seventy-five Italian organizations in Boston, only thirty-four actually participated. This picture was misleading—as indicated by one organization that had donated money to help victims of the 1905 earthquake but had never received a satisfactory accounting of how the money was used.[4] Many cities in Massachusetts with an Italian enclave—such as Revere, Waltham, Marlboro, and Lawrence—reported their own fundraising efforts, as did ethnic communities in Providence, Rhode Island, and Portland, Maine.

THE WORKFORCE

Collaboration between American and Italian authorities was established with regard to employment of local personnel. It was deemed desirable that in the house-building operation, the navy employ as many native workers as possible at the American Village construction site, a goal that was facilitated by engaging Genio Civile, an Italian government agency. Together they worked out a plan whereby native workers were to receive higher daily pay than elsewhere, excepting unsatisfactory workers who were to be weeded out. Accordingly, the local Messina prefect or Simonetti, his deputy, assumed the responsibility for establishing wages for various categories of workers depending on skills, while American officers held the authority to engage or discharge employees—usually those who exaggerated their skills or were outright incompetent. Thus the prevailing market rate of pay became standard, even when some workers fell short of expectations. There was a constant need for capable native (Sicilian) supervisors. Naval officers quickly learned that those Sicilians who had spent some time working in America generally made for better managers. Thus, in general, esteem for Italian workers tended to be perceptibly higher if such workers had been exposed to American ways, as in an instance when the person employed was "an Italian who had worked in Brookline, Massachusetts, and is fully competent to build more houses of the same type."[5] In general, Americans preferred Calabrian to Messinese workers. Whatever these critical views and purported shortcomings, Americans believed that earthquake victims eventually would benefit. Consequently, the navy became adept at finding more than a few whose assets included being able to speak the local dialects in addition to English—albeit sometimes with a Harvard accent, as in the case of an Italian immigrant who had worked in the Boston area.

Employment of hundreds of local workmen was very important in helping constructing the needed shelter, as well as helping the economic revival of everyday life in Messina. Within eight weeks, the workforce grew to over 800, with a payroll of 25,000 lire in Messina alone. The importance of such employment to the local community's social and economic welfare is readily evident in the fact that there were no absentees among workers at payday—5:30 on Saturday afternoons—and none failed to be in the queues before Paymaster Buchanan's office to receive his salary. Because of the obvious temptation on the part of some of the unscrupulous to receive more than they were entitled, Buchanan learned to exercise great care and became very proficient in doling out pay, making certain the men before him were who they claimed to be and simultaneously turning away repeaters.

Necessary steps were taken to screen out possible frauds. For instance, Italians hired as carpenters were required to possess and to bring their own tools to the job and were warned severely not to sell their names to others. All workmen were required to wear a yellow band on their left arms at all times while working and when ready to be paid. On occasion, arguments ensued around the paymaster's shack. In one instance in Reggio, a clamorous group of workers crowded around the pay room, charging that they were not being paid agreed-upon wages. The problem revolved around two contrary concepts of wages. The American view was to pay Italian carpenters up to five lire day, while supervisory Italian engineers argued that except for the very best carpenters, the salary was excessive. Belknap supported the American concept, maintaining that "under our superintendents, the Italians worked more industriously and better than they did elsewhere."[6] By contrast, performance results were deemed inferior under native Italian superintendents "who did not drive and keep after their workmen as constantly and energetically as our American carpenters did." On another occasion, the problem at the payroll office stemmed from an insufficiency of money on hand because the funds were late in arriving from Naples. Fortunately, Tenente Brofferio was able to resolve the contretemps by arranging for supervisors to provide money from their own holdings as loans until money from Naples reached Messina.

When it came to evaluating the work performances of Italian workers, there were decidedly negative opinions from American supervisors who tended to belittle the quality of the Sicilian work ethic. The assessment revealed a less than harmonious relationship between native workers and American supervisors, and not surprisingly led to some problems between the Americans working in Italy and their native counterparts. In the judgment of Americans, many Sicilians who claimed to be carpenters lacked ordinary basic skills of the trade; however, because of the attractive wages involved, very many Sicilians were tempted to pass themselves off as skilled carpenters when, apparently, many were not—rendering some validity to the negative evaluation.

The pessimistic attitudes about the supposed inferiority of Sicilian work performances were perhaps a reflection of an initial superciliousness that was tantamount to condescension. "Few of our Sicilian carpenters really deserve to be so called, and those who did were not the kind our American carpenter were accustomed to dealing with: yet by a division of labor, teaching one man only one thing, instead of building a whole house, we managed to control a large force, who produced a gratifying amount of work."[7] In the judgment of American overseers, "under our superintendents, the Italians worked more industrially and better than they did elsewhere. There was no doubt about this, because elsewhere the superintendents or foremen were all natives, who certainly did not drive or keep after their workmen as constantly and as energetically as our American carpenters did."[8] Fortunately, in time, these attitudes changed after Americans taught Italian natives American house-building skills and worked side by side with them.

Local masons also proved disappointing to Belknap. "To me the most discouraging of all experiences in Messina was to find that so terrible a lesson as the earthquake had given, of the crime of dishonest masonry work, was absolutely lost upon the local workmen."[9] The results were different and better, however, when skilled and conscientious Italians like engineer Pella made the selection of masonry workers, whom he supervised.

Payrolls of those engaged in house building proved to be significant in helping the local economy inasmuch as for many this was the only source of income because the earthquake had severely disrupted their normal occupations and livelihoods. The presence of hundreds of Americans in the stricken area of Messina also served as a boon to the local economy since American sailors spent their money purchasing local goods. For example, they bought clothing that was manufactured in small Messina sewing factories, including one cited by the media that was started by an English woman to provide additional employment for the local populace.

Specialization was established as the expeditious model in the house-building project. Belknap's plan was to build twenty-four houses a day—although with allowance for bad weather and other delays, it was hoped that an average of one hundred houses per week would be erected. Rather than have individual workers trained to construct all aspects of home building, workers were put into teams, essentially "gangs" of four men each to perform specific tasks such as framing, sheathing enclosers, brickwork for kitchens, and so on. The American Village architect, Elliott, provided a graphic description of the steps required to build the houses, beginning with the first gang on the ground.

> They cleared the land: (the peasants had previously cut down the lemon trees), smoothed and leveled the soil, drove the foundation posts, laid the sills.
> Second…gang of framers. They put up the side studs, the roof frame, the gable ends (made in the shop), and laid the floor joist.
> Third…gang. They placed the end studs, the door and window frames, their "cripples" and the kitchen framing. When the work of these two framing gangs was done, they passed on, leaving a skeleton house behind them.
> Now came one of the four enclosing gangs…They took a skeleton house and clothed it with clapboards and floors; so that the

roofers—who came next with their Sicilian capo (boss), Ferrara—
found something that looked a good deal like a house. After the
roofers had put on the roof, the finishers came. They hung the
doors, fitted and glazed the windows, put on locks and fasten-
ings, added the steps. When the carpenters were done with the
house, the bricklayers and masons took hold and built the famous
kitchen, putting in a stovepipe to make it all complete, and in their
turn making room for the painters. These men gave each cottage
two coats of white paint, green doors and trimmings.[10]

The enclosers were the most critical of the work gangs because they set
the pace for house-building completion and required the closest supervision. To speed things up, a one-lire (twenty cents) bonus per man
in enclosing gangs was established with immediate favorable results.
Instead of enclosing only one hundred houses a week, enclosing gangs
were then able to complete one hundred and seventy-six in a record-
setting week.[11]

THE ROOSEVELT VISIT

Within weeks of the navy's arrival in Messina on February 22, its house-
building project had proceeded at such a pace that the contours of an
amiable community were clearly discernible, although far from finished.
Construction had progressed to a point where distinguished visitors,
including outgoing President Theodore Roosevelt, expressed interest in
inspecting the work. With the completion of his term at noon on March 4,
1909, Roosevelt planned to indulge in one of this favorite sports: big-game
hunting in Africa. It was rumored that en route, Roosevelt might stop to
visit the earthquake site to personally see the extent of the devastation
and also review the rate of rebuilding progress underway by Americans.
Italians were no strangers to Roosevelt or his wife, who cherished their
previous visit to Italy. Interaction with Italian immigrants as neighbors in
the vicinity of his Oyster Bay, Long Island, home is even more revealing
with regard to his association with the ethnic group. By the early twentieth century, Italians had developed significant ethnic enclaves in Oyster

Bay and its vicinity where they constituted a distinctive and vital low-cost workforce in the region, with many of them working on Roosevelt's estate. Roosevelt continued to interact with them in his postpresidential career.[12]

The former president sailed from New York to Naples on board the Hamburg-American liner *Hamburg*. The mere suggestion of a possible Roosevelt visit prompted Griscom to send a wireless telegram to the former president via the America-bound Italian liner *Duca Degli Abruzzi* that communicated with the *Hamburg* in the midst of the Atlantic Ocean. Griscom's wireless message implored Roosevelt not to decline to make the prospective visit since it would be a positive step for both Italy and the United States.

> I deeply regret that the essentially private nature of your journey makes you decline all honors and prompts you to avoid the public enthusiasm which would have had such an admirable effect in emphasizing the good relations between Italy and the United States.
>
> I profit by the inventive genius of a great Italian to send you while you are at sea a welcoming message from Italy.[13]

However, a potentially disastrous incident on board the *Hamburg*, in which an Italian deportee from the United States had threatened to assail Roosevelt, endangered the visit. Although no violence ensued, it brought distress, especially to Italian authorities whose condemnation of the Italian perpetrator was unmistakable.[14] Upon reaching Naples, Roosevelt then embarked on the German–East Africa steamer *Admiral*, whose regular schedule did not include a stop at Messina; however, given Roosevelt's wish to stop at the site, the *Admiral* went out of its way in deference to such a distinguished passenger. It was to be a short diversion of three hours.

Meanwhile, navy personnel—who by April 6 supervised some 1,200 workers at the American Village, as well as at other construction locations—were thrilled even at the rumor of a possible Roosevelt visit. For Belknap and other American civilian and naval administrators, this was especially welcome news, which afforded the opportunity to demonstrate unmistakably the value of their endeavor. Although the portended visit would interrupt the work schedule and, thus, retard the desired building pace, the positive aspect, according to Belknap, was that "the rumor that Mr. Roosevelt was coming spurred every man to his best pace...We must have something worthwhile to show him."[15]

As the German steamer *Admiral* entered the Messina Harbor, one could see the royal standard flying masthead of a man-of-war nearby bearing the Italian king and queen. The monarchs were preparing their own inspection of the recovery rate of progress and were ready to alter their course to greet the ex-president. The Italian monarch proceeded to send a launch to the *Admiral* for Theodore Roosevelt, with Ambassador Griscom and other officials to board in order to come to his ship and join them in visiting Messina. It was an acknowledgment that although Roosevelt was no longer in office, the visit represented a fine occasion as a goodwill tour. Indeed, it inspired Maud Howe Elliott to expressions of an overstated but deeply felt sense of solidarity between Italians and Americans. To her, Roosevelt's visit was important because

> in the eyes of the Italians, he represented the American people. It was under his administration that the earthquake occurred, that the relief work was planned and started; he himself had given the impetus. Morally, if not technically, this was a meeting of the representatives of two great allies, Italy and the United States, bund together by the strongest of alliances, the need of each other's help.
> What would America do without the skill of the Italians? What would Italy do without the gold of the Americans? May neither ever have to stand the test.[16]

For his short stopover in Italy, Roosevelt was attired in his recognizable "rough rider" garments with the familiar soft hat that he took off only to kiss the hand of Queen Elena.[17] In his diary, John Elliott remembered the warmth and cordiality of the visit as he portrayed Roosevelt's words of praise to officers, sailors, carpenters, and volunteers engaged in the philanthropic work. He also recorded the remarkable Italian response as men and women—who apparently had still not yet finished with dressing and the act of doing their hair—nevertheless rushed outdoors and ran along his carriage, shouting, "Long live our President." This was undeniably the highest tribute the destitute population could pay to him. One commentator provided a singular, if unusual, explanation of the phenomenon: "Unconsciously the Sicilians proclaimed the fact that Mr. Roosevelt, having ceased to be President of the United States, will remain a kind of spiritual President of the unfortunate island. It has already decided that the main square of the new Messina should be called Piazza Roosevelt, in the same way that one of the principale thoroughfares of Catania is called Via Lincoln."[18] With cries of "Viva l'America" rending the air, the Roosevelt party's attempt to visit the ruins of the former American Consulate were frustrated because of narrow roads, ruins, and large crowds. Roosevelt was able to see, however, the ruins of the cathedral where debris was piled up halfway to the second-floor windows.

Notwithstanding the torrents of rain that accompanied Roosevelt and his entourage as they drove up the Viale San Martino to the camp, the road was nevertheless in good condition. Lt. Buchanan, Tenente Brofferio, formations of sailors, along with officers, volunteers, and carpenters, as well as representative naval officers from camps in Reggio and Taormina and Italian officials were present to greet them at the camp.

> The visitors walked through Viale Taft, Viale Roosevelt and Viale Stati Uniti (the streets in the American Village are all named for men who had some part in building it). Mr. Roosevelt was keen to see every detail: the ice house, the kitchen, the neat offices, the comfortable bedrooms, and finally the "mess-room," gay with bunting. Gasperone had set the tables with fresh linen, and decorated them with wild hyacinths and acanthus. Such hospitality as the Camp could afford was offered...Mr. Roosevelt made a short speech, then, raising his glass, gave the toast: "To every man of every nation engaged in this great work!"[19]

Although the heavy rain that marked the Roosevelt visit might have seemed a negative, it was perhaps fortuitous because it provided vivid example of the kind of weather that Belknap and the naval officer repeatedly encountered in their house-building project, a challenge presented by nature, threatening to thwart the completion schedule. Ironically, after the end of Roosevelt's visit on Good Friday, the day dawned bright and sunny. Sicilians, however, refused to work on the solemn religious day.

Roosevelt clearly was proud of the humanitarian work that Americans undertook in Messina both at the time of his visit and years later. In a 1916 talk he gave to Boy Scouts in his hometown, he cited the American military men who came to the aid of earthquake victims as models for the young scouts. "Those stalwart jackies were as fine a type of fighting men as there are in the world," he declared, saying that Americans should be proud of the army and the navy who, although the finest fighters in the world, "yet they were incapable of the brutalities…If they are given half a chance by the men above them they will always take care of women and children and see that no harm comes to noncombatants."[20]

ARCHBISHOP D'ARRIGO OF MESSINA

A notable relationship between officials at the American house-building site was that between Belknap, Elliott, and other Americans with Archbishop D'Arrigo of Messina. Since the cathedral had suffered only partial damage, a priest on the archbishop's staff was able to show Elliott rooms in which the cathedral valuables were kept, primarily gold and silver mantas that were royal gifts from the queens of Spain and Italy. There was a fear that valuables might be lost or stolen because some of these rooms had suffered earthquake damage. However, in a wonderful display of honesty and integrity, soldiers and people from Messina recovered and brought in all the valuable items—nothing was missing.

When it came to the question of what the American naval officials could do for the church, the archbishop asked for the building of a church and a barracks for eighteen priests. The earthquake had destroyed the priests' home and killed eighty of 105 priests. In response, architect Elliott presented his plans for a church to the archbishop that elicited deep interest and enthusiasm. The cleric also responded affirmatively to Elliott's request that the church be named Santa Croce in recognition that it was to be built by donations from the American Red Cross. Archbishop D'Arrigo also consented to a request that one of the old church bells be used to assemble men to work. This bell was brought into camp on an ox cart to "Belknapoli," as Mrs. Griscom unofficially christened the camp. The importance of the bell was a characteristic steeped in "campanilismo"—an ancient Italian tradition in which the town church bell tolled to assemble town folk on important occasions. From that day forward, the Italian workers responded to the bell as the call to work.

Letterio D'Arrigo, who served as archbishop of Messina, was a truly outstanding churchman, one whose demeanor deeply impressed keen observers. Born of a wealthy family, he cheerfully used his assets to assuage the afflicted. Immediately after the earthquake struck, he unhesitatingly converted his palace into a temporary hospital for injured victims and the homeless and made available ground for the burial of those who had perished. He also resolutely opposed a scheme to obliterate Messina even in the face of many townspeople who were prepared to comply with General Mazza's extreme proposal that the city be abandoned, bombarded, and destroyed in a move to prevent epidemic. The archbishop stated that even if there was no bread to eat, he would eat herbs but stay at his post in Messina and continue to succor the tormented populace and help rebuild the city. He averred emphatically that as long as there was a place called Messina he would remain. Thus he remained and then proceeded to build a new chapel, a library, and, subsequently, sixty-seven parishes. For this energetic devotion, he became known as "the Archbishop of the Earthquake," the symbol of Messina's rebirth.

EASTER 1909

Easter time in 1909 in Rome was busy with numerous tourists from many countries, some of whom would expect to have audiences with Italy's monarchs. However, these meetings were suspended in keeping with the period of mourning because of the earthquake disaster. There was one exception to this rule, as both Queen Elena and Queen Dowager Margherita personally welcomed Americans. "The two Queens said that they felt as though they could refuse nothing to Americans after their splendid generosity and kindness in the work of relief in Sicily and Calabria."[21] Among those received in audiences were Mrs. Winthrop Chanler whose husband was still working in Sicily, and William Hooper of Boston who also had a role in the aid effort. For his part, King Victor Emmanuel met with members of American Committee of Relief Work in Calabria and Sicily to discuss the rapid work of recovery.[22]

The celebration of Easter in Messina on April 11, 1909, against the backdrop of the horrendous natural calamity, provided a timely occasion to measure the degree of recovery that had taken place. From Maud Howe's writing, who was present on the scene, one can glean a sense of the impact made by her depiction of the Easter services presided over by Archbishop D'Arrigo as "more impressive than any I ever saw at Rome or even Seville." Howe stated that Messina then housed 40,000 and that many of them were in the congregation, including the maimed and crippled. In the afternoon, images of the Savior and of Mary the Mother were carried in procession through Messina, evoking heartfelt and emotional responses recalling the earthquake. "A poor old woman cried, Ah, Santissima Maria you nave nothing, not even a drum, to do you honor! Ah! The band that went before you a year ago! The musicians are all dead. I lost my two daughters. They are under the ruins; may I meet them in Paradise."[23]

All the while, tremors continued. Indeed, earthquake shocks that caused frame structures to quiver persisted in the Messina region until the middle of May—somber reminders to people of the morning of December 28. Understandably, they also caused near panic among workmen, some of whom did leave their jobs, saying they would not go back to Messina. These concerns notwithstanding, the Catholic populace displayed a muscular fidelity.

For the religious faithful in Reggio, recovery was evident in the midst of ruined churches and shrines. On May 9, 1909, Fr. Giuseppe Filianoti led a solemn procession to worship at a shrine on a nearby hill—using a makeshift shed as the chapel. By September, worshippers in Reggio were prepared to venerate Maria della Consolazione, the city's patron, attending services at a shed that served temporarily as Reggio's cathedral. It was a solemn occasion that was interrupted periodically by the traditional cry of "Viva Maria."

GRISCOM'S DEPARTURE

As these events were transpiring in Messina, some of the principal American participants in the rescue efforts were in Rome winding up their affairs. Ambassador Griscom, who had actually been on the verge of ending his diplomatic tour prior to December 28 but stayed on to supervise the American aid effort, was now preparing to depart. The rate of progress in home construction had proceeded on schedule so satisfactorily that it allowed him to begin shipping household items from his beautiful home in Rome to New York by the third week of March. Ironically, the shipment was carried on the USS *Celtic* that had rendered invaluable aid to devastated areas.

After leaving the diplomatic corps, Griscom took up residence in New York City where he had earned such profound debt among Italian Americans for his earthquake work that it would soon become a factor in municipal electoral politics. The 1909 race for mayor of New York City found three men running for office: William J. Gaynor, Democrat and Tammany Hall candidate; William Randolph Hearst, who broke with Tammany Hall; and Otto T. Brannard, the Republican/Fusion candidate. Griscom, chairman of the Executive Committee of the Business Men's Municipal Association, became heavily involved in the campaign on behalf of Brannard. Realizing that Griscom's admirable record in directing the American aid during the Messina Earthquake rendered him an unusually trustworthy figure, Brannard called upon him to campaign on his behalf in Italian American enclaves. Although not a practitioner of elective politics, Griscom heartedly complied by endorsing Brannard in the heavily Italian Lower East Side—the district led by James March (Maggio). Griscom's role in the campaign was rather meaningful

> among Italians on the east side. He speaks Italian fluently, and can even make speeches in the vernacular of the southern provinces which are so largely represented on the east side. He is also popular on account of the prominent part which as Ambassador he took in the relief work at Reggio and Messina after the earthquake in. Calabria and Sicily, and has stirred the Italians to great enthusiasm.[24]

Griscom's role angered powerful Tammany Hall leaders who reacted sharply by ordering their henchmen to terrorize proprietors by tearing down Brannard posters that storeowners had put in their windows. Tammany Hall emissaries threw up a picket line a half-block away from where Griscom was to speak in a futile effort to discourage potential Italian American voters who defiantly crowded the meeting hall. Although Gaynor won the general election in a three-way race, Griscom's efforts were so very effective in the Italian areas that the district straw poll showed that Brannard gained 2,732 votes to Gaynor's 289 and Hearst's 120—a total of 409 for his opponents.

Griscom made other personal appearances in which his background in Italy came to the fore. On November 28, 1909, for instance, he addressed the First Annual Meeting of the Italian Medical Society at the Astor Hotel where he spoke about his experiences in Sicily during the earthquake, saying that much could be expected from people who were able to withstand such a blow. In December 1909, President William Howard Taft, who continued to serve as president of the American Red Cross, appointed Griscom to a subcommittee charged with reorganizing and making more efficient the charitable organization. The American Red Cross awarded Griscom a gold medal in its appreciation of the work that he had done for Italy's poor people who were subjected to the crushing and terrible natural disaster.[25]

READY TO EXIT

By mid-April 1909, the first of the homeless were already moving into the American Village, a firm indication that the project was keeping up with Belknap's ambitious schedule. It was his intention that naval personnel attempt to complete their stay in the work sites even before all inhabitants had moved in because "the presence of such an emergency organization as ours would be out of place."[26] The plan was for the various work projects to be accomplished virtually simultaneously, thus allowing the main American body to depart. The remaining work would be finished under Italian foremen, leaving only a small American party to tie up loose ends. One of the latter tasks was that of preparing contracts for those moving in, obliging them to maintain houses in the "best condition" and provide assurance that family members adhere to "good behavior." There was great concern regarding cleanliness and misuse of facilities. Inhabitants could keep neither in their houses nor in their vicinity sheep, pigs, cows, oxen, horses, asses, mules, or poultry. They were also to agree to use latrines strictly for latrine purposes, not as places to discard rubbish. In addition to the American Village, homeless Sicilians were also moving into Villaggio Regina Elena. Indeed, there was a kind of competition between expectant mothers housed in each of the villages as to who would give birth to the first baby born in an American house. On May 17, it was reported that Teodoro Lloyd Belknap Paratore was the first to claim the honor.

At the outset, Belknap aimed to complete all work by June 15, if not sooner. The rate of progress on the remaining houses had indeed been so rapid that he advanced the departure date to June 12. However, he was almost stymied because he had not counted on so many people coming to look at the houses and, indeed, to occupy them—it slowed down work somewhat and jeopardized the departure date. Nevertheless, the schedule was achieved.

As American naval personnel planned to take leave of their house-building project, the issue of the disposition of the American camp in Messina arose. After discussions with Elliott and others, Belknap determined that the best use of the camp would be to turn it over to the Little Sisters of the Poor. The sisters' former home had been so completely demolished that it would take considerable time to rebuild, thus "if they want this camp and its equipment as a temporary dwelling, it would be suitable and available. I know of no other charitable disposition equally as good as the Little Sisters are indeed poor. It would trouble them little to move what little they own in, as we move out."[27] The superior provincial of Little Sisters of the Poor was very grateful "for the kindness shown our sisters in that unfortunate country...Gentlemen, you may rest assured that your benevolence will never, never be forgotten; you will always be considered as our first benefactors and our prayers and the prayers of our dear poor will follow you everywhere."[28]

In Celebration of Departure

June 4, 1909, the last Sunday for most U.S. Navy personnel workers in Messina, was also the great Italian National Festival and appropriately the occasion on which they opened the bridge connecting Villaggio Regina Elena and the American Village, which had been jointly built by Italian and American workers, respectively. Led by the queen, a group of students waving flags in which the American stars and stripes were prominent marched before the guests—American naval officers and Italian officers and soldiers, who were treated to a great big dinner. On June 11, Commodore Belknap hosted a lunch for Italians and Americans who had worked on the house building project. It was the opportunity for a warm exchange of greetings and gratitude as the prefect of Messina spoke about the "beginning of a new life in Messina, where until now there had been a banquet of death."[29] That afternoon, throngs of people enthusiastically waving flags and bands lustily playing accompanied the main body of Americans who departed Messina on the 5:00 p.m. ferry to Naples. By his account, Belknap estimated that Americans had built or provided material for the construction of 3,171 cottages—at a cost of $235 per domicile—a hotel, church, monastery, laboratorio, and two schools. He further estimated that these cottages accommodated up to

18,000 people. Although the bulk of American Navy and civilian personnel left Sicily at this time, a small cadre under Ensign Spofford stayed on until July 1 to see to the completion and painting of kitchens.

Italy's earnest and heartfelt gratitude for what the Americans had wrought was offered in informal and formal ways. There was, for example, a spontaneous demonstration of appreciation for Americans in a small town adjoining Messina in which music accompanied townspeople who welcomed American workers in the locality with "Long live the American carpenter!" Thanks were also registered on another authorized level. The Messina municipality was especially profuse in its official message that cited the United States for taking its "part in this great manifestation of the solidarity of humanity by means of enduring works." It singled out "the gallant officers and sailors of the glorious American Navy"[30] and conferred honorary citizenship to Belknap, Buchanan, Wilcox, Spofford, Donelson, and Elliott. Upon his departure, Belknap ruminated on the aid experience and recorded his sense of satisfaction that was, in truth, a reflection of all engaged in the house building enterprise.

> Before leaving Messina, we had the satisfaction of seeing many of them filled, by needy families of all degrees of life. I have since learned from time to time of the continued usefulness of the cottages: of the wholesome influence of their orderly arrangement and attractive appearance. The church and the schools are in constant use: the hotel has become the center of the better class of life. But better than all that was the vitality that our enterprise contributed toward the restoration of the city.[31]

Merle Curti, an eminent historian of American philanthropy, cited the navy's labors in Messina as America's finest example of philanthropy.

> The outstanding example of initiative and sustained supervision on the part of foreign service officials was, however, in the Messina earthquake catastrophe, when Consul Bayard Cutting and Ambassador Lloyd Griscom organized resident Americans in relief committees, hastened to the scene of disaster, and directed the use of American unofficial as well as official contributions.[32]

LINGERING ECHOES

Reminders of the earthquake in the form of refugees continued to be manifest in New York City for many months, sometimes in spectacular ways. One instance was that of a young stowaway Maria Cavallero, evidently the youngest ever girl stowaway, who entered New York on the Italian liner *San Giorgio*. Hers was an astonishing saga. She had lost her mother, sister, and brother in the earthquake. Her father had survived, but decided to leave her in the care of relatives while he embarked for America. Tired of life with her relatives, she ran away—actually walked from Messina to Palermo and found the ship *San Giorgio* just ready to depart, whereupon she sneaked on board. She got along well with streams of emigrants traveling in steerage, playing with other children and sharing their food. Crossing the Atlantic Ocean, in time, she was found out to be a stowaway when a ship officer realized that she was alone and had slipped on board; however, ship authorities were perplexed over what to do because they had no experience with a female evader. Temporarily, they listed her as passenger/stowaway until she could be rejoined with her father, a situation complicated by the fact that she did not have her father's address, remembering only that he worked in Brooklyn. A newspaper reported that the task of locating the father would be referred to the Italian Society, otherwise she would have to be deported. A more sorrowful case was that of Charles Barbara who was sixteen years old and in Messina when the quake struck. He was injured after jumping out of a second-storey window, but, ignoring his injuries, he returned to the house and rescued his mother—his sister was killed, however. Together with his mother, he came to America and lived in Brooklyn. Unfortunately, in February 1910, Charles, now eighteen, succumbed to the earthquake injuries.[33]

Episodes of ongoing hardship for those who fled the earthquake in Italy for America were found in other parts of the United States. The United Charities of Chicago interacted with a family of survivors from the Messina Earthquake—parents and eight children who faced difficult economic times because the father and the oldest daughter were out of work. In desperation, the family tried to send younger children to work but ran afoul of the compulsory education law. Public school authorities rejected an effort to obtain working papers for a younger daughter, asserting that their records indicated she was only thirteen years old, not fourteen, as claimed by the family. To resolve the matter, the charitable agency wrote to Messina where, surprisingly, the family's records had not been destroyed, as assumed, and confirmed that the girl was, in fact, underage.[34]

Members of a Protestant church in Massachusetts heard firsthand accounts of clergymen who visited the earthquake site. Thus, on April 18, 1909, the congregation was made more fully aware about the calamity by Rev. H. Pullen, director of the Spezia Mission in Italy, who had just returned from the Messina Earthquake scene where he had been caring for Protestant victims and bringing them their due share of the relief funds. Rev. Pullen had a special permit from the Italian government to enter the forbidden zone and command whatever help from officials he desired. He showed the congregation visible evidence of the tragedy via two postcards—one was titled "Messina. Le rovine della Palazzata," and the other, "Messina—La catastrophe—Imbarco lugubre." He also provided two photographs showing ruins of Messina. "He was therefore able to give us firsthand intelligence. We are sure his story will not soon be forgotten. All were profoundly impressed, and some completely overcome by the pathos of the narrative, especially as he told of some, reduced to absolute destitution, dazed morally and spiritually as well as physically, yet returning to faith in God."[35]

RATE OF RECOVERY

It did not take very long—only a matter of days—before serious proposals for rebuilding Messina surfaced. By January 4, 1909, detailed plans with specific amounts of money needed were reported. In retrospect, these optimistic projections were unrealistic and probably were uttered to counter fears of despair and hopelessness that had gripped many. By mid-January 1909, there were reports that many who had fled the earthquake-ravaged area were returning to Messina, and discussions were underway as to the type of construction that could best resist earthquakes. To be sure, there were indications of an early comeback; as has been discussed, signs of recovery in the earthquake-stricken area were visible very early in the form of makeshift shops reopening, resumption of port traffic in Messina, the remarkably rapid construction of temporary homes, and the return of thousands of former residents.

However, there would remain for years indelible signs of the ferocity of the disaster. On December 28, 1910, exactly two years following the great catastrophe, a devastating fire struck Messina, destroying wooden buildings around the harbor including the post office, the telegraph office, and the railway station. It was a calamity described as "the final coup de grace to any plan to rehabilitate the town." Fortunately, the American quarter was not harmed. At the time, a spectator described the city's appearance as

> practically what it was the day after the earthquake. Foreign observers declared when they saw the ruins that it was extremely unlikely the city would be rebuilt, at any rate at the same site, and so far their predictions have proven correct. And yet about fifty thousand persons have been living in or near the old Messina.[36]

It was explained that these were survivors who may have fled initially, but who

> returned, driven by that strange nostalgia that makes human beings desire to go back to their native place, though it be a desert; of many others who huddled together because the villages and farms in which they existed were quite wiped out; or still others, and a good many of them, who belong to the Sicilian "loafing" class and were attracted to Messina by the prospect of obtaining charity.[37]

The area remained vulnerable to seismic upheavals for years, with earthquake shocks visiting periodically. On December 22, 1912, for instance, ominous earthquake tremors were reported in Messina and Reggio Cal-

abria. Although walls of unfinished houses collapsed, little real damage was done, owing to the fact that most of the buildings destroyed in
1908 had not yet been rebuilt. Nonetheless, the frightened inhabitants
of those locales camped outdoors in fear of future shocks. Earthquake
shocks in Calabria on June 28, 1913, were such forcible reminders of
the 1908 disaster that terror-stricken people rushed out of their homes
screaming and asking for mercy as they spent the night in open fields.
Meanwhile, earth disturbances accompanied by a hurricane that struck
Messina in August 1913 destroyed some of the American-built wooden
shacks, thereby causing panic among people living in them. Furthermore, a November 24, 1914, tremor that caused a 1908-damaged palace in Messina to collapse—claiming the lives of three people and
injuring others—led authorities to demolish similar unsafe structures.[38]
While traveling in Italy for his masterful study *The Italian Emigration in
Our Times*, Robert Foerster bluntly asserted, "Today, ten years after the
demolition of Messina, the city, its little wooden suburb notwithstanding, still is a pile of ruins."[39]

The slow pace of recovery was borne out in the writings of prolific English author David. H. Lawrence, who traveled extensively
in Italy several years after the earthquake and wrote more than one
volume about that country. In 1921 he published his famous work *Sea
and Sardinia* which, while primarily a fascinating memoir about his
travels through Sardinia, nevertheless, provides insightful reflections
regarding the effect of the earthquake upon Messina that he found vile
and depressing.

> Oh, horrible Messina, earthquake-shattered and renewing your
> youth like a vast mining settlement, with rows of streets and miles
> of concrete shanties, squalor and a big street with hops and gaps
> and broken houses still, just behind the tram lines, and a dreary,
> squalid earthquake-hopeless port in a lovely harbor. People don't
> forget and don't recover. The people of Messina seem to be today
> what they were nearly twenty years ago, after the earthquake;
> people who have had a terrible shock, and for whom all life's
> situations are really nothing, neither civilization nor purposes.

The meaning of everything all came down with a smash in that shuddering earthquake, and nothing remains but money and the throes of some sort of sensation. Messina between the volcanoes, Etna and Stromboli, having known the death's agony. I always dread coming near the awful place, yet I have found the people kind, almost feverishly so, as if they knew the awful need for kindness.[40]

The description of Francis B. Clark, who visited Messina several years after the Great Earthquake, further underscored the reality that recovery was a long way off.

We reached there after dark, and as we walked through the deserted streets and great stone business blocks and warehouses seemed substantial and untouched as they loomed above us. But the next morning we saw they were tenantless in the semi-darkness. And that there was no light in the eyeless sockets of the windows, for they were mere shells. Everything within them was but dust and ashes, and there had been no attempt to rebuild these splendid blocks. The citizens, evidently discouraged by repeated earthquakes, were living for the most part in the Campo Americano, so called, the settlement of wooden houses which had been transported ready made from benevolent America at the time of the earthquake.[41]

Thus, notwithstanding some notable signs of recovery, the revival effort would take many years. Such was the case regarding the reconstruction of the Shrine of St. Anthony of Padua that was started as a chapel by Fr. Annibale in a poor Messina neighborhood in the 1880s. Fr. Annibale sought to construct a major church on the site that had been heavily shattered by the December 28 catastrophe. However, in 1910 Pope Pius X provided him with an edifice on the place that allowed a resumption of work. Recovery came slowly. On April 26, 1919, a mysterious fire destroyed the building. Messina's faithful continued to support the new edifice, seeing its completion as a providential sign of recovery for the city as a whole. On June 13, 1922, rebuilding had advanced sufficiently that mass could be celebrated amidst a joyous and thankful congregation. The sanctuary was finally blessed on Easter, April 4, 1926, bringing jubilation throughout Messina as not only a notable religious development but also one that symbolically advanced Messina's restoration. Well into the twenty-first century, the Shrine of St. Anthony continues to attract 100,000 people on the saint's feast day.

ECONOMY

The fact that the Italian economy, especially in Sicily, was based largely on agriculture meant that the extensive earthquake-generated disaster would have deleterious impact on the economy for years to come. The effect on prices of certain agricultural products customarily derived from Sicily included lemons, from which lemon oil was produced. Since the earthquake-stricken districts around Messina normally produced more than half of the lemons consumed in American markets, the destruction of the product—an estimated 200,000 boxes had been destroyed in Messina warehouses—and consequent severe shortages were expected to lead to sensational price jumps for Americans. Compared to the 1,500,000 boxes supplied annually by California, the United States normally imported 2,000,000 boxes of lemons from Sicily. Within two weeks, lemon prices had tripled. Although Antonio Zucca, a major New York importer and Italian American political leader, predicted that the price increase would soon be over, the situation would, in fact, worsen— as evidenced by the fact that by the autumn, lemon oil that had sold for $0.75 per pound pre-earthquake had jumped to $5.00 per pound. The high cost of the product found an increase in misbranding watered products.[42] The market for bergamot, a citrus fruit used to manufacture flavoring extracts and perfumes and produced primarily in Reggio, faced a similar fate, as prices jumped fourfold in a short time.

> The bergamot trees which grew round Messina take three years to become fruitful…The earthquake first directly destroyed many of the young trees, and in the second place destroyed many indi-

rectly by causing their cultivation to be neglected. This produced a serious shortage in supply, which will probably continue for a year or two yet. In reaction to this, manufacturers turn more and more towards synthetic odorants. However, a perfumer comments: "The public simply gets more of the synthetic perfume nowadays, but, of course, there is a difference, and for the superior perfumes the essential oil must still be used. People who want the real thing must simply be prepared to pay a high price for it."[43]

There was an irony regarding the relative paucity of these agricultural items at this time because since the late nineteenth century, the United States had begun to increase substantially its production of fruits and nuts. Italy, which had previously been a major supplier of citrus fruits such as oranges and lemons, would eventually be impacted negatively, although it still exported such items to this country in lesser amounts. [44]

EXAMPLE OF REVIVAL

Notwithstanding the aforementioned problems regarding citrus fruits, other signs pointed to a rather rapid economic recovery. This was the conclusion of Giorgio Mortara, who in 1913 wrote glowingly about Messina's economic revival. "In less than five years Messina is reviving,"[45] wrote Mortara, citing the substantial return of the city's population, which now had 130,000 residents in the commune (75,000 in the city itself), compared to 160,000 in the commune (100,000 in the city itself) in 1908. In his analysis, there had to be a sufficiently mature, vigorous, and mixed economy to sustain such large numbers. Mortara referred to agriculture and fishing as mainstays of Messina's economy, maintaining that they had not seriously suffered as a result of the earthquake and, accordingly, accounted for the livelihood of 25,000 people. Orange and lemon production continued to be remunerative as was a simple form of fishing. Although there was a relative absence of large manufacturing establishments, and even though the earthquake had demolished virtually all manufacturing establishments, many already had been rebuilt, enabling 60,000 of Messina's inhabitants to derive their incomes from small manufacturing activities. It was estimated that from ten to twelve thousand people earned their incomes from local retail and foreign trade. Professionals (doctors, lawyers, engineers) and those in public offices provided living expenses for their families—about 25,000. Mortara stated that educational facilities and government offices had reopened.

Mortara depicted resumption of business that was brisk and growing in the port of Messina, which served as the main link between Sicily and the Italian mainland. The shipping business from Messina, for example, was 467,000 tons in 1913, compared to 500,000 tons in the year prior to the earthquake, while the value of goods approximated 40 million lire, as opposed to 50 million lire in 1907. Messina once again rivaled Palermo and Catania as major Sicilian export centers, mostly in the form of citrus fruits, vegetables, nuts, wine, and olive oil. Banks had resumed business, leading to sufficient capital on hand for further development. This was, to be sure, a stunning revival in so short a time, one that Mortara explained as follows:

> The revival of Messina which, at first sight might appear strange and inexplicable, is partly due to the tenacious attachment of the people of Messina to their home; but to a greater degree is the necessary consequence of economic conditions. The existence of a large natural harbour at the most suitable point for the passage of the railway between Sicily and the mainland, a port of call for ships crossing the straits, where emigrants from Eastern Sicily to America may embark and where the produce of the region maybe accumulated for export abroad calls for a city at this point.[46]

Even as he described the revival in optimistic terms, Mortara issued a sober caveat that underscored how much remained to be done before full recovery was achieved.

> The economic revival is now almost complete. But before the life of the city can resume its ordinary course, permanent dwelling houses must be built. Up to the present very few had been erected. Most of the people live in wooden barracks, only to be put up as temporary dwellings, and now, after exposure for three

or four years to a very variable and in rainy climate, in fairly bad condition.[47]

The reality was that great difficulty was encountered in moving toward rebuilding the city's residences to approach anything close to pre-earthquake numbers. The absence of a detailed municipal map to tackle the problem was lamentable, as was the existence of large piles of debris that still had to be removed. The sluggish rate of progress was attributable to inaction, want of those administrators entrusted with the task, lack of funds, and serious technical problems, but most of all to the interminable delays and official formalities that unfortunately characterized operations of the Italian national government. The situation led Mortara to conclude that it would be at least three to four years before Messinese could leave the wooden barracks for regular homes, and only then would Messina begin to appear like its former self. Regrettably, that was an overly optimistic assessment; it was estimated that fifty years later, 10,000 people still lived in the shacks and, according to certain accounts, some wooden barracks remained on location eighty years later.

The Teatro Vittorio Emanuele, the city's beautiful opera house, offers another example of the lengthy period of time that passed before before some pre-earthquake Messina fixtures were restored. Suffering extensive damage because of the earthquake, the edifice remained in partial ruins for years and suffered further damage due to bombardments during the Second World War. Finally, when, in April 1985, the rebuilt opera house was reopened, and under the esteemed conductor Giuseppe Sinopoli, it fittingly offered Verdi's *Aida* as its return bill of fare.

ENDNOTES

1. *La Gazzetta del Massachusetts*, January 9, 1909.
2. Albert Nelson Marquis, *Who's Who in New England* (Chicago, A. N. Marquis & Co, Publishers, 1916), 116.
3. *La Gazzetta del Massachusetts*, February 27, 1909.
4. Ibid., February 13, 1909.
5. Belknap, *House Building*, 215.
6. Ibid., 133.
7. Ibid., 108.
8. Ibid., 108–109, 133.
9. Ibid., 181.
10. Howe, *Sicily* in Shadow, 438–439.
11. Belknap, "Earthquake Relief Work at Messina and Reggio," *The Survey*, May 2, 1914, 115–119.
12. See Salvatore J. LaGumina, *From Steerage to Suburb*, 86, for an example of Roosevelt's personal involvement in a 1916 health issue that centered around an Italian American locale in his community.
13. *New York Times*, March 31, 1909.
14. Ibid. Identified as the assailant was Giuseppe Tosti, described as a dangerous character. Apparently, he was under the delusion that Roosevelt wanted to injure his son. No physical harm was done, but Italian government officials and the Papacy apologized to the United States.
15. Belknap, *House Building*, 427–428.
16. Howe, *Sicily* in Shadow, 429.
17. *Il Movimento*, April 8, 1909.
18. *New York Times*, April 18, 1909.
19. Howe, *Sicily* in Shadow, 431.
20. *New York Times*, May 6, 1916.
21. Ibid., March 21, 1909.
22. Ibid., March 21, 1909.
23. Howe, *Sicily* in Shadow, 455–456.
24. *New York Times*, October 30, 1909.
25. Ibid., December 7, 1909.
26. Belknap, *House Building*, 188.
27. Ibid., 222.
28. Ibid., 222–223, 485.

29. Ibid., 242.
30. Ibid., 251.
31. Belknap, "Earthquake Relief Work at Messina and Reggio," 115–119.
32. Curti, *American Philanthropy*, 220.
33. *New York Times*, February 25, 1910; March 20, 1910.
34. During this period, many Italian immigrant parents took their children out of school and sent them out to work in the hopes of augmenting meager family incomes. See Edith Abbott and Sophonisha Breckinridge, "The Special Problem of the Immigrant Child," in *Truancy and Non-Attendance in the Chicago Schools* (Chicago: University of Chicago Press, 1917), 264–286.
35. *Echoes of the Earthquake*, Baptist Church, Bristol.
36. *New York Times*, December 29, 1910.
37. Ibid., December 29, 1910.
38. Ibid., December 23, 1912; June 29, 1913; November 25, 1914.
39. Robert Foerster, *The Italian Emigration in Our Times* (Cambridge, MA: Harvard University Press, 1919), 63.
40. David H. Lawrence, *Sea and Sardinia* (Garden City, NY: Doubleday & Company, Inc., 1954), 17–18.
41. Francis E. Clark, *Memories of Many Men in Many Lands: An Autobiography* (Boston: United Society of Christian Endeavor, 1922), 490–491.
42. *New York Times*, September 30, 1913.
43. Ibid., November 26, 1911.
44. See Joe Morilla Critz, Alan L. Olmstead, and Paul W. Rhode, "Horn of Plenty: The Globalization of Mediterranean Horticulture and the Economic Development of Southern Europe, 1880–1930," *Journal of Economic History* 59, no. 2 (June 1999): 316–352.
45. Giorgio Mortara, "The Economic Revival of Messina," *Economic Journal*, 23, no. 91 (September 1913): 438–442. *See esp* p. 438.
46. Ibid.
47. Ibid.

Chapter 8

The Legacy

There is probably no person alive today who experienced the events of December 28, 1908, and was old enough to have a clear memory of what took place in Messina. However, there are still many who have memories and recollections of relatives who endured the calamity and for whom the events of a century ago still resonate. A number of testimonies are available on Web sites, while others volunteered the experience of their families for this study. Now in advanced age, Frank Cama recalled that his mother Madeline, born in 1894, was fourteen years old when the earthquake struck her town Gallico Marino, Calabria, with lethal fury. She was asleep when water suddenly rushed in and swept her out of bed and out the window. The force of the water kept pulling her farther and farther away from her house for about a half a mile until she grabbed for a tree trunk and held on for dear life, awaiting rescue. Injured, she carried the scar on her back from the ordeal for the rest of her life. Palma Cama remembered that her aunt was a victim of the earthquake that took the lives of her whole family. She was left an orphan and raised in an orphanage. Memories of such horror were so agonizing that decades later, neither Frank's mother nor Palma's aunt was inclined to talk about the event.[1] Louis M. Chibbaro Jr. recalled the event as told by his grandmother:

> My grandmother lived through the 1908 earthquake in Messina as a child, helping her mother care for survivors in the small town of Salice, located on a mountainside just outside Messina. Her father (my great grandfather) was in New York arranging to bring his family to America when the earthquake struck. As a child, I listened with great interest as my grandmother recounted the trials and tribulations of the townspeople at the time of the 1908 quake. My grandmother's house was among the few that remained standing and in good condition.[2]

Even more intriguing is the phenomenon that the Messina Earthquake remains a subject of fascination for many who were not directly or even indirectly connected to the catastrophe. The fascination runs the gamut from hobbies and interests to religious meanings and scientific inquiries.

GOLD

As previously discussed, when the *Republic* was sunk off the Nantucket coast in January 1909, an unconfirmed report had it that a large sum of money was on board the vessel—it was even speculated that it was one of the reasons the captain of *Republic* remained on his ship. Although denied by various officials, newspaper after newspaper carried the same story that a large sum of money destined for earthquake survivors had gone down with the ship.[3] The irrepressible rumors from that time continue to this day—becoming a veritable legend in lost-treasure lore. It has been asserted that on board the ship was a $265,000 U.S. Navy Payroll intended for delivery to the Atlantic fleet at Gibraltar—its estimated contemporary value is perhaps $50–70 million. Additionally, the *Republic* was said to have carried thousands of dollars in relief monies destined to aid the earthquake survivors, several hundred thousand dollars of silver ingots, hundreds of thousands of dollars of personal jewelry and other valuables of wealthy passengers, and also a politically sensitive and secret shipment of $3 million in gold destined for the czar of Russia that altogether constituted a five-ton shipment of mint-condition American Gold Eagle coins. Denials aside, the staggering amount of suggested wealth was more than enough to stir the imagination of would-be finders of sea wrecks.

Proponents of the gold theory in the wreckage of the *Republic* attempt to bolster their view by bringing up the fact that there was never an official inquiry into the disaster. They further rationalize that, given the enormous amount of wealth involved—worth today as much as $5 billion—its reported loss, had it been revealed at the time, would have caused public panic in the world financial markets as well as a destabilization of the government of the czar of Russia.

In 1981 Captain Martin Bayerle discovered the wreckage of the *Republic*. He maintained that "there is a high probability that the gold is there," and has since dedicated much of his adult life to recovering the gold. While there are many naysayers who categorically dismiss Bayerle's claims as preposterous—one calling him a boisterous, big-talking entrepreneur—he asserts that he is determined to salvage the greatest treasure recovery in history.[4] In 2005 a federal district court in Boston gave him the sole salvage rights to the *Republic*, and he has embarked on a fundraising effort to accumulate $20 million to lift the wreck in pieces from the bottom, 270 feet down. He further declares that some people have indeed invested in his venture. In 1997 a scuba diver testified that he dived in search of the *Republic*. "During the next two weeks there were some false alarms but no Gold Eagles…In the last ten years no one else has launched such a major operation on the Republic. Maybe the Gold does not even exist."[5] Into the twenty-first century, the legend of the elusive gold endures.

RELIGIOUS MEANING

Times of apocalyptic natural disasters have ever been periods of philosophical and religious introspection. This certainly has been the pattern in Italy, which frequently has been visited with malevolent occurrences—events that usually evoked religious responses. Processions in which the faithful carried the statue of St. Agatha through the streets of Messina and similar spiritual expressions were definitely in evidence following the December 28, 1908, catastrophe. From the outset, the earthquake became the backdrop for religious sermons elsewhere. In the United States, Fr. John Montgomery Cooper used it as the basis for his January 3, 1909, sermon in which he exhorted his congregation to extend kindness to the suffering. Employing a vivid description of the earthquake at Messina that he undoubtedly extrapolated from newspaper accounts, he emphasized the occurrence of terrifying alarums such as the trembling earth, collapse of buildings, cries of the injured, clouds of dust, people rushing into the streets, and the tidal wave that struck in the middle of the night. He reminded people of the great pain and agony suffered by victims without medical help—the hardship of survival amidst menacing conditions. These events, he preached, provided serious lessons: "1. Be prepared always for death 2. Render aid when called on 3. Kindness to sick and suffering."[6]

Another example of utilizing the Messina Earthquake as a backdrop for a sermon is that of Congregational minister Raymond Calkins of Cambridge, Massachusetts. Several years after the event, he referred to the Messina quake as one of a number of similar disturbances that were then shaking the earth as reminders that things that are made are temporary, imperfect, and undesirable. They are removed in order to strengthen a dependency on unshaken faith.

> Now we are living in earthquake times. Within the memory of all of us the ground has shaken all over the world with terrible effect. Martinique, Messina, San Francisco, Japan, Italy—the stories of these catastrophes are in all our minds. But again it is not the ground only that has shaken. Everything has seemed to be shaking. Governments have been tumbling all around us; old things have passed away. Behold all things are becoming new. Ancient and venerable religious ideas have been shaking under the impact of modern science and knowledge. The social order

is trembling. No one imagines for a moment that we are on solid foundations there. The whole question of property ownership, the whole relation of labor and wealth, the whole system of production and distribution—it is all shaking and trembling in the new world of ideas in which we live. And the civilization of a whole continent, which involves practically the civilization of our whole planet, has been shaken to its very center by terrible international collisions; and people are wondering whether there is any solid foundation upon which civilization can be rebuilt, and if so, what and where it is.

What we need then, evidently, is the recovery, if we are able to recover it, of the calm and exalted mood of the New Testament. Our most desperate need at such an hour is a sense of assurance, born of the deep spiritual persuasion that underneath all the rocking surface of things there is a foundation of God that standeth sure.[7]

Speaking at the YMCA in New York City a few days after the disaster, Dr. Lyman Abbott voiced a similar message, namely, that although natural disasters are horrendous, they are transient and outweighed by the spiritual.

You read how the king and queen immediately went to the aid of the unfortunate peasants. You also read that immediately—in the fraction of a half second—the thought occurred to the peasants to turn to the Almighty. Skeptics laugh at their falling on their knees in prayer at their procession with the cross; but through their tears the peasants saw more than the laughing skeptic; they saw the eternal spirit.[8]

To many Italians, disasters regularly visited upon the populace were essentially deserved chastisements because of sinful conduct—calamities meted out as punishment. This understanding was unacceptable to some, like Italian Socialists who belittled "the hand of God" explanation as too casual and, even more, as a ridiculous superstition. Causal interpretations of the Great Earthquake became staples of contemporary political wrangling.[9] In contradistinction to right wing political groups including clerical parties, those of a left wing persuasion emphasized political, economic, and social reform as the rational way to deal with natural disasters. Because these differing ideologies were expressed within the context of political infighting, the situation became more exacerbated.

Even more disturbing was the attitude of zealous and aggressive atheists who mocked the religious expression that a natural disaster of this magnitude produced. What followed was a wave of religious excitation in the form of millenarianism which, in Messina, took the form of competing ideologies that pitted the spiritual versus secular—specifically, the disaster prediction a year before it occurred, versus a challenge to God. Thus, in October 1907, the archbishop of Messina had prophesied the ruin of the city—a surprising prophecy rendered even more startling when it was juxtaposed with that of an atheist's impudent boast daring God to inflict such a catastrophe. Significantly, almost a century after the Messina eruption, religious leaders continue to refer to the earthquake phenomenon as an unerring lesson of divine intercession. In one instance, a Presbyterian minister recounted the tale of Johnson, a man on a scaffold who nearly fell to his death and in that instant saw his whole life flashing before him, before escaping from the peril.

> Now transport yourselves to the beautiful city of Messina, Italy. In the early morning hours on Dec. 28th, 1908, an earthquake struck that city and 84,000 people were killed. Three days before, on Christmas day, the local newspaper, El Telefono, actually published a blasphemous parody of Christmas and as a part of that parody they mocked God and actually dared God to make himself known by striking the city with an earthquake.
>
> Coincidence or was God taking them up on their dare? Did God save David Johnson's life or is he just an extremely lucky guy?[10]

In 2003 a Protestant Evangelical radio program titled *The Quiet Hour* broadcasted "The Four Cities," an episode that detailed the destruction that visited four sinful cities, one of which was Messina. It cited the abominable resolution of some "wicked inhabitants" who rejected God and led to the largest devastation and destruction in a Christian nation.

> God doesn't always settle His accounts so quickly. But Scripture warns us that someday soon the entire earth will be destroyed. God

has in His mercy given us a few more moments of time to prepare for His coming. I think of the words of that old gospel song: "Oh my lovin' brother, when the world's on fire, don't you want God's bosom to be your pillow? Hide me over in the rock of ages. Rock of ages, cleft for me." Isn't it wonderful to know that those who love God have a refuge in the day when Jesus comes to claim His own? Won't you let Him be your hiding place?[11]

The non-Christian Theosophic cult also referred to the Great Messina Earthquake in communicating its belief. Its proponents wrote that although self-preservation is a natural instinct,

the brave man is always ready to risk pain and danger and even life itself for higher objects...We know that death is not the end of everything, as people so often think, and for us a catastrophe like that of Messina is not terrible simply because a large number of people were suddenly thrown out of their bodies on to the astral plane...So we should not regard that great earthquake as an evil, merely because it suddenly threw a number of people on to the astral plane. The cases of those who were imprisoned and died slowly were comparatively few. There were some who were burned to death, and some who were buried among the ruins. Those would seem to us cases of very terrible suffering, but even then we must apply our Theosophy in- the extreme cases as well as in the ordinary cases and realize that the great suffering of an occasional individual probably wiped out from his account karma which might have taken twenty ordinary lives to cancel. Therefore, while we should feel the greatest pity for the people who suffered in that way, and should do all in our power to help them, still we are not to mourn over them.[12]

BOOKS, NOVELS, AND MOVIES

Not surprisingly, the greatest of Europe's natural disasters spawned a number of popular re-creations of the phenomenon in the form of the printed word in Italian and other languages, as well as film. There are many Italian novels such as Leonida Rèpaci's *I Fratelli Rupe* (Milan: Ceschina, 1933) that contains an episodic description of the earthquake, and Mercadante's *L'omu e la terra* (Man and Land) that was inspired by the Messina Earthquake of 1908. While there will be no attempt to survey English-language novels in a comprehensive fashion, mention will be made of one novel in which the earthquake served as the central theme. In *Flag of Her Choosing*, novelist Derek Hart told his story by employing the background of the Messina Earthquake, including a mixture of fictional characters and bona fide historical figures such as Admiral Sperry, Captain Bowyer, and Ambassador Griscom. For the most part, he adhered to the historical record because, in fact, there is little need to invent horrors, given the sweeping drama of the catastrophe that provides an abundance of material for the writer to develop in the telling of awesome action, factual adventure stories, heroics, and romance.[13]

The 1908 earthquake became a subject treated in a variety of ways by a number of authors who exploited it for their own purposes. The prolific author Upton Sinclair, who wrote in many genres, provides an unusual illustration. An advocate of strenuous dieting as a health benefit, he exhorted followers not to be fearful of going without food for extended periods. In encouraging the practice of lengthy fasting, he sought to counter the fear of starvation by convincing them that diets or starvations of modest durations do not in themselves cause people to die of starvation—rather, he maintained, they die of fright. He fastened on the Messina tragedy as an example.

> The first time I fasted happened to be at the time of the Messina earthquake. I was walking about, perfectly serene and happy, having been without food for three days, and I read in my newspaper how the rescue ships had reached Messina, and found the population ravenous, in the agonies of starvation, some of the people having been without food for seventy-two hours! (It sounds so much worse, you see, when you state it in hours.)[14]

Poetry

The cataclysmic event of 1908 inspired its share of poetry. One example is that of Hâfiz Ibrâhîm, born in 1872 of an Egyptian father and a mother of Turkish origin, who wrote "The Earthquake of Messina." An excerpt of the poem that captured the emotion and feeling that it evoked follows:

> Tell me o stars, if you know, what is happening to the universe:
> Is it the wrath of God or a plot of land to punish the man?
>
> God forgive me, it is not one or the other, but the very nature of things:
> In the belly of the earth there is a riot
>
> That releases and upsets the sea and the volcano.
> O Lord, what is the chance if sea and land conspire against man?
>
> I was afraid of the seas, since the death you waited a minimum of distraction captain:
> (Here) creep under us, (threatening us) wrapping ourselves, now more forthcoming now more distant.
>
> So land and sea have arisen both (betray)
> What has happened in Messina, doubly killed in the prime of his youth?
>
> His incomparable beauty came less the arrival of the two disasters.
> In a moment was sucked from the ground and covered by the waters,
>
> Its beauty is perished at once and has made his fate.
>
> His incomparable beauty came less the arrival of two disasters.
>
> Perhaps the time had granted at least from friends and neighbours, leaving it to fellow joy to meet, the lovers meet.
>
> Earth and mountains have prevaricated on it and how arrogance has done the sea!
>
> The soil is bursting with resentment against her
> and splits so it spatters.[15]

SHAPED BY THE EARTHQUAKE

It is obviously self-evident that anyone who experienced the horror of the December 28, 1908, cataclysm would be deeply impacted by the event. This not only was unquestionably the case for those directly involved, but also proved to have influenced those who were indirectly affected. One noteworthy example was that of Salvatore Quasimodo, Nobel-Prize-winning writer and poet whose father, a government railroad administrator, was transferred to Messina to help the population following the earthquake. Hence, although born in Modica, Sicily, Salvatore grew up in the devastated city and acquired strong impressions of the power of natural forces, which would have a great impact him. This impact is evident in his writing, as follows:

> **"To My Father"**
> Where Messina lay
> violet upon the waters, among the mangled wires
> and rubble, you walk along the rails
> and switches in your islanders'
> cock-of-the-walk beret. For three days now,
> the earthquake boils, it's hurricane December
> and a poisoned sea. Our nights fall
> into the freight cars; we, young livestock,
> count our dusty dreams with the dead
> crushed by iron, munching almonds
> and apples dried in garlands. The science
> of pain put truth and blades into our games
> on the lowlands of yellow malaria
> and tertian fever swollen with mud.
> Your patience, sand and delicate,
> robbed us of fear,
> a lesson of days linked to the death
> we had betrayed, to the scorn of the thieves
> seized among the debris, and executed in the dark
> by the firing squads of the landing parties, a tally
> of low numbers adding up exact
> concentric, a scale of future life.[16]

Evoking World Sympathy

More so than any natural disaster in recent history up to that time, the Great Earthquake evoked deep and genuine interest throughout the world. It was manifestly unlike any other catastrophe, wrote a compassionate reporter. "One fact stands out vividly. Of all the calamities, so far as I know, this is the only one which has been found to be more appalling as time went on."[17] I have already recounted the exceptional aid rendered by a number of nations whose naval forces were among the first in the destroyed region, and the generous help tendered by the United States government and the American Red Cross. Even small countries contributed. For example, Switzerland's Red Cross built a village for the victims in Sicily—a series of typical Swiss-style chalets, with characteristic architecture of sloping roofs, to house forty-two families. There were, in addition, a number of fundraising efforts, such as opera performances and concerts, in various European countries: Bronislav Hubermann, the Polish-born violin virtuoso who became celebrated throughout the world, played in a 1909 Milan fundraising concert for Messina Earthquake victims, while Sicilian-born classical musician Francesco Paolo Neglia organized a fundraising grand-concert effort in Germany that raised some 5,000 francs.

One of the more unique steps to augment fundraising that occurred shortly after the tragedy was the publication of a book of empathy that featured original autographs, letters, poems, and music from over 200 leading international luminaries in a variety of fields. Actresses of the caliber of Sarah Bernhardt, poet Gabriele D'Annunzio, and writer Anatole France contributed to the volume with messages of sympathy conveyed in an assortment of languages. The English writer Thomas Hardy, for instance, used the Latin language of the Roman poet Horace: "Incedimus per ignes, Suppositos cineri doloso" ("We march through fires, hidden beneath deceptive ashes," Hor. Od. 2.1).

MOVIES AND DOCUMENTARIES

As the most destructive natural disaster in European history, the Great Earthquake of Messina attracted the attention of many cinematographers. Cameramen from various nations immediately rushed to the scene to chronicle the event by taking gory shots of collapsed buildings, rubble on the streets, and half-clad survivors. Sometimes, the photographers had to run for their lives in the face of still-collapsing walls, while leaving behind their cameras to be destroyed. The scope and scale of natural disasters with concomitant human suffering and physical devastation were said to hold a strange fascination that would attract many paying customers to graphic film retelling. Ironically, the presentations may have been too gruesome—there were reports that films of the earthquake scene including macabre twisted naked corpses were so explicit that many exhibitors returned them, deeming them "too terrible to show."[18]

There are two interesting documentaries of more recent vintage. One is *The American Experience: Rescue at Sea*, produced by Ben Loeterman, which was presented on television in 1999. It deals with the inherently dramatic event that revolved around the collision of the *Florida* and the *Republic*, the former bringing to America earthquake survivors, while the latter was bringing supplies and material to the Great White Fleet. The engrossing tale recounts the 1909 collision between two ships carrying thousands of passengers and the first use of the new Marconi wireless radio to prevent further disaster. The most recent documentary is *Messina: City without a Memory?*, produced by John Dickie for the British Arts and Humanities Research Council. The film investigates the relationship between memory and place in Italian cities—which, for Messina, is about the legacy of the 1908 earthquake. At the time of this writing, the film is to be shown in Messina in 2008 to mark the centenary of the disaster.

PSYCHOLOGICAL EFFECTS

As the twentieth century unfolded, major strides were made in the field of psychology that facilitated objectivity in the examination and analysis of the effects that natural disasters have on those directly affected. Thus, whether it is in the form of hurricanes, floods, storms, cyclones, or earthquakes, psychologists have studied the traumatic effects of grief and loss not only regarding the immediate impact but also the post-traumatic stress disorder that evidences itself in the long term. There is awareness that natural disasters can be especially traumatic for children and youth caught up in a dangerous calamity—experiences that are frightening even for adults.[19] There is also recognition that devastation to the familiar environment can be long lasting and distressing often to an entire community; one study indicates that while most go through months of grief, about 5 to 10 percent experience long-range psychological symptoms, sometimes appearing months later.

This raises the question about the psychological consequences of the Great Earthquake of 1908. Extant newspaper coverage, interviews of survivors, and other reports of the Great Earthquake clearly indicate that disaster and death threatened the entire community and resulted in mass emotional disturbances based on a sense of helplessness, disorientation, and personal guilt. Unfortunately, analysis of the psychological impact of such phenomena was then merely in its earliest stages, with (at best) only truncated versions of what had transpired. This was essentially a time of minimal sophisticated epidemiological studies on the topic. Nevertheless, there was at least one study—a PhD dissertation written by Eduard Stierlin (1909) at the University of Zurich in Switzerland who wrote on the psychological and psychiatric consequences of disasters, using data from 135 persons caught in the earthquake in Messina in Italy in 1908, as well as data from 21 survivors of a mining disaster in 1906. This work was said to focus on the psychological negative shock to the earthquake victims and found that 25 percent of the victims suffered from sleep disturbance and nightmares. The observations of historian Robert Foerster corroborate the psychological impact.

"Of all consequences however the most serious is probably psychological, the creation of a mood of helplessness, or even worse, of apathy, restraining at once the impulse to progress and the energies needed for accomplishment."[20] At the same time, there were indications that many individuals reacted well. In his study of the event, Alexander N. Hood observed.

> The immediate and almost universal effect of the earthquake had on those who escaped death at Messina was of stupefaction, almost of mental paralysis…Lamentation was infrequently heard except when caused by physical suffering. Tears were rarely seen. Men recounted how they had lost wife, mother brothers, sisters, children and all their possessions, with no apparent concern. They told their tales of woe as if they themselves had been disinterested spectator's of another's loss.[21]

Writing about another earthquake of exceptional violence that killed his mother and five brothers and destroyed a large part of his province in thirty seconds, the Italian novelist Ignazio Silone expressed astonishment at the reaction.

> I was surprised to see how much my fellow-villagers took this appalling catastrophe as a matter of course. The geologists' complicated explanations, reported in the newspapers, aroused their contempt. In a district like ours, where so many injustices go unpunished, people regard recurrent earthquakes as a phenomenon requiring no further explanation. An earthquake buries rich and poor, learned and illiterate, authorities and subjects alike beneath its ruined houses. Here lies, moreover, the real explanation of the Italians' well-known powers of endurance when faced with the cataclysms of nature. An earthquake achieves what the law promises but does not in practice maintain—the equality of all men.[22]

Commenting on this research, one contemporary scholar has opined, "As far as we can see, this outbreak of systematic studies never was built upon and they seemed to have disappeared from the awareness of later scholars."[23] And thus, we are left to extrapolate from research essentially subsequent to Messina the psychological impact of the earthquake.

SCIENTIFIC EXPLANATION: ZEBROWSKI

Italians who lived in earthquake-prone areas had long resorted to using stone construction for their houses in the belief that sturdy, solid rock could better resist the earth's periodic upheavals. By strange irony, students of earthquakes maintain that this was a fatally erroneous view. One engrossing study comparing the Messina Earthquake with the San Francisco Earthquake of 1906 raised some intriguing questions with regard to their similarities and differences. In both San Francisco and Messina, the earthquakes struck when most people were sleeping, approximately at the same time: 5:13 a.m. in San Francisco and 5:23 a.m. in Messina. The earthquakes in both cities were similar in geographic events, geographic features, and loss of personal property; however, the results were drastically different when it came to the loss of life. Whereas only 700 out of 355,000 San Franciscans died, 83,000 of 150,000 in the city of Messina alone perished—considered one of the lowest survival rates for all earthquakes. Another way of measuring comparable survival rates shows that 98.8 percent of San Francisco residents survived (that is, for every 1,000 residents, around 2 perished), while at Messina, only 33 to 45 percent survive (that is, for every 1,000 Messina residents, between 553 and 667 perished).[24]

Further comparison reveals that whereas the Messina Earthquake measured 7.5 on the Richter Scale, by contrast, San Francisco's measured 8.25—thereby releasing five times more seismic energy. Fire raged in San Francisco for three days, while in Messina the fewer smaller fires were extinguished by rain. Although few residents had actually experienced a serious earthquake, the populations of both cities were generally familiar with the phenomenon. Whereas San Francisco functioned as a major city for little more than a half a century, Messina enjoyed a history that stretched back 2,000 years and, accordingly, had a long record with earthquakes. Why, then, did the Messina disaster cost the lives of so many more people?

Zebrowski's answer involves types of construction that housed people, attributing the differences in mortality rates to the strength of building material—namely, how well these materials perform when deformed by tension, compression, shear, and torsion.

> In San Francisco, most of the structures were wood, a cheap and plentiful building material for that rapidly growing city. In Messina, houses were predominantly masonry, with massive stone floors and brick tile roofs supported by timbers set into niches in the granite walls. When Messina's walls began to wiggle in the earthquake, timber joists all over town slipped from their wall niches and allowed the heavy masonry above to crash onto the occupants below. The unsecured walls then fell in on top of the rubble. There wasn't much of a fire because there was so little to burn; nearly everything was stone. In San Francisco most occupants therefore had plenty of time to get out well before the inevitable fire.
>
> The message is clear: The death toll from an earthquake has more to do with the type of building construction that with the intensity of the earthquake. Earthquakes themselves seldom kill people; for the most part, it is our buildings that kill people.[25]

Zebrowski concluded that it was the plastic behavior of wood versus inflexible stone that explained the dramatic difference in earthquake survival rates. San Francisco's houses were built of wood, which will bend and twist and will allow its occupants time to escape during a quake. The houses in Messina were built of stone.

In actuality, Hobbs had arrived at a similar conclusion soon after the earthquake as he predicted a return of people to the area. It was his hope that a new era was dawning for Calabria and Sicily and the inhabitants would learn the lesson that proper construction was an absolute necessity.

> Calabria and Sicily as a whole are still in the age of masonry with which their history began; but the age of wood and reinforced concrete has now been inaugurated, and the American villages which have been and are still being constructed at Messina, Reggio, and San Giovanni and in scores of other communes, with groups of from

20 to 1500 cottages each, cannot but greatly hasten the dawning era when all of Calabria and Sicily shall be protected from its greatest scourge…It is vain to hope against hope that earthquakes will not return to regions which they have already visited in the past.[26]

OTHER SCIENTIFIC INTERPRETATIONS

Systematic investigation and analysis of earthquakes has undergone impressive development in the last century as volcanologists, engineers, and physicists seek to bring an objective scientific methodology into study of the phenomenon. Seismologists systematically examine oceanic and continental plates, the earth's crust, faults, tectonic stress, and ocean waves. They provide data about the motion of a deeper part of the earth and predict when earthquakes are likely to occur. Because of earthquake prevalence in the region, Messina had established a Seismological Observatory in 1887 that was destroyed in 1908. It resumed activity after a number of years and eventually was annexed to the Geophysical and Geodetic Institute of Messina University that was reformed in 1998. In its publications about earthquake research, it frequently refers to the 1908 occurrence as its pivotal point of reference.[27]

Earthquake engineering, a relatively young science, was given strong impetus by the Messina Earthquake because "it led to the first earthquake-resistant construction methods and, therefore, the science of earthquake engineering." Following the disaster, the Italian government established a team of practicing engineers and engineering professors that studied and recommended construction principles in earthquake-prone regions that, in time, would lead to other research that slowly led to policy recommendations that became integrated into building codes. Accordingly, this earthquake was responsible for the birth of the practical antiearthquake design of structures, and the commission's report appears to be the first engineering recommendation for earthquake-resistant structures by means of equivalent static method.[28]

A quick survey of the latest scientific theory about the causation of the Great Earthquake maintains that it was due to a massive underwater landslide in the Ionian Sea rather than an earthquake. A March 10, 2008, report told of a new study conducted by researchers at the University of Rome, headed by geologist Andrea Billi, and at the University of Messina. This study concluded that a landslide occurred along the undersea shelf in the Ionian Sea about fifty to sixty miles east of the Sicilian town of Giardini-Naxos and that it traveled at a speed of at least sixty miles per hour across the Straight of Messina.[29]

MESSINA AS A REFERENCE POINT

Few natural disasters of a century ago remain as ongoing reference points, as commentators and government officials regularly refer to more recent events in stressing their messages. Thus, in criticizing Myanmar's (Burma) military junta for refusing foreign aid in the face of a cataclysmic cyclone in May 2008, for example, an official said he had never before seen such delays. He cited the establishment of an air bridge of daily flights to Indonesia within forty-eight hours after the tsunami in 2004 as a reference point.[30] However, in recent years, top American officials have indeed used the Messina Earthquake to underscore or buttress policy recommendations.

In January 2005, the then secretary of defense Donald Rumsfeld argued on behalf of an increase in naval appropriations, specifically calling for a fleet of sixty small ships to shallow-water operations. He asserted that in addition to bolstering military strength, the naval force would be better able to assist in humanitarian work, citing the navy's Indonesia tsunami response as an example. Rumsfeld stated that his vision of the future American navy stressed important nonfighting goals as part of its historic and noble role. He referred to the 1907 expedition of the Great White Fleet sent out on a world cruise by President Theodore Roosevelt as a specific illustration of utilizing the military for diplomatic and humanitarian gain, and recounted the story of the fleet's presence in the Mediterranean Sea when the earthquake ripped into Messina and inflicted major damage. In the face of this tragedy, America rushed to help—the first American assistance being a navy supply ship, soon augmented by marines and crew from naval auxiliaries who lent a hand in recovery work. In this work of mercy, newly arriving supplies of food and medical supplies meant to prepare the fleet of 14,000 sailors for an Atlantic crossing were diverted directly to the disaster zone. The contributions from the low-profile auxiliaries made a great impression that redounded to the image of the battleship flotilla as an image-enhancing humanitarian triumph.[31]

Enduring reference to the Great Earthquake was included in a June 2007 speech before the War College when Secretary of the Navy Donald Winter had occasion to speak about successful cooperation and communication among the navies of the world, especially during times of distress. Contending that this collaboration bore fruit first and foremost at the time of the Messina Earthquake of 1908, he portrayed Roosevelt's idea to send a fleet of sixteen U.S. battleships on a world tour as

> a dramatic gesture aimed at audiences both at home and abroad. To the world, the message was that the United States had arrived as a significant world power, outward-looking, and filled with goodwill towards every nation. To the public of this great country, the message was that you have a Navy to be proud of, and that the strength of the U.S. Navy is a primary source of our status as a nation of influence and power.[32]

Secretary Winter reflected on the enormous impact the Great White Fleet had on audiences all over the globe that, in effect, caused the U.S. Navy to play a leading role in promoting the nation's diplomatic goals.

> The cruise also established a precedent for responding quickly to disasters to provide humanitarian assistance. As the Great White Fleet was taking on fuel in Port Said, Egypt during December 1908, the fleet commander received word that a terrible earthquake had struck Messina, Italy. Four of the ships were then immediately dispatched to Messina. The Sailors and Marines who arrived at the scene of devastation then rendered assistance in every possible way to the survivors, making a strong, positive impression on not only the Italian people but on world opinion at large.

At home, the impact of our historic world cruise was equally momentous. President Roosevelt's Great White Fleet had an enduring influence on the attitude on the people of the United States toward their Navy. The impressive display of seapower helped to impress upon the minds of the public an understanding that their country's security and place in the world required a strong Naval capability.[33]

ENDNOTES

1. Interview with Frank Cama and Palma Cama, December 20, 2007.
2. Letter from Louis M. Chibbaro Jr., editor and publisher of SicilyToday.net.
3. *New York American*, January 25, 1909; *New York Sun*, January 25, 1909.
4. Stan Freeman, "Finder of Wreck Aims for Gold," *The Republican*, January 26, 2006, www.rms-republic.com/in_the_news/.
5. Joseph M. Cocozza, *The Republic*, Pod Diver Radio & Pod Diver Tv, 1997, homepage.mac.com/josephcocozza/poddiver/page18/page22/page 22.
6. John Montgomery Cooper, sermon, "Messina Earthquake," John Montgomery Cooper Papers, Catholic University of America, Archives.
7. Raymond Calkins, "The Things That Remain." www.bestsermons.net/1926/The_Things_That_Remain.
8. *Brooklyn Eagle*, January 4, 1909.
9. See "Dio e disastri," *Il Savio*, Gennaio, 1909, N. 4, for examples of the ongoing debate between Socialists and Catholic.
10. Ronald W. Scates, "Father God, Mother Nature, and Our Salvation," www. HPPC org/sermons (accessed October 10, 2004).
11. "A Tale of Four Cities," 2001–2003, The Quiet Hour, nc, www.thequiethour. org/cgi-bin/pastsrmns/sermons04.
12. Annie Besant and C .W. Leadbeater, *The Light on the Path* (Wheaton, IL: The Theosophical Publishing House, 1926).
13. Derek Hart, *Flag of Her Choosing* (N.p.: iUniverse, 2003). English language publishers sought to capitalize on the timely event. Macmillan immediately advertised an old novel of Marion Crawford and sold an appreciable number. The earthquake figured as accessory in a number of short stories and novels of the period such as Frank Saville, *The Pursuit* (Boston: Little, Brown, and Co.), 1910.
14. Upton Sinclair, *The Book of Life*, (Girard, KS: Haldeman-Julius Company, 1921), 170.
15. Il terremoto di Messina in un poeta egiziano moderno di *Paolo Branca, Il Soldo On-Line* 1/6/2005.
16. Salvatore Quasimodo, "To My Father," The Jackdaw's Nest March 2007, hedgeguard.blogspot.com/2007_03_01_archive.html.
17. *New York Times*, January 10, 1909.
18. Rachel Low, *The History of the British Film*, vol. 2 (New York: Routledge, 1995), 29.

19. Interestingly, Carl Jung, eminent psychiatrist, studied the effects of the Messina Earthquake on a four-year-old child just after it occurred, who had learned about the event when it was discussed at the table. She became so preoccupied with the destruction of houses and the many people who lost their lives that she had nocturnal fears, was afraid to remain alone, and was in constant dread that an earthquake would kill her. Carl G. Jung, "The Association Method," *American Journal of Psychology* 31 1910: 219–269.
20. Foerster, *Italian Emigration*, 63.
21. Charles Rycroft, *Anxiety and Neurosis* (London: Maresfield, 1988), 23.
22. Quoted in Charles E. Fritz, *Disasters and Mental Health: Therapeutic Principles Drawn from Disaster Studies*, DRC Historical Comparative Series no. 10 (N.p: Disaster Research Center, 1996), 68.
23. E. Quarantelli, "The Earliest Interest in Disasters and the Earliest Social Science Studies of Disasters: A Sociology of Knowledge Approach" (Preliminary Paper 349, University of Disaster Research Center, 2005).
24. Ernest Zebrowski Jr., *Perils of a Restless Planet* (Cambridge, Cambridge University Press, 1997), 53.
25. Zebrowski, *Perils of a Restless Planet*, 5.
26. Hobbs, "The Messina Earthquake," 420–421.
27. Bottari, Antonio, Mayer-Rosa, Dieter, Ibanez, Jesus, and Maugeri, Michele, eds., *Messina Seismological Observatory Memorial*, Basel, Birkhause Verlag, Reprint from Pure and Applied Geophysics (Pageoph) Vol. 162, (2005) No. 4. See Gianluca Valensise, Daniela Pantosti, "A 125 Yr-Long Geological Record of Seismic Source Repeatability: The Messina Straits (Southern Italy) and the 1908 Earthquake," *Terra Nova* 4, no. 4 (1991): 472–483. See also Pino, Nicola Alessandro, Giardini, Domenico, Boschi, Enzo, "The December 28, 1908, Messina Straits, Southern Italy, Earthquake: Waveform Modeling of Regional Seismograms," *Journal of Geophysical Research* 105, no. B11 (2000): 25473–25492.
28. Andre Filiatrault, *Elements of Earthquake Engineering and Strucural Dynamics* (Montreal, Canada: Polytechnic International Press, 2002), 1–2. A publication by the Consortium of Universities for Research in Earthquake Engineering, 2000, states that the work of Italian engineers after the 1908 earthquake was the effective origin of the equivalent static lateral force method.
29. "Undersea Landslide Caused Messina Devastation in 1908, New Study Says Sicily at Risk for Killer Tsunami," *Sicily Today*. SicilyToday.net.
30. *New York Times*, May 9, 2008.
31. *International Herald Tribune*, January 5, 2005.
32. Remarks by Donald C. Winter, Current Strategy Forum, US Naval War College, Newport, RI, June 12, 2007.
33. Ibid.

CHAPTER 9

CONCLUSION

The century that has passed since the Great Earthquake devastated Messina provides an opportunity to review many aspects of the calamity and measure its subsequent impact. The first feature to note is a comprehension of the enormity of disaster itself, which cost so many lives. Since the destruction of Messina's municipal archives renders exactness impossible, we continue to rely on estimates of casualties—approximations that vary and range from 60,000 to 200,000, which the passage of time has not been able to verify. Approximation is not unusual since, notwithstanding all the expertise and sophistication of the twenty-first century—current natural disasters from Katrina to the Indonesia tsunami, as well as those in Myanmar (Burma) and China in 2008, have also defied accuracy in tallying casualties, leaving little better than educated guesses.

A second feature was the response of various nations and people to the Great Earthquake of 1908 that was verily remarkable and attested to a welcome sense of cooperation and brotherhood among competing nations. Huge natural disasters frequently result in instances where assistance is rendered by nations extremely hostile to one another—witness the aid offered by the United States to Iran at the time of a violent earthquake on December 26, 2003, that killed an estimated 43,000 people. The American Red Cross deployed a relief emergency response unit to Bam, Iran, where team members worked with Red Cross partners to distribute relief supplies to those in need and also to assist in recovery operations. Aid shipments were facilitated after highly unusual direct communications between Iran and the United States, which otherwise maintain no formal diplomatic ties. Indeed, Iran remains on the State Department's list of sponsors of terrorism. The dichotomy confirms a truism, namely, that in times of major tragedy people are inclined to extend themselves beyond the limitations of national, ethnic, racial, religious, and political borders.

It is upon occasions such as this that the kinship of nations and the brotherhood of mankind are convincingly and practically demonstrated. The willingness of great powers to interrupt their normal pursuits—even, at times, in the face of fatal danger to their own personnel—was especially noteworthy and a testimony that in the face of stunning natural disasters, there can be a solidarity, even if only temporarily. That Italy, the recipient beneficiary of aid in the wake of the 1908 catastrophe, continues to remember and thank the rescuers underscores the durability and sincerity of its gratitude.

Another feature was the use of military might that saw navy fighting vessels converted into instruments of compassion—an outcome that might be regarded as the equivalent of the biblical expression, "They will hammer their swords into plows."[1] It constituted a unique instance of employing instruments of war not as means of destruction but as creative tools for mankind. In the context of the Great Earthquake, mighty warships were used extensively for worthy purposes of rescue and supplying food, shelter, and clothing, while military personnel who had trained for combat now exerted themselves—even at physical risk to themselves—to aid unfortunate victims. It is a worthy mission that continues to be highlighted by military spokesmen.

Quickness of response in the face of horrendous natural disasters is bound to elicit diverse reactions: from the expeditious to the unhurried and obtuse. The Great Earthquake was a major test for a recently unified nation struggling for inclusion among the great world powers. The Italian government responded within its means, although it absorbed severe criticism over the paucity of aid, the sluggishness of its delivery, and the favoritism it showed in aiding Messina while ignoring Reggio. While the criticism was warranted, allowance must be made for the fact that the disaster was so massive that it would have been beyond the resources of all but a few nations. The criticism, moreover, was much milder by comparison to the American government's response to the Katrina Hurricane of August 2005. Aside from some perfunctory, face-saving steps, the fact that the Italian government was open to aid from other nations suggests that under the dire circumstances, it was willing to forego overly politicizing the event. The genuine solicitude displayed by Italy's king and queen won universal approval and led to their acclaim among the world's most admired monarchs.

The national disaster had a political influence of no small import for Italy's future. Only two months previously, Italy was said to be on the brink of a great European war, a situation that changed drastically due to events of December 28, 1908. Preoccupation with the catastrophe meant distraction from any consideration of foreign affairs; it temporarily forgot the European crisis, "and Italians from all parts of the peninsula proved the solidarity of the Kingdom in their efforts to help their hapless brethren of Sicily and Calabria." Italy had become aware that during the crisis Austria was trying to take advantage of its problems thereby lessening Italy's international influence. It left in the hearts of Italians a profoundly anti-Austria mindset."[2]

Avoidance of extreme measures was another feature of the Great Earthquake. Because of its location in a zone that was prone to earthquakes, and in view of the severity of the latest array of earth tremors, some advocated drastic measures. As we have seen, Italian General Mazza was prepared to bombard the city into smithereens to prevent people from ever inhabiting it again. This radical view was also endorsed by

Americans such as Rufus Leavitt, a member of the Consolidated Stock Exchange, who was in Taormina at the time of earthquake. He not only thought that the generosity shown by the United States and other nations was excessive, but also doubted the wisdom of rebuilding it. "I do not think, from what talks I had with Italians and others, that Messina will ever be rebuilt." He thought the risks were too great and that many better sites for new city were available.[3] That Messina shunned the awful notion was a testimony to determination and resiliency.

Learning from the disaster was an important feature of the earthquake— likewise, the utilization of the army for humanitarian civilian needs proved to be a valuable lesson. The 1908 Messina Earthquake marked the first time the Italian military was given major responsibility for responding to civilian disasters. It was the beginning of an evolutionary development in the area of civil protection involving both the military and civil defense along with the Red Cross. Another notable lesson was that of enacting a rigid building code that approved of mandatory construction regulations in the building of new homes and other edifices. These and other developments seemed to advance the notion of a unity of national purpose that was alien to Italian customs and history, and indeed, this was the result for a period of time. Alas, the duration of solidarity was, in fact, temporary—Dickie asserted that it lasted only for several weeks and that, in the long run, it failed to develop national identity.[4]

Nevertheless, adversity had led to unity—at least for the interim. Sociologist Edward Banfield, who studied a "typical" backward and poverty-ridden southern Italian town, rendered his view that because they were "amoral familists," Italians were impervious to the welfare of groups beyond their immediate nuclear families. This made them unable "to act together for their common good or, indeed, for any end transcending the immediate, material interest of the nuclear family."[5] Regardless of whether it was a valid interpretation, this became the prevailing view about Italians. Nonetheless, the Great Earthquake had the effect of bringing about unanimity of purpose among people in Italy, a unity that was demonstrated by numerous instances in which cities and towns assembled economic, social, and religious resources to find pragmatic ways to aid victims, even to the extent of housing and nursing them. For a society in which regionalism and localism were predominant, and one in which there remained reluctance to accept the concept of a unified nation, this was an accidental but significant development—that of lending their efforts toward a common goal. The Banfield perception that Italians were disinclined to bestir themselves on behalf of community enterprises was a widely held judgment that found ready acceptance by scholars of the Italian American experience.[6]

Notwithstanding the prevailing view, reaction among Italian Americans to the Italian ordeal was parallel to that in the Italian homeland. In their response to appeals for clothing, medicine, supplies, and monetary donations to aid earthquake sufferers, Italian immigrants coalesced and worked together to alleviate their pain and distress. The New York Italian American community—representing disparate political and social class views—on this occasion revealed an early if infrequent example of cohesion. It was another inadvertent but significant step toward concord. The large and growing Italian immigrant population in New York clearly was able to influence American political and business leadership to play a large and meaningful role in assisting Italy. Because their ancestors have coexisted all their lives in areas frequented by earthquakes and volcanoes, southern Italians have developed a fatalistic yet resilient attitude. Some maintain that this psychological background explains "the Italian American spirit of quiet determination, love and awe, hope and guardedness in the face of life."[7]

Cohesion and unity among turn-of-twentieth-century Italian Americans was only in its infancy. Emanating from a background where regional ties were strong, preoccupied with earning a living, and having a high rate of return migration, Italian Americans did not form an interconnected and organized bloc. When they joined organizations, they were likely to become members of mutual aid societies that provided sick and death benefits and that reflected their local Italian regions and towns. It must be remembered that the Order of the Sons of Italy, which sought to form an umbrella coalescence that went beyond localism, was then in its infancy—it was organized in 1905. Accordingly, for small, provincial, Italian American organizations to join in broad efforts beyond their immediate purview—as, for example, unifying to aid earth-quake sufferers—was an unusual undertaking. Banding together for the purpose of aiding fellow Italians against the horrendous natural disaster constituted one of the first effective instances of moving outside of their traditional provincial circles for a universal goal.

As for the role of the United States in the wake of Hurricane Katrina—the most horrifying natural disaster to strike the United States—it is fit-ting to make epigrammatic comparison. Whereas huge controversy has swirled around the inadequacy of the federal government's reaction to the colossal damage inflicted on New Orleans and the Gulf Coast in 2005, the United States' response to the Messina tragedy was virtually the opposite. It was exemplary. The prompt reaction by the U.S. Navy exemplified by its warships laden with ample food, medicine, and medi-cal personnel, the extraordinary manual work undertaken by hundreds of navy members within the stricken areas, the proficiency exercised by Ambassador Griscom and other United States representatives, the gener-ous and unprecedented congressional approval of substantial amounts to help the afflicted, the unparalleled amounts of voluntary contributions by prominent and working-class Americans, and Roosevelt's personal visit to the disaster scene—all of these actions and more elicited astonishing commendation. They won profuse and profound praise from Italy, from other nations, and from Italian Americans.

The outpouring of aid to poor, beleaguered Italians in the wake of the disaster prompted the writing of an extensive and absorbing article in the *New York Times* that portrayed the generous aid extended as a wonderful repudiation of a long-time detractor, Ouida (Louise de la Ramee). In her novels, English author Ouida championed the cause of harshly exploited Italian peasants so vigorously that it led to her reputation as their fore-most defender as she regularly inveighed against their bitter oppression at the hands of an unresponsive government. How would one—who was said to know the soul of the peasants more than any other writer—have written about the disaster? The speculation was, however, a literary device that the *New York Times* writer employed to declare that if she had been alive, she would have been forced to change her views in the light of the munificent aid extended by forces Ouida constantly attacked. "No writer who ever lived in her time hated governments more, more bitterly assailed the plague of modernity, and more openly despised America, than Ouida. What would she have said had she seen the rest of the world as now, led by America—coming to the rescue of the country-men she most loved."[8]

The *Times* writer wondered how Ouida—who loathed all governments, monarchs, and democracies alike for their neglect of the peasantry—would react to the present spectacle, and in the process of that wonderment, provide a sturdy apologia for America's role.

> What would she have said had she seen the rest of the world, as now led by America, coming to the rescue of the countrymen she most loved?...
>
> Today she would see the greatest Republic in the world hurrying relief to Sicily: a King, a Queen, Dukes, Marquises—they have all been doing what they could, not by sitting at home and writing orders, but there on the spot, in the flesh...
>
> What then, would she have said to the spectacle of America voting nearly a million dollars to the stricken country; of the nations and the individuals of almost all civilization joining in this great relief? Would she again have written the grim sentence—
>
> "There is no true compassion in that crowd of opposed yet mixing races which, for want of a better word, we call the modern world"?
>
> That crowd opposed yet mixing races—we can take that title to our very selves, to America, and then ask, all the more pointedly, would Ouida have still hated us, had she lived to-day and mean the relief we send?[9]

Contrasting the Messina postearthquake experience with the aftermath of Hurricane Katrina is instructive for a number of reasons; one is that hopelessness and despondency, which were manifested immediately after the cataclysms, may not be accurate forecasts for what will follow eventually. Thus among the suggestions proposed to deal with the Messina 1908 catastrophe was one that would have bombarded the remains of the city before abandoning it—an interesting parallel to the gloom and doom that have been predicted for the New Orleans of the future. Nevertheless, it was only a matter of a few short years before Messina started to come back, although it would take decades before substantial recovery was accomplished.

Messina, a hundred years after the Great Earthquake, stands as Italy's fourth greatest port. A quick survey of population statistics reveals that whereas the population of Messina proper decreased in the wake of the earthquake from 147,589 in 1901 to 128,121 in 1911, within a few years, it rebounded. Statistics show a population of 177,196 in 1921; 254,603 in 1961; 231,693 in 1991; and 252,026 in 2001. The city's population approached pre-earthquake numbers within a few years, the citrus trade was restored, commercial activity rebounded to 1908 levels, and Messina reestablished itself as Italy's fourth port.

Students of the Messina Earthquake cannot fail to take into account the role of religious organizations that saw American groups from Christian to Jewish respond generously to appeals for aid. In Italy, where the Catholic Church represented the overwhelming portion of the population, the church's response was particularly noteworthy. The historical record demonstrates that members of the clergy and religious suffered and died along with laypeople. It illustrates also that although battered, the church placed all of its resources at the disposal of the sufferers, thereby providing hospitalization, shelter, and prayerful encouragement. Messina's Archbishop D'Arrigo, moreover, became a leader in keeping the city alive and in its restoration by steadfastly opposing the city's destruction by bombardment. He and his successor Archbishop Angelo Paino played an important role in helping the city recover. It was Archbishop Paino who was credited with promoting the University of Messina to take a prestigious position in academia. The heroic works performed by Fr. Annibale and Fr. Orione in helping victims to survive, as have been already narrated, were among the important background factors in their subsequent canonization.

Messina in the twenty-first century shows few signs of its turbulent earthquake past. Physically, it is a modern city of modest size and population consisting of descendants of the earthquake and those who moved in after the turbulence of December 28, 1908. The city is a "gate to Sicily" that houses many historical treasures. It boasts of an outstanding museum, the National Museum of Messina; the Norman cathedral, now mostly rebuilt; and the Church of Santa Maria Alemanna (Saint Mary of the Germans), which retains part of its original Gothic splendor, one of the best examples of the architectural standard not widely found in Sicily. Today, Messina impresses people as a beautiful and charming city, rich by nature and also, thanks to what the people have succeeded in preserving and reconstructing, rich in heritage. Albeit much of the valuable works of antiquity have been destroyed, the remaining ruins provide valuable vestiges of Sicilian Gothic architecture.

The Messina Earthquake was a brief but absorbing chapter in the history of the Italian and American encounter—one that prompted individuals from both countries—from presidents and popes, from kings and queens, from military personnel and working proletariat, from the unassuming and the intelligentsia—to combine forces in remarkable and praiseworthy efforts to bring succor to a suffering people. It energized activity on the part of Americans and recent Italian immigrants who harbored a concern for Italy and contrawise stimulated more Italians to look for their future in America. There is also a paradox: the limited knowledge—the virtual ignorance about the event. The notion is perhaps best reflected in the following melancholy account of Giovanna Jackson who grew up in a wooden "barracks" built by Americans that served a necessary purpose:

> My mother grew up and I was born in an American shack and I can barely remember the two rooms and the kitchen. The bedroom was large and served the whole family; the other room served as the dining room and its door went out into the street that divided the barracks. The kitchen was a small thing with a door that took one outside to a garden no larger than a handkerchief. Yes, because the American sailors cut a corner of the shack to

make room for a garden. In this way every family could grow
basil, parsley, two plants of tomatoes or a rose bush. The barrack
had a wooden floor and a front door opened to a porch where the
people used to sit. In the evening in bed you could hear the sea
and at times it sounded angry. The families had a roof over their
head and a door to shut; only in the winter was it bad because the
north wind would rush in without hindrance between the slits of
the clapboards.[10]

Jackson also wrote in a melancholy vein about the receding memory
and impact of the American rescue experience.

[T]he neighborhood began to thin out. Little by little the neighbors moved away and so after a few years the shacks were abandoned. Now in Messina the American bridge has been replaced
by the Via Europa that goes from the sea to the mountain. And the
Church of the Madonna has been replaced by a public park, and
the neighborhoods of Maregrosso are all new.

Of that American ship no one knows the name, and not even
the memory of one of her sailors who helped the unfortunate people of Messina remains. Many people were born and grew up in
the American barracks and now only a few remain to remember
this experience.

Note: Nowadays, only very old people remember something
about the shantytown that was home to the survivors of the great
earthquake for many years. The rich found shelter in the villas outside the devastated city, and they quickly had their homes rebuilt
with modern seismic ideas. Later public housing was made available to all, but all was lost again in WWII [sic] Messina is now a
very modern city with rare historic buildings; it is the memory of
survivors, that writes her history.[11]

ENDNOTES

1. Micah 4:3, *Good News Bible*, 1976, American Bible Society.
2. William Kay Wallace, *Greater Italy* (New York: Scribner's Sons, 1917), 100–105.
3. *New York Times*, January 31, 1909.
4. Dickie, "Timing, Memory and Disaster," 163.
5. Edward Banfield, *The Moral Basis of a Backward Society* (New York: The Free Press, 1958), 10.
6. Joseph LoPreato, for example, in *Peasants No More* (San Francisco: Chandler Publishing Co., 1970), 107, likewise concluded, "[C]ooperative ethnic activity comes hard to Italian Americans." Richard Gambino, in his popular work *Blood of My Blood* (New York: Anchor Books/Doubleday, 1975), 325, cited statistics from Andrew Greeley, indicating Italian Americans score high in percentages (62 percent) among those who do not belong to any organization as proof of the disinclination of the group to join with others in synergetic activities.
7. Richard Gambino, *Blood of My Blood*, 65.
8. *New York Times*, January 10, 1909.
9. Ibid.
10. Giovanna Jackson, "The American Barracks in Messina," *Arba Sicula*, 20 nos. 1–2 (Spring and Autumn, 1999), 51, 53, 55.
11. Ibid.

PLATE 1. Beautiful Messina. Il Corso Vittorio Emanuele col Nettuno before earthquake. (Photo courtesy of the Messina Public Library.)

PLATE 2. Via Garibaldi e Porta Marina before earthquake. (Photo courtesy of the Messina Public Library.)

PLATE 3. Panoramic view of destruction following the earthquake.

PLATE 4. A view from the port of majestic facades still standing in Messina. (Photo courtesy of the Messina Public Library.)

PLATE 5. A scene at the juncture of the four fountains. (Photo courtesy of the Messina Public Library.)

PLATE 6. Interior of destroyed Duomo, Messina. (Photo courtesy of the Messina Public Library.)

PLATE 7. Visible signs of destruction on Corso Garibaldi. (Photo courtesy of the Messina Public Library.)

PLATE 8. The scene on Corso Garibaldi and Villa Mazzini. (Photo courtesy of the Messina Public Library.)

PLATE 9. Earthquake and fire struck Corso Vittorio Emanuele. (Photo courtesy of the Messina Public Library.)

PLATE 10. Barges with bodies of victims of earthquake. (Photo courtesy of the Messina Public Library.)

PLATE 11. Damaged Teatro Vittorio Emanuele would take decades before being rebuilt. (Photo courtesy of the Messina Public Library.)

PLATE 12. Palazzo della Costa after earthquake hit. An example of one of palaces destroyed. (Photo courtesy of the Messina Public Library.)

PLATE 13. Setting up medical facilities on Corso Vittorio Emanuele. (Photo courtesy of the Messina Public Library.)

PLATE 14. Italian military encampment set up in Messina. (Photo courtesy of the Messina Public Library.)

PLATE 15. Italian police set up outdoor kitchen amid ruins. (Photo courtesy of the Messina Public Library.)

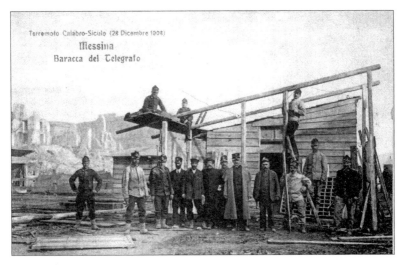

PLATE 16. Italian Army Telegraph company constructing its barrack. (Photo courtesy of the Messina Public Library.)

PLATE **17.** Destruction along shore in front of Messina's Customs House. (Photo courtesy of the Messina Public Library.)

PLATE **18.** What remained of the Customs House in Messina. (Photo courtesy of the Messina Public Library.)

Reggio Galabria dopo il terremoto del 28 dicembre 1908.
Nave apportatrice di soccorsi in attesa d'imbarco di profughi e feriti per Napoli.

PLATE 19. Italian navy personnel removing victims of the catastrophe in Reggio Calabria.

Photo # NH 2359   USS Culgoa at Messina, Italy, December 1908

PLATE 20. The USS *Culgoa*, a refrigerated supply ship of the "Great White Fleet," was among the first American ships to enter the distressed Messina area.

PLATE 21. Admiral Charles Sperry, commander of the Great White Fleet, went to Italy where he conferred with the king over plans to assist Italy.

PLATE 22. Officers of the United States Great White Fleet that diverted many ships to aid earthquake victims.

PLATE 23. The American flag rises in unusual collaboration wherein Italy agrees to the establishment of an American base within its borders to aid in recovery efforts. (Reginald R. Belknap, American House Building in Messina and Reggio)

PLATE 24. Under U.S. Navy supervision, Italian workers build barracks for homeless survivors. (Belknap)

PLATE 25. Row of houses built with American funds for victims of the earthquake. (Belknap)

PLATE 26. Two-storey barracks, one of thousands built under U.S. Navy supervision.

PLATE 27. King Victor Emmanuel of Italy provided extraordinary leadership in dealing with the earthquake disaster.

PLATE 28. Queen Elena of Italy won the admiration of people for her personal efforts in helping earthquake victims.

PLATE 29. Memorial Card that showed scenes of Messina before and after earthquake along with the King and Queen of Italy and American presidents Theodore Roosevelt and William Howard Taft. This was used to raise funds for victims by the American Italian Relief Committee.

INDEX

Printed in the United States
143634LV00001B/69/P

9 781934 844069